THE ATLAS OF
SCIENTIFIC
DISCOVERY

THE ATLAS OF
SCIENTIFIC
DISCOVERY

COLIN RONAN

CRESCENT BOOKS

A QUILL BOOK

This edition published by Crescent Books,
distributed by Crown Publishers, Inc

ISBN 0-517-421690

Library of Congress Number 83-72742

This book was designed and produced by
Quill Publishing Limited
32 Kingly Court
London W1

Art director Nigel Osborne
Editorial director Jeremy Harwood
Senior editor Liz Wilhide
Editor Joanna Edwards
Designers Alexander Arthur   Paul Cooper
Illustrator Steve Braun
Picture researcher Veronique Mott

Filmset by QV Typesetting Limited, London
Origination by Hong Kong Graphic Arts Service Centre Limited,
Hong Kong; Rodney Howe and Co Limited, London; Speedlith Photo
Litho Limited, Manchester
Printed by Heraclio Fournier SA, Vitoria, Spain

Quill would like to extend special thanks to David Worth at
Line and Line

Contents

Introduction

Aristotle, who lived almost 2,500 years ago and was the most influential of Greek philosophers, claimed that the difference between people and animals lay in what he called the 'rational soul': people possess this noble attribute, animals do not. Certainly, over the ages, it is intellect that has lifted human beings above other creatures, who spend most of their waking life hunting for food and shelter. People have developed cultures, become able to control nature, to some extent, for their own benefit and have even begun to fathom its inmost workings. Further, human beings are characterized by an abiding curiosity, an inbuilt urge to enquire into the world, exercising imagination as well as powers of observation.

The examination of nature is something of a cumulative process. Observations are amassed and studied; explanations and theories are proposed and put to the test. Today, this process is known as 'science', though in past ages it was called by different names. But whatever it is called, it is not only cumulative but creative. Ideas must be proposed before they can be rejected or accepted. We are now aware of a far more complex universe than our ancestors were; the whole of creation has been found to be more astounding and awe-inspiring than ever imagined before.

This slow climb from ignorance to enlightenment is not the usual stuff of history, which concerns itself with the rise and fall of empires, the struggle not to comprehend nature but to control people and territory. Yet the history of scientific discovery is as much a part of our civilization as an account of power politics and, because it involves the creative imagination, it is as truly cultural as any history of the arts. The gradual growth of natural knowledge is the theme of this atlas.

The beginnings of science are lost in the mists of prehistory. Precisely when human beings began to enquire into the nature of things no one can say for certain, but it was certainly a very long time ago. The carefully observed cave paintings of animals at Altamira in Spain and Lascaux in France date from Paleolithic or Old Stone Age times, from at least 18,000BC. Why the paintings were made is not certain but there seem to be three possible reasons. One could have been the age-old desire for self-expression. Another may have been to record nature; such would be the natural motive of a proto-scientist. But the third possibility, and probably the most likely, was that the intention was to make magic. There was a belief, which is not completely unknown today, that drawing a likeness of someone, similar to taking their photograph, captures something of their soul. In this way, the painter, or photographer, is believed to gain power over the person. And what applies to an individual, applies also to an animal: in days when man had to hunt for his food, depicting his prey may have been thought to ensure success for a hunting expedition. Similar magical ideas lie behind the animal dress worn sometimes by shamans and witch doctors. Yet though magic is not science, magical practices enshrined some knowledge of the surrounding world; the compounding of herbal remedies, with or without casting spells, showed an acquaintance with simple chemistry and basic medical treatment. By trying new things and observing

UNDERSTANDING NATURE Man's involvement with science as the key to his understanding of the world and the universe around him began for very practical reasons. The Ancient Egyptians, for instance, began their observations of the heavens and the development of a calendar in order to predict the time at which the Nile would flood *(right)*. This enabled them to plan their harvests accordingly. Slowly they built up the corpus of knowledge that enabled them to construct the Pyramids *(far right)* to geometric accuracy.

the consequences, 'scientific' experiment began.

Another aspect of prehistoric science, or proto-science, was a natural interest in the skies. The moon was an obvious object of curiosity; it appeared regularly like the sun, but changed its shape from night to night. This waxing and waning held further interest — the cycle coincided with certain periodic physiological changes in women and, it was later discovered, with behavioural changes in some marine life, for example, the sea urchin. At times close to full moon, there was enough light even to hunt at night. Moreover, the cycle of the moon's phases took no more than 29 days — 29½ to be more precise — a period short enough to count with ease. It is no wonder then that a lunar calendar became the universal method of time-reckoning. It was only replaced by a solar or seasonal calendar when people ceased to be nomadic and settled down to cultivate the land.

To devise a solar calendar, however, required some degree of sophistication. It meant knowing where the sun lay with respect to the stars but, since the stars cannot be seen when the sun is above the horizon, the problem of determining the sun's position was fraught with difficulties. In due course the problem was solved, but its very solution had forced a close observation of the skies and a growing familiarity with the patterns or constellations of stars. This was the true beginning of astronomy as a science.

The heavens had always exerted a particularly strong fascination for the enquiring mind; in the lands where civilizations first seem to have flourished — in Arabia and the Mediterranean — the night sky is a marvellous sight and so

this interest was, in a sense, natural enough. Moreover, the sky produced an ever-changing pageant. Not only the sun and the moon but also a number of bright 'stars' wandered in and out among the constellations; to account for this motion was a perpetual intellectual challenge.

Astronomy was a constant occupation of every civilization; as a result, it acts as a continuous thread running throughout the whole history of scientific development. The different and changing views of the universe particular to each civilization reflect the awareness of nature and the degree to which natural forces could, and can, be explained in that civilization. This is why astronomy must occupy the prime place in the chapters that follow.

Other matters also stimulated interest from the beginning. Why were there so many different kinds of plants and animals? What relation, if any, did they bear to one another? How did plants and animals differ in essence? At the outset, attempts to solve these questions took the form of exercises in natural history rather than biological science, more a process of collecting facts and simple observations than a disciplined experimental analysis.

Another focus of curiosity was the study of natural substances: minerals, ores, plants and deposits. By experimenting with these materials, mixing and heating them, the beginnings of scientific chemistry came about. But this was a very long and difficult process, diverted at times by magical bypaths like alchemy, and the fully scientific process of experimental investigation and analysis was not reached until about two centuries ago.

WONDER OF THE WORLD The lighthouse at Pharos *(left)* was built by the Egyptian Pharoah Ptolemy II around 280BC to guide ships entering Alexandria's harbour. The city was one of the greatest scientific centres of the ancient world.
BASIC REQUIREMENTS Science and technology developed hand-in-hand with the growth of urban, organized communities. Tolland man, preserved for centuries in a Danish marsh, was a hunter-gatherer, without any such sophistication *(below)*.

EGYPT

Although science was slow to start, its beginnings can be seen very clearly in the first great civilizations which grew up on the east and southeastern edges of the Mediterranean, in Egypt and in Mesopotamia, the land which lay between the Tigris and Euphrates rivers in what is now Iraq. In Egypt, a land centred on the Nile and with borders naturally protected by high ground and desert, a complex civilization grew up. By 3100BC the country was under dynastic rule and, though political upheavals and power struggles gave rise to new dynasties as well as periods of instability, the nation lasted for over 2,000 years before it decayed and came under foreign domination. In one sense Ancient Egypt was like an island, insulated from its neighbours; this is evident in its use of hieroglyphics for writing, a method that differed substantially from other early scripts and could not be used for diplomatic correspondence. Hieroglyphics were, however, ideally suited for writing on papyrus sheets, prepared from the pith of a tall grass found in the marshes of the delta at the mouth of the Nile, and they had been in use from at least as early as 3500BC. The country was run by a large but efficient administration.

Today, the Ancient Egyptians are remembered mainly for their burial customs and for their monumental buildings. These last, epitomized by the giant pyramids built some 4,500 years ago, must have demanded not only a vast practical knowledge of civil engineering but also a knowledge of hygiene and dietetics to keep so large a workforce — anything up to 100,000 men — free from epidemics. Egyptian burial customs are well known; the bodies of the poor were dealt with simply but those of the nobility were elaborately treated, with certain organs being removed

before the corpse was soaked in a nitrate solution. Whatever the treatment, it is clear that the Egyptians must have gained some knowledge of the human body; nevertheless, although they practised surgery and amassed a wealth of practical medical facts, there was no attempt at systematization. The Ancient Egyptians seem never to have felt the need to take a general philosophical view of what they knew.

What was true in medicine was true in other fields of endeavour. The civil engineering carried out by the Egyptians led to no science of mechanics and was therefore limited in its development. Their surveying, especially after the annual flooding of the Nile, was achieved by rule-of-thumb methods; when they wanted to divide an area of land into square fields, they laid out the corners of their square by using a loop of rope, the length of which was such that it could be laid out in a triangle with sides in the ratio of three, four and five. Yet they did not develop this practical knowledge into a general theorem about right-angled triangles. Indeed, their mathematics, efficient and eminently practical though it was, was hindered by the fact it had no formal basis. Egyptian astronomy suffered from the same limitations. Like the astronomy of every other civilization, it grouped the stars into artifical patterns to make recognition easier. However, the Ancient Egyptian constellations were so large that even now their detailed identifications elude scholars. On the practical side, they applied their astronomy with brilliance, devising the first satisfactory seasonal calendar system. Ancient Egyptian life centred round the flooding of the Nile, which occurred every 360 days or so; it was with this in mind that they developed a calendar of 12 30-day months, which was easy to administer, with five extra days added at the end of each 360-day period.

MESOPOTAMIA

The other early Mediterranean civilization, that of Mesopotamia, was rather different in attitude. Its people faced a harsher world than their naturally protected Egyptian contemporaries, who were almost insular in outlook. The Mesopotamians suffered numerous attacks from outside; they were also the victims of a somewhat irregular water supply and of two rivers which slightly changed their courses from time to time. Despite these hardships, permanent settlements grew up on the banks of the Tigris and Euphrates, and by 3000BC the area between the rivers was peopled by the Sumerians, who drained the marshes, domesticated animals such as cattle, sheep and goats, constructed chariots and used mud bricks for building.

The Sumerians devised a form of writing which was suited to the one natural substance they had in abundance: clay. They made clay tablets and wrote on these by using a wedge-shaped stylus which made triangular impressions. The earliest types of cuneiform ('wedge-shaped') writing, dating from before 3000BC, probably featured picture symbols, but it was the Sumerians who identified sounds with symbols and thus developed a written vocabulary. Writing is, of course, vital to science, because it allows for the transmission of information from one generation to the next.

The Sumerians were conquered but their culture, which was well advanced in the field of natural science, lived on, especially in the cities of Lagash and Ur (the city said to be Abraham's birthplace). Although these centres lost their importance to Babylon, which reached the height of its influence by the middle of the eighteenth century BC, the spirit of Sumerian culture could not be suffocated: the Babylonians simply became the Sumerians' successors. Sumerian attempts to describe animals and plants systematically were continued; not only were the flora and fauna noted but also attempts were made to classify them. Marine animals were separated from those on land and then both were subdivided into various types, and plants were treated in a similar fashion. The rudiments of plant sexuality were also discovered.

As in Egypt, a system of standard weights and measures was introduced; it seems, however, to have predated the Egyptian system. In mathematics, the Sumerian-Babylonian culture surpassed that of Egypt. The Sumerians adopted a basis of 60 for counting — still with us in the division of angles and of units of time such as the hour and the minute — and developed a kind of algebra which allowed them to solve mathematical equations, the results of which they applied to the solution of practical problems such as building and surveying. They also worked out the relationship between the sides of a right-angled triangle, and in these and other ways displayed a truly mathematical approach.

This difference in attitude between the two civilizations is evident in their astronomy and conceptions of the universe. Both peopled the universe with gods and goddesses but the Mesopotamians brought a physical approach to bear, which was lacking in the Egyptian picture. Although the Egyptians were aware of the brighter planets, it was left to the Mesopotamians to study their motions which, characteristically, they expressed in mathematical form, laying the foundations of what was to be the main subject of astronomy for the next 3,000 years and more.

GREECE

In the sixth century BC Babylon was conquered by the Persians. Scientific development continued, but now in an extraordinary civilization that grew up among the islands of the Aegean Sea and on the neighbouring mainland area, which we now call Greece. Here a rational approach to the natural world was cultivated by a few men who were able to spend time philosophizing about nature, but who rejected any mythical stories about gods and goddesses, seeking instead natural, physical explanations. Their views were often coloured by the Greek love of symmetry and form, a love that was channelled by the more mathematically minded into developing the formal study of geometry. It was this inherent feeling for symmetry that, in the ninth century BC, led the poet Homer or, rather, the school of poetry that was named after him, to imagine the universe as a vast sphere instead of a dome as the Mesopotamians had done.

Greek philosophers considered the earth to be a globe at the centre of the celestial sphere. In the sixth century BC, the mathematician Pythagoras, who was also a religious and political leader, suggested that the sun, moon and planets all move round the earth in circles at an unchanging pace. It fell to his successors to devise mathematical explanations to account for the observed behaviour of the planets on this basis. Yet it must be remembered that the Greeks were nothing if not independently minded when it came to matters of 'natural philosophy' and, although Pythagoras believed the earth to be stationary at the centre of the universe, a later disciple, Philalos, suggested that the earth, sun, moon, planets and stars all orbited a central fire. His reason for such a suggestion was a somewhat mystico-religious one based on the belief that there should be 10 moving bodies, yet his reasoning from then on was scientific enough. Again, 200 years later, a moving earth, this time orbiting the sun, was suggested by Aristarchos of Samos as a better way to account for observed planetary movements, but this was rejected, mainly because it seemed at the time to make nonsense of the laws of physics.

Physics was another subject which the Greeks studied. In the fourth century BC, Aristotle (384-322BC), a pupil of Plato and the tutor of Alexander the Great, worked out a self-consistent scheme of physics which accounted for the behaviour of moving bodies of every kind, explained why heavy bodies fell to the ground, why water spread outwards 'to find its own place' and why flames always burn upwards. Although it was not without its faults, it was a magnificent intellectual feat, the more astonishing since, as a scientific observer, Aristotle was most at home in the biological field. He studied bees and their diseases (a subject of great practical importance since honey was the substance used for sweetening), cattle and, above all, marine life, carrying out dissections to help him in his work. Aristotle did not stop at

9

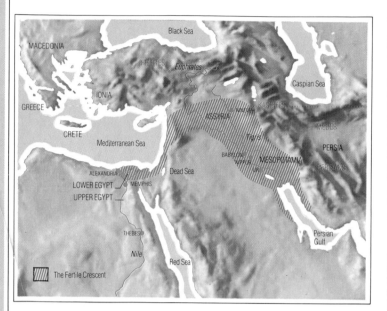

mere observation; he devised his own classification system — his 'scale of nature' — and discussed the essential dissimilarity between non-living things and those that are alive, as well as the underlying differences between plants, animals and man. Aristotle has sometimes been called the 'father of marine biology' just as Theophrastos (371/370-288/287BC) his successor at the Lyceum in Athens — the educational centre Aristotle founded — is known as the 'father of botany'. Theophrastos classified plants according to their branches, stems and roots, he named their component parts and discussed their habitat as well as their structure.

The Greek attitude to science and the true philosophical approach to nature is revealed in a story Aristotle told about Thales, one of the original 'seven wise men' of Ancient Greece. Taunted that he was not clever enough to make money, Thales, believing the signs of a good olive harvest were evident, bought every olive press he could find in the vicinity; at harvest-time he hired them out at high prices, confounding his critics. But the moral of the story was that, as Aristotle put it, a philosopher can make money if he so wishes, 'but his aims are of a different kind'. To the Greek mind the philosopher, or scientist, had a noble calling in his own right.

When, in 323BC, Alexander had conquered the whole of the Middle East as well as part of the Indian continent, he set about building a seaport in the north of Egypt. Although Alexander's kingdom was divided into three parts after his death in 321, Ptolemy Soter, one of his generals, was appointed ruler of Egypt and decided to complete the project. Ptolemy Soter was a patron of learning and established a vast library and museum close to the royal palace in Alexandria, a place which soon became a centre of advanced scientific research. Founded with the help of two of Theophrastos' pupils, it drew learned men from all over the world, including Jews and, later, Christians. Here Euclid taught and worked, systematizing Greek geometry, Archimedes (c 287-212BC), the great mechanician and mathematician, stayed for a time with his friend Eratosthenes (c 276-c192BC) who had been appointed head of the library. Eratosthenes was also engaged in research; as a geographer and mathematician, he measured the size of the earth with an astounding degree of accuracy. It was at Alexandria, too, that in the second century AD, the astronomer Ptolemy, who was no relation to the ruling family, produced his great mathematical synthesis of all Greek astronomy. This astonishing compendium, now known by its Arabic title *Almagest*, contains not only Ptolomy's own research, but is also the main source of information on the work of Hipparchos, the greatest observational astronomer of Ancient Greece who lived in Rhodes during the second century BC.

The library and museum at Alexandria provided a centre for advanced Greek medical research. In Greece, tradition held that medical treatment had been founded by the god Asklepios, who is mentioned in Homer's *Iliad*, but whether or not he was a real person we do not know. What is

certain is that a cult was centred on him and temples associated with this cult existed where medicine was practised. Treatment consisted of herbal drugs, rest and consultation with the priests, so forming a psychosomatic approach. There was no surgery. However, by the fourth century BC two major medical centres had become established, one at Cnidos on what is now the southwestern Turkish coast, and the other on the nearby island of Cos. The Cnidos school concentrated on certain diseases and also specialized in obstetrics and gynaecological problems, but the school at Cos was broader in its approach. The physician Hippocrates (who, according to one source was born in 460BC) taught at Cos and organized the Greek medical knowledge of his day into a coherent system there. In his work diseases were carefully observed and detailed case histories compiled; he

considered the effects of climate on diseases which, he thought, were due to a lack of balance of the four qualities — cold, dry, hot and wet — and the four 'humours' of bodily fluids — phlegm, black bile, blood and yellow bile. It is to Hippocrates of Cos that we owe the basic moral attitude of the medical profession, enshrined in the Hippocratic Oath. The medical school at Alexandria was a direct descendant of the Hippocratic one at Cos; its founder, Herophilos, was trained in Hippocratic medicine.

Herophilos went to Alexandria at the request of Ptolemy Soter. He was a competent and successful physician, an inspiring teacher and followed up research on his own account. The study of anatomy was not well developed at Cos, but Herophilos redressed the balance at Alexandria. He distinguished the veins from the arteries, traced the optic nerves from the eye to the brain, studied the whole nervous system with immense care and concluded that the brain, not the heart, was its centre. This was a revolutionary idea at the time. He also carried out other anatomical work and discovered the Fallopian tubes which connect the ovaries to the womb, although this was one of many discoveries to be lost; the tubes were rediscovered 1,900 years later by the Italian Gabriele Fallopio, after whom they are now named.

A successor to Herophilos at Alexandria was Erasistratos, whose work was mainly carried out in the middle of the third century BC. An author of many medical books, he too carried out much original research, which included what were probably the very first experiments on the way the body copes with and reacts to different substances; this was the study of what is now known as 'metabolism'. He also instituted the practice of carrying out post-mortems and these gave him a further insight into human anatomy. He realized that all living parts are made of a tissue of veins, arteries and nerves, and he distinguished between sensory and motor nerves. It was Erasistratos who first showed how the larynx closes during swallowing and that digestion is not a process of fermentation or of 'cooking' the food in the body, but is due to the working of the stomach muscles. Finally, he came to the conclusion that the heart is a pump. Unfortunately, he did not take the next step and discover that blood circulates around the body.

The medical work at Alexandria, as well as the mathematical and astronomical research, shows very clearly the scientific peak reached by Greek culture more than 1,800 years ago. These people laid out a very broad basis for the future development of science but, after the time of the astronomer Ptolemy, who was certainly working in Alexandria between AD127 and 145, progress became very slow. In AD269, the library at Alexandria suffered damage when the Syrian queen Zenobia captured Egypt, but this was only the beginning of what was the library's disintegration. Early in the fourth century AD, Cyril, patriarch of Alexandria, incensed at the outlook and behaviour of the museum's director, the woman mathematician Hypatia, encouraged a mob to storm the buildings. The mob got out of hand, a fire was started and Hypatia was lynched. A little over two centuries later the final destruction occurred when the Muslim armies conquered Egypt. Scholars had, however, fled long before, with some of the manuscripts; these were cared for in centres of learning in Persia and neighbouring lands.

CHINA
Recent research has shown that the Mediterranean area was not the sole domain of early science. In northwest and southwest Britain and in Brittany evidence still stands of a civilization that built stone observatories some 4,000 years ago. These observatories enabled them to devise a seasonal calendar and, perhaps, even predict eclipses of the sun and moon. At present, however, little else is known about these megalithic builders or their culture. Stone observatories of a different kind were also built in Europe and later in South America by the Mayan civilization.

In China a complex civilization flourished from about 2500BC which developed its own independent scientific outlook on the world, in almost complete isolation. The belief that the whole universe was one vast organism, of which man was part, was the basis of the Chinese outlook; this led to extensive records of natural events being kept and collated. If the universe were one organism, signs would be expected if the emperor and his officials failed in their duties, for this would be similar to a disease in one part of nature. Therefore nature could, in one sense, provide a guide to official policies, as long as suitable evidence was collected. The result was that records of celestial events, the weather, and natural catastrophes, were kept continuously from early times by an efficient bureaucracy, and this evidence has proved of great benefit to modern science when gradual, long-term changes are being investigated.

Yet Chinese science was not merely a passive observation of natural events. Although the Chinese were masters of technology of every kind, they also possessed a lively curiosity about nature itself. They made notable advances in mapping the earth and the skies, devising ways of representing both on a flat chart which pre-empted some similar achievements in the Western world — notably Mercator's method of map projection — by some six centuries. They also devised an advanced form of support for their sighting instruments, used to observe the skies so that only one movement was required to follow the curved path of the stars as they rose and set. In this, too, they were ahead of the West by at least 300 years. Chinese astronomers also seem to have been the first to conceive of an infinite universe of stars stretching throughout space with the earth, sun, moon and planets floating within it, borne along by a force they described as a 'hard wind'. This view is as advanced as any Greek thinking and, although the date of its origin is obscure, it was certainly current in the first century AD.

The Chinese probably also studied rock formations and fossils earlier than the West; their concern with natural catastrophes and the practical steps necessary to minimize their effects, led to the development of the first seismograph, or earthquake recorder. But perhaps one of their most important discoveries — certainly their most significant contribution to physics — was that of the earth's magnetic field and the development of the magnetic compass. People in the West derived their first compass and an introduction to magnetism from China, but not until the fourteenth century.

In the biological sciences the Chinese, like other nations in antiquity, described animals in some detail but they also carried out much work on selective breeding, notably with the water-buffalo and the Pekingese dog. It was the Chinese, too, who specialized in the domestication of insects, beginning some time around 1500BC with the breeding of silkworms and then the cultivation of scale insects for white wax and different species for dyestuffs. From as early as the third century AD, they also used ants as a form of biological plant protection against other pests; the Chinese were the first to do so in known history.

In their studies of plants, the Chinese not only prepared detailed scientific descriptions, but with the advantage of a wider range of species and an efficient feudal bureaucracy that required the full and correct use of land, they laid the foundations of the study of plants and their environment — geobotany — making the first detailed studies of soils. Moreover, the need to make use of wild plants for food during periods of famine led to a new form of applied botany that was the forerunner of our present concern with expanding the sources of the food supply. As we might expect, the Chinese also paid particular attention to the medicinal use of plants — although they did not restrict themselves to herbal drugs alone — and in medical treatment developed unique techniques of which acupuncture is the best-known example.

Although this book is concerned with the history of science, not the history of technology, some technological innovations must be mentioned because they have had so profound an effect on the progress of science. One was certainly the invention of the mechanical clock, which was devised by the Chinese some 600 years before it became known in the West. Even more significant was the Chinese invention of paper and printing. Techniques of papermaking took some 12 centuries to reach the West from China and printing, using wooden blocks, took more than 400 years to arrive.

To some extent, Chinese science was carried out in isolation. What was discovered in China filtered through to the West very slowly, either by sea or, more often, overland by way of trade routes through central Asia and Arabia. Often, as in the case of papermaking, it was the Arabs who made the invention first — in this case the time-lag was some seven centuries. Not until the seventeenth century did China come fully into contact with Western science, and the transmission of information was not just in one direction; early on, the Chinese appear to have learned and, for a time, to have adopted, the Mesopotamian picture of the nature of the physical universe.

ARABIA
When the Alexandrian library and museum were destroyed, the development of science moved east into Arabia and central Asia. This migration was a result of the fact that the new Mediterranean religion of Christianity was primarily concerned with matters other than the nature of the physical world, and, indeed, like Cyril of Alexandria, inimical to it. Not all Christian leaders took this view however; St Augustine proclaimed early in the fifth century AD that a study of the natural world revealed more of God's glory. But the urge for independent enquiry, so characteristic of the Greeks, was gone. What little Greek science that survived in centres like Byzantium (present-day Istanbul) was taken by the Western Church as a basic authority for the physical world, in much the same way as the Bible was for the spiritual. In the West, then, science became ossified. But in the Arab world a different attitude of mind grew, covering practically all fields of scientific achievement. It is to the Arabs, for instance, that we owe our system of numbers, even though this originated in India.

The development of science in Arabia occurred mainly during the Islamic era. That period is usually taken to have begun in AD622 when Mohammed went from Mecca to Medina, as after this date the drive to unite the various people of Arabia began. With their religious zeal, the Islamic armies made wide conquests that even took them far into Spain. Yet despite their religious motivation, the Muslim conquerors showed astonishing tolerance to those cultures which they brought under control. By the time the period of expansion was over, the Muslims had inherited knowledge from Alexandria and other Hellenistic centres, as well as learning that had been amassed over the previous centuries in Persia. Islam, in this way, acted as a transmitter of Greek science to the West, but also made some important contributions of its own.

In astronomy the Arabs made no great theoretical advances; they were content with Ptolemy's work, to which they gave the title *Almagest*, meaning 'the greatest'. They did believe, however, that they had discovered a slight oscillation of the heavens which they called 'trepidation'. The existence of such a phenomenon had been hinted at by some Greek astronomers and seemed to be confirmed by the more precise observations the Islamic astronomers were able to make; only some centuries later was it to be disproved.

There is no doubt that the precision of astronomical measurement was increased in the Islamic world, partly due to the feeling that the more observations were made, the smaller the amount of random errors that would occur, and partly due to the instruments they used. Islamic astronomers believed another way to reduce error was to build giant instruments. Graduated scales on these instruments would be correspondingly big, making it possible to read them to a far higher degree of precision. Many such instruments were built, most notably in Rayy in Iran and at Samarkand in the Uzbekhistan region of what is now the USSR. One of the notable products of such observational activity was the production of a considerable number of astronomical tables, each one more accurate than the last, giving positions of the stars as well as the sun, moon and planets. The astronomers and mathematicians of Islam also developed the astrolabe which was a handheld observing instrument and calculating device.

Modern mathematics owes a great debt to Islamic mathematicians. In the ninth century AD, Abu al-Khwarizmi invented a development of arithmetic now known as 'algebra' (the word itself is Arabic) and adopted the use of Hindu numerals which are still known in the West as 'Arabic' numerals. These were a great improvement on previous methods of writing numbers and, together with the development of trigonometry by Abu al-Khwarizmi's contemporary Abu al-Battani, helped to develop the nature and scope of mathematics.

In physics, Islam is noted for the original work of Ibn al-Haytham on optics. He studied the eye and concluded that light was received by it from every object observed; although this may seem obvious, it was a great step forward from Greek ideas which had assumed things were only seen because something emanated from the eye itself. Al-Haytham also discussed the behaviour of light emitted from objects and the nature of colours.

Their approach to the biological sciences, despite careful descriptions of animals and developments in veterinary knowledge, was primarily practical, as it was in botany where interest centred on the agricultural and medical aspects of plants. In medicine itself the Arabs made some progress, but were hampered by their bias towards the Greek surgeon Galen, who had worked in Rome in the second century AD. Although Galen was a man of great erudition, with a practical knowledge of anatomy based on his work as a surgeon to gladiators and an immensely successful medical practice as a physician, his work was hampered by a lack of human bodies available for dissection, which forced him to work on the bodies of animals. A believer in the earlier Greek idea of three souls — nutritive, animal and rational — originally proposed by Plato, he also thought that the blood flowed through the heart from one side of it to the other. Thus the blood was believed to 'ebb and flow' like a tide through the body, not to circulate.

Islamic physicians were not alone in following Galen's system; in medieval times in Western Christendom, Galen's scheme was also adopted. However, a physician named Abu Bakr al-Razi did question Galen's theories, and also many other beliefs including the Islamic faith. His contributions to knowledge, which included an attempt to revive the Greek atomic theory, were not, however, pursued.

THE RENAISSANCE AND EUROPEAN DEVELOPMENTS

For a time Islam enjoyed a monopoly over the scientific knowledge of the Ancient Greeks, but the situation changed remarkably in the twelfth century. From the ninth century onwards, after the Islamic conquest of Sicily and the eastern Mediterranean, trade began between the two areas and, by the twelfth century, some Western scholars were well enough acquainted with Arabic to be able to turn Arabic translations and commentaries of Greek works into Latin. Toledo in Spain, which had become a famous city of learning and research, was one of the centres for this work. Greek texts, hitherto unknown, were made available, while those few which had been available as commentaries could be read in full, either in translation or in the original. The arrival in Western Christendom of this Greek learning was intellectually stirring. It also became clear that the Greeks had differed in their opinions and that they had not considered everything to be eternally fixed as did Western thinkers.

There were problems because much that was rediscovered was coloured by an Islamic interpretation which the Western Church felt it necessary to expunge. Such a task was carried out by a number of scholars, most notably St Thomas Aquinas in the thirteenth century. Scholars had therefore to pick their way with care, but the new sense of enquiry could not be stifled. The comparatively safe field opened up by al-Haytham's optical research was pursued early on, while later, Aristotle's laws of motion were attacked on a mathematical basis, which was again a reasonably safe area for new and independent thinking.

Gradually, this new movement gained ground and its influence widened. There was a 'renaissance' or rebirth of the human spirit of independence; horizons were extended — explorers took routes to Africa and India, and Columbus set sail to discover a western route to the Far East — and scientific problems were considered in a fresh light, based upon a startling new awareness of the world. The consequences of this feeling of emancipation gave rise not only to the questioning of authority but also to a break with traditional religious and scientific concepts leading, again in the fifteenth century, to the Reformation and the disintegration of Western Christendom into two camps, Catholic and Protestant. The outcome was the further questioning and fragmentation of the authority of old ideas and this, in its turn, helped strengthen the freedom to propose and test new ones.

Perhaps the best example of these developments occurred in 1543 when two important and revolutionary scientific books were published — *De Humani Corporis Fabrica (On the Fabric of the Human Body)* by Andreas Vesalius (1514-64) and *De Revolutionibus Orbium Coelestium (On the Revolutions of the Heavenly Spheres)* by Nicolaus Copernicus (1473-1543). The first was an illustrated description of the human body, based on Vesalius' dissection of human corpses, shown in detail never before achieved. The study corrected some errors in Galen's teaching, which was still accepted as standard, and later, in 1555, Vesalius totally repudiated Galen's anatomy when the second edition of the *Fabrica* came out; this marked the beginning of the modern science of medicine. The book by Copernicus heralded a revolution in astronomical thought, for he countered Aristotle's 'reasons' for the earth being fixed in space, and presented in detail a new scheme of the universe with the sun not the earth at the centre. No longer did the earth hold a position of special privilege in the universe; it was relegated to the status of a mere planet. This view had significant religious and philosophical implications as well as being of immense scientific importance.

SPREAD OF KNOWLEDGE The scientists of the Renaissance did not work in isolation to develop those theories which laid the foundations of modern science. They were not only the heirs of Greek science, but also of the science of Arabia and China. The Chinese pioneered the domestication of insects, such as the silkworm, as early as 1500BC; the secret of the compass, which made the great Renaissance voyages of discovery possible, also came from the Chinese, via the Arabs.

SCIENCE AND SUPERSTITION Even with the advances of the Renaissance, common superstitions continued. The old belief that the mandrake, with its fork-shaped root resembling the human form *(left)*, screamed as it was pulled from the earth, still persisted.

THE SCIENTIFIC REVOLUTION

With the advent of the seventeenth century, the basis of modern scientific endeavour became firmly established. In Italy, Galileo (1564-1642) began to conduct experiments in motion and in other areas of physics, analyzing his results mathematically. This was an extension of the work of Archimedes some 1,800 years before, based on a scientific approach that was to become universal in the physical sciences. It was Galileo, too, who made extensive use of the telescope, an invention that had just become widely known, to make observations of the skies. Without any doubt, these observations showed celestial bodies of which the Ancient Greeks simply could not have had any knowledge. This was another blow to the orthodox opinion that Greek science was the ultimate authority on matters concerned with the physical universe.

Galileo was only one of many scientists open to new ideas. In every western European country, the new and powerful method of observing, theorizing and then testing by experiment was being carried out. In the physical sciences it was to reach a peak in 1687 when Isaac Newton (1642-1727) published *Philosophiae Naturalis Principia Mathematicae (The Mathematical Principles of Natural Philosophy)*, which was one of the most important books ever to be written.

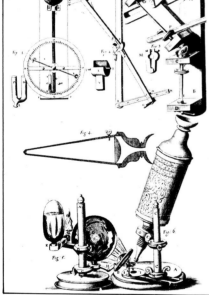

SCIENTIFIC REVOLUTION The epic voyage of Christopher Columbus (1451-1506) across the Atlantic *(top)* not only revealed a New World; it was also one of the practical discoveries that confirmed the theory of a round earth. Through his microscope *(above left)*, the English scientist Robert Hooke examined the inner world of plants. The enormous telescope at the Lick Observatory, California *(above right)* is part of a process that started with the observations of Galileo. Newton devised the theoretical model *(right)* to demonstrate his third law of motion.

Fig. 1.

Within the pages of one volume was a mathematical analysis not only of the laws of motion of bodies on earth, but also a solution to the problem that had vexed and challenged astronomers ever since the days of Pythagoras: the motion of the planets in space. In brief, Newton brought the whole universe within the framework of one set of laws, guided by the principle of universal gravitation.

The new spirit of experimental enquiry was also evident in the biological field. This began with the classification of plants and animals but, in addition, scientists began compiling detailed and exact drawings showing, for instance, plants as they are, not as they were supposed to be. Animals were dissected and compared — in one case the human skeleton was compared with that of a bird — and similarities were noted. A different attitude to the human body emerged and it began to be seen as an animal.

A new look was also taken at chemistry. There was a desire to avoid the mysticism and deliberate obscurity that surrounded alchemy, and to think anew about chemical substances. Thus chemistry became characterized by careful experiments in which the products were precisely weighed at every stage; the old idea of the four elements was discarded and a new definition of elements attempted.

In all this work, the new breed of 'natural philosophers', as they called themselves, formed learned societies, groups where they could meet, experiment and discuss the new results. The French *Académie des Sciences* and the British Royal Society were the two foremost examples, founded in the seventeenth century. These bodies were centres in which scientific discoveries could be communicated and results published. Thus it was that the Royal Society publicized the discoveries made with the newly invented microscopes, especially the outstanding work of the Dutch microscopist Anton van Leeuwenhoek (1632-1723), and it was the Royal Society that published Newton's *Principia*.

Once the new 'scientific revolution', as it is sometimes called, had begun and people began to question and experiment, the movement gathered momentum. The pace of scientific research which had moved slowly in Greek times and in Islam, and not much faster before the Renaissance, now began an accelerated progress.

Heat was a popular matter for scientific study in the seventeenth century when it became possible to measure degrees of heat by thermometers, because this gave some precision to questions such as how heat is exchanged between bodies and the amount of heat required for a body to change state, for example, from ice to water, or from water to steam. In the late seventeenth century, these investigations led to new concepts, some of which had immediate practical consequences, like James Watt's efficient steam engine. Practical experience of the effects produced by new machinery — the heat generated when boring the barrels of cannons, for example — led to the idea that heat existed because of the motion of the particles of a body. As chemistry developed and a new atomic theory arrived in the early 1800s, so the idea of heat as a motion became more acceptable, although proof only came later.

The study of electricity had never been followed up in the ancient world. The Greeks knew that if amber was rubbed against fur it attracted small objects, but it was not until the seventeenth century that a machine for the generation of electricity by friction was devised. In this and the following century, other machines of a similar kind made it possible to study such 'static' electricity, and means were even devised for storing as well as measuring it. Soon it became identified with the electricity associated with lightning discharges during thunderstorms. Then a new form of electricity was discovered, this time one that could be generated simply by placing two different metals in a container filled with a weak acid. Later research was to show that this chemically made electricity was precisely the same as the old static electricity, while there was also found to be an intimate link between electricity and magnetism. Still later, mathematical analysis was to show that light itself was an 'electromagnetic radiation' which included other radiations that we now call gamma-rays, X-rays, ultraviolet light, infrared and radio waves.

MODERN SCIENTIFIC DEVELOPMENT

This new subject of electricity brought together various studies that had hitherto been quite separate: electricity and magnetism, chemistry and the study of light. In this it was typical of the way science progressed in the nineteenth century and has continued to develop in the twentieth, where research continually illuminates links between one aspect of the natural world and another. This has become evident in the fields of biology, chemistry and geology.

In the late seventeenth century, a scientific study began on the way the earth's geographical features had been formed, and in the West it became appreciated that fossils were indeed the remains of extinct animals, a fact apparent in China centuries before but unknown elsewhere. By the time the nineteenth century dawned, much geological evidence had been amassed and it seemed clear that in spite of disasters like earthquakes and volcanic eruptions, geological changes occurred only very slowly. Meanwhile the study of plant and animal life was also progressing. In the mid-eighteenth century a vast new classification of living things had been drawn up by Linnaeus (1707-78) in Sweden. Linnaeus felt that he had at last uncovered the divine plan of creation, but many others disagreed. In France there were some who believed that the species of animals were not fixed once and for all and this idea gathered force although there was no agreement about how these changes occurred. Some thought they were due purely to inherited characteristics, or to the effects of the environment. It was not until the mid-nineteenth century, after his five-year voyage on the *Beagle*, that Charles Darwin (1809-82) was able to gather sufficient evidence from the way species were distributed over the earth's surface to propose that species changed, and did so by a process of natural selection. This view was to have immense repercussions.

Another nineteenth-century development that opened up a new aspect of science in the twentieth century was the study of organic chemistry. When the nineteenth century arrived chemistry was entering a new phase, to be extended even further by the adoption of an atomic theory to explain the nature of matter. By the middle of this century it was discovered that some substances present in living things were ordinary and familiar chemicals. Previously it had been thought that living materials were totally different. A new field of research opened up; on the one hand, there was 'organic' chemistry which led to the development of a new generation of synthetic materials, including dyes and, on the other, the science of biochemistry which has reached a peak in the discovery of the double helix of DNA and the mechanism of genetic coding. Medicine, closely married to explorations in physics and chemistry, is being transformed.

In the physical sciences there have been immense strides forward since the end of the nineteenth century, speeded by the development of microminiature circuits and the computer. The nineteenth-century atomic theory led to experimental work which in its turn generated theories about the nature of the atom and, in the end, the appreciation that atoms are themselves compounded of still smaller particles that behave in a way best described in terms of statistics; this study is now known as quantum theory. It has led to an understanding of the nature of stars and nuclear energy.

Our quest to discover more about the universe has led us into strange new realms. In the first quarter of this century, Newton's ideas of space, time and gravitation were seen to be only a special case of a more general theory: relativity. Our sun was found to be part of a star island, one of billions of such islands existing in an expanding universe. Advancing technology has brought about both manned lunar landings and the near observation of planets by equipment sent to probe deep space. As history continues, these and other progressive techniques open new chapters in our scientific adventure.

SCIENCE AND TECHNOLOGY Today, though the subjects are still separate, scientists and technologists work together to produce the advances which influence every aspect of our daily life. The car assembly lines *(below* and *bottom)* are largely automated, the manufacturing process being initiated by computer. Computer science, too, has been the vital catalyst in man's conquest of space *(right)*.

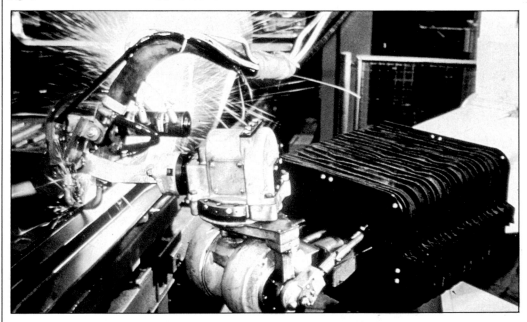

Astronomy

Curiosity about the heavens seems to have existed as long as human thought; it is found wherever we uncover evidence of civilization, back beyond the bounds of written history. Yet, although the history of astronomy is many centuries old, it falls into four distinct observational phases.

The first and longest phase is that without optical aids, astronomy by direct observation using only the eye. This was primarily an era of plotting the skies and watching the movements of the sun, moon and planets. It lasted for thousands of years, from the distant past until the beginning of the seventeenth century. Only then, a mere 38 decades ago, did astronomy's second phase begin; this was the age of the optical telescope. To an extent, this second phase is still with us: modern astronomers continue to use optical telescopes and are planning new and more advanced instruments. The stars and planets are still plotted, but ever more precisely, while the telescope has also opened up new fields of study that had been impossible before.

Astronomy's third phase was the development in the 1950s, after the Second World War, of radio astronomy. This revealed new vistas of the universe because radio telescopes could detect objects in space which could not be seen optically. It next became clear that observations in types of radiation other than light were important, and this gave impetus to the use of rocket technology as an aid to scientific research. Advanced engineering techniques that had been developed first for military purposes found great peacetime applications, and ushered in phase four. This last phase has had spectacular results including the landing of men on the moon and the production of extraordinary pictures of Mars, Jupiter and Saturn. It has also had a less glamorous but no less fascinating aspect: the launching of special telescopes into space. In the long term, the orbiting optical telescopes and telescopes specially designed to see the universe at X-ray, gamma ray, ultraviolet and infrared wavelengths will probably prove the more significant. The reason for this is that X-rays and gamma rays never reach earth; they are blocked out by our atmosphere. Ultraviolet and infrared radiation only fare a little better: some of it reaches ground-based observations but much does not. Thus space-telescopes are capable of revealing a myriad of previously undetected events.

Yet astronomy is not, and never has been, a totally observational science. Even in very early times, observations were analyzed mathematically; the derivation of a lunar calendar is the simplest example. But as early as Babylonian times, some 2,300 years ago, a highly developed mathematical astronomy had already been devised for describing the movements of the sun, moon and planets. This mathematical aspect had two important effects. First, it laid stress on the need for accurate measurement and, in a sense, the history of astronomy is

also the history of a growing ability to position the celestial bodies precisely. This developed a little in the hands of the Greeks and still further some 1,300 years later with the giant instruments devised by Islamic astronomers, but it was in the late sixteenth century that much smaller instruments were first constructed with immense precision by the Danish astronomer Tycho Brahe. It was Brahe, too, who discovered that further accuracy could be obtained if the errors inherent in an observing instrument were determined before use, and in due course this technique was adopted by all scientists who used measuring equipment.

The second effect of the mathematical aspect of astronomy has been its power to help in understanding the universe itself. The most famous example of this is Isaac Newton's solution of the problem that had puzzled all the earliest astronomers: the full explanation of why the moon and planets move as they are observed to do. More recently, Einstein's theory of relativity (1915), in which all motion is relative and there is no fixed point in space, has

DISCOVERIES, CENTRES OF LEARNING AND OBSERVATORIES A fundamental curiosity about the heavens seems to be common to every civilization. Astronomy's beginnings can be found, therefore, in the early cultures of Mesopotamia, Greece and Egypt, as well as China. At least some of the ancient sites around the world were used either to observe or record celestial movements; since the development of the telescope in the seventeenth century, observatories such as those at Greenwich and Paris have been the sites for major discoveries which have radically altered our perception of the universe. Today, with the invention of radio astronomy, we are able to observe a host of events in our own Galaxy and beyond.

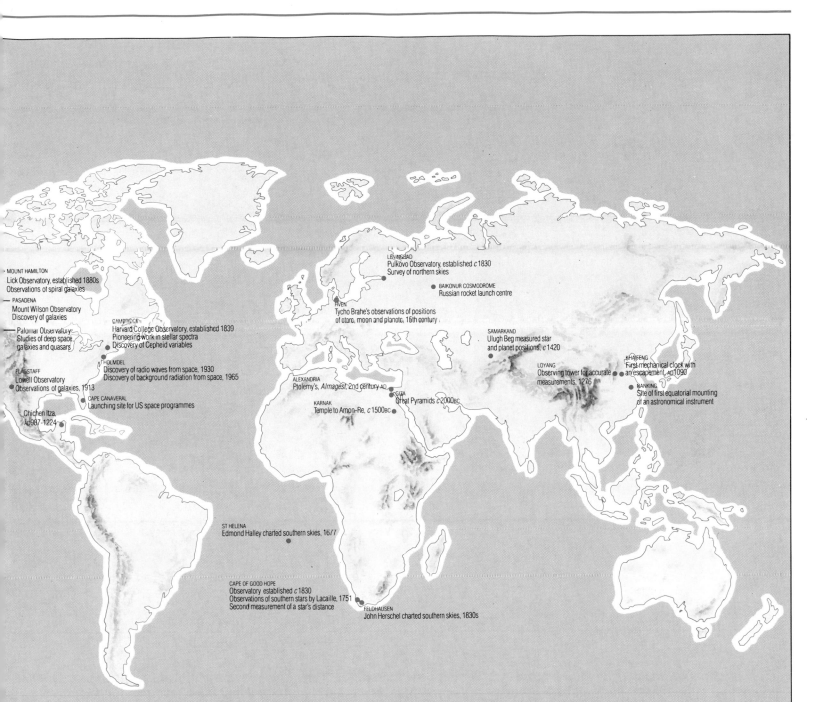

MOUNT HAMILTON
Lick Observatory, established 1880s
Observations of spiral galaxies

PASADENA
Mount Wilson Observatory
Discovery of galaxies

Palomar Observatory
Studies of deep space,
galaxies and quasars

CAMBRIDGE
Harvard College Observatory, established 1839
Pioneering work in stellar spectra
Discovery of Cepheid variables

FLAGSTAFF
Lowell Observatory
Observations of galaxies, 1913

HOLMDEL
Discovery of radio waves from space, 1930
Discovery of background radiation from space, 1965

CAPE CANAVERAL
Launching site for US space programmes

Chichen Itza,
AD 987-1224

LENINGRAD
Pulkovo Observatory, established c 1830
Survey of northern skies

BAIKONUR COSMODROME
Russian rocket launch centre

HVEN
Tycho Brahe's observations of positions
of stars, moon and planets, 16th century

SAMARKAND
Ulugh Beg measured star
and planet positions, c 1420

ALEXANDRIA
Ptolemy's, Almagest, 2nd century AD

KARNAK
Temple to Amon-Re, c 1500 BC

GIZA
Great Pyramids c 2000 BC

LOYANG
Observing tower for accurate
measurements, 1276

KHAIFENG
First mechanical clock with
an escapement, AD 1090

NANKING
Site of first equatorial mounting
of an astronomical instrument

ST HELENA
Edmond Halley charted southern skies, 1677

CAPE OF GOOD HOPE
Observatory established c 1830
Observations of southern stars by Lacaille, 1751
Second measurement of a star's distance

FELDHAUSEN
John Herschel charted southern skies, 1830s

also had a profound effect on modern concepts of the universe. Calculations based on it have shown some strange results which experiments and observations have confirmed, despite the fact that these results were neither expected nor noticed before the theory had been proposed. What is more, the use of relativity theory has made it possible not only to develop detailed theories about the nature of the universe, but also about its beginning and likely end.

The theory of relativity is not primarily a theory of astronomy but a theory about the whole physical world. It is a study of the universe which does, however, show its effects very clearly and allow many of its conclusions to be checked. That such a theory should be important in the scientific examination of the universe underlines an important factor which has come increasingly to the fore during the last 150 years or so: the way physical science and theories about physical science can be applied to astronomy. Indeed, things have gone so far in this direction that some scientists now consider astronomy to be a branch of physics!

Quantum theory was devised in 1900 to explain the way atoms radiate energy. Its formulation laid the foundations of nuclear physics and it has helped to explain much in astronomy that was previously obscure. It has proved vital in discovering the sources of radiation of the sun and others stars. Considered with relativity, quantum theory has also allowed astronomers, in the last 60 years, to work out the events likely to occur in the later stages of a star's life. Current theories consider that at such a time stars become superdense bodies, known as 'white dwarfs', 'neutron stars' or 'black holes', depending on how massive they are to begin with. Once again we see the interplay of what were once quite separate disciplines.

These various strands in the development of astronomy often run concurrently, overlapping and interweaving from time to time. It would, therefore, be confusing to give a purely chronological description of the discoveries that have been made; in what follows, the progress of each aspect of the subject has been considered separately.

Pyramids and Megaliths

Astronomy began when people first started to notice regularities in the heavens and the demand for accurate observation was evident very early in the history of mankind. Once the regularity of the moon's phases was measured — and this was comparitively easy because no special equipment was needed — observations requiring more precision were soon in demand. Instruments were devised; the Egyptians, for instance, used a forked stick, carrying a cord with a weight at its lower end, to mark the moon's rising and setting points on the horizon. Using their knowledge of the stars and the sequence in which the constellations follow each other around the heavens, they could use heliacal risings and settings — risings and settings of the stars just before sunrise or just after sunset — to determine where the sun might be.

In Egypt the annual flooding of the Nile was the most significant factor of the seasonal year and it came at about the time of the heliacal rising of Sothis (now known as Sirius), the brightest star in the northern skies. It was reasonable, then, that some tomb buildings such as the Great Pyramids should be so built that one part of them was aligned on Sothis' rising-point on the horizon just before dawn. Certain other buildings were also astronomically orientated, like the temple to the sun god Amon-Re at Karnak where the sun shone directly down between the colonnades at the midsummer solstice. Such orientations of buildings indicates some astronomical knowledge as, of course, does the preparation of a solar calendar, but it must be appreciated that the reasons for making the orientations in the first place may have

CHARTING THE HEAVENS Early Egyptian cbservations of the stars were based on the heliacal principle *(bottom right)*. By observing the rising and setting of the stars immediately before sunrise, or just after sunset, they were able to calculate the position of the sun in the sky with a fair degree of accuracy. In northern Europe, sighting stones *(below* and *below right)* were used to mark the extreme positions of sun and moon. Stonehenge *(far right)* is thought by some astronomers to be the most sophisticated example of this system. It has been argued, notably by the astronomer Gerald Hawkins, that Stonehenge was planned as a huge astronomical instrument to measure accurately the movements of the sun and moon, together with eclipses.

been religious or magical, and had little to do with a curiosity about the heavens themselves.

The construction of astronomically orientated buildings was to be adopted long after Egyptian times by some of the Meso-American civilizations, especially the Mayan. At Chichen Itza in Yucatan, Mexico, an observatory building was aligned with extreme positions of the planet Venus on the horizon. Clearly, the building was used to observe the times when Venus reached such extreme points, for they were concerned with a long cycle of time (65 years) based on the appropriate returns of Venus (584 days). But this was some 3,000 years

later than the period of the great burst of pyramid building in Egypt.

In Europe, particularly in Brittany, the west of England and in Scotland, there are many stone circles and some astronomically orientated tombs. In these more northern countries, the acute sloping angle of the rising and setting sun against the horizon, together with a long period of twilight, prevented heliacal risings and settings being used because observers were unable to see close enough to the horizon at sunrise and sunset. They had therefore to use sighting stones to mark the extreme positions of the sun and moon. Between at least 2500BC and 1500BC many stone circles were erected; Stonehenge, near Salisbury, England, is the most famous. Some seem clearly to have been used for religious ceremonies but this does not mean they were not also used as observatories for noting extreme points. What is yet to be investigated is the motive; were they merely markers for determining a seasonal calendar or were they also used to enquire into the motions of celestial bodies, in other words for pure astronomy? Was Stonehenge used for predicting eclipses, or are we imagining this because of our more detailed knowledge of the skies, some 4,000 years later?

Early Ideas

THE EGYPTIAN COSMOS Two views of the Egyptian cosmos *(above* and *right)* both show the importance the Egyptians gave their gods and goddesses in their view of the heavens. In the top picture, Shu, the god of the air, is taking the weight of Nut, the starry goddess of the sky; in the second picture, the reclining figure accompanying Nut is the god Qeb, representing the earth.

In open country, away from city lights, the heavens appear to stretch overhead like a giant dome. This is how they must have seemed to the earliest peoples, wherever they may have been, and it is interesting now to look at the way they interpreted what they saw, to find out how they integrated this evidence into a concept of the universe. The earliest records of this are from Egypt and Mesopotamia, and the way in which these civilizations tackled the question shows immense differences in outlook. One was far more 'scientific' than the other.

The Egyptian picture of the universe was essentially an expression of their belief in a host of gods and goddesses. To them, the dome of heaven was the star-spangled body of the goddess Nut, goddess of the sky. She was imagined standing on both hands and feet, her body stretching in one long line. Of course, it is clear that this picture is of the skies having an elongated shape rather than the shape of a dome. At the same time, Egypt is a long narrow land, centred on the Nile; in other words it runs very nearly north and south, and spreads out only a little way to the east and west. In consequence, the long body of Nut would satisfactorily cover Egyptian skies.

Although Nut supported herself by standing on hands and feet, she was nevertheless helped by the god Shu, whose upstretched arms took some of the weight. Shu was the god of the air and we can, perhaps, perceive behind this sym-

bolism a belief that the sky was supported by the air beneath it. Below Nut and Shu was the reclining figure of the god Qeb (or Geb), the earth-god. He is often shown lying partly on his side with one leg bent upwards.

It was not the case that the Egyptians imagined the earth to have arms, legs, a torso and a head, yet this is how they depicted it. Nor did they believe the air took the form of Shu, or even that the heavens took the exact form of Nut. Obviously, the aim behind the scheme was not an attempt to draw a scientific picture of the cosmos. Rather, the Egyptians were drawing a symbolic picture which expressed their belief that the gods ruled every aspect of creation, and at the same time to depict something of the relationship between them — Nut, for instance, was Qeb's sister and wife — with only an echo of the natural world about it.

The Mesopotamian picture was a very different one: their dome of heaven was solid and a true dome. It was supported at its rim by a ring of mountains and the earth lay beneath it. The earth was not flat but had a bulge in the centre and within the earth itself were nether regions; these were the abode of the dead. The shape of the earth, like that of the heavens, was circular, and around its rim lay a great trench filled with water. Partly because of the mountains near Sumer, and partly due to the fact that in every direction overland from the Tigris and Euphrates valley travellers eventually reached

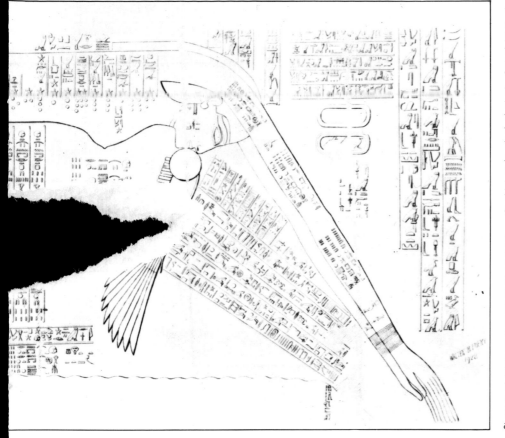

water, geographical facts were well accommodated in this conception of the universe. Moreover, the Mesopotamians believed there was water above the dome of heaven; this came through openings in the dome to fall as rain. This may now seem a very simplistic explanation, but it was nonetheless effective. Incidentally, it is referred to in the Bible (*Genesis* 1:6), where God is described as dividing '... the waters which were under the firmament from the waters which were above the firmament ...'; Abraham, it should be remembered, came from the Mesopotamian city of Ur and thus it is quite possible that Mesopotamian views coloured the view of Creation developed by the Jews as part of the Old Testament.

The Mesopotamian picture of the universe is physical, based on the observations of the everyday world. The supporting ring of mountains is a case in point. Mesopotamians were aware of the fact that no solid dome of heaven stretching down into the water could be supported on air alone. At the same time, gods and goddesses were present; there was a passage along the tops of the mountains within the dome through which they could pass. Yet these broad conceptions illustrate a giant step forward. Here, for the first time, was a description of the universe that elevated physical facts above everything else. In brief, it was a far more rational and 'scientific' approach than that adopted by the Egyptians.

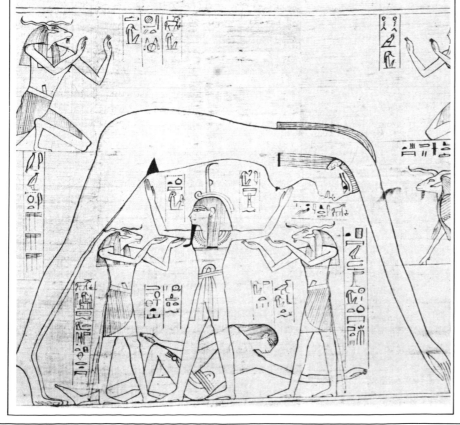

THE BABYLONIAN UNIVERSE The Babylonian view of the universe *(above)* was more sophisticated than the Egyptian prototype, based on physical observation more than mythological beliefs. The Babylonians saw the dome of heaven as having real and solid existence, supported at its rim by a ridge of mountains. Between the ridges lay the circular earth, slightly bulging at the centre. Both heaven and earth were surrounded by water; in the first case, this penetrates to the earth in the form of rain.

The Greek Universe

The Greeks inherited ideas from surrounding areas of the Mediterranean and the Aegean. They were influenced by the Egyptians and by the contemporary civilizations that grew up in the Cyclades — the islands to the southeast of the Greek mainland — and in Crete. Trade existed among these communities and with Mesopotamia, whose influence on Cretan jewellery, for instance, can be seen as early as 2500BC. Greek culture was also affected around 2300BC by the arrival of invaders, first from west Turkey, the Balkans and south Russia when the Cyclades were overrun; then 1,000 years later, when the Cretan civilization was destroyed. Moreover, as the seas were for a time controlled by the maritime power of the Phoenicians who came from the Lebanon and parts of Syria and Israel, this civilization also played its part in the formation of what we now know as Greek culture. It was the Phoenicians who introduced an alphabetic script that was modified and used by the Greeks and, incidentally, later became the basis of our own alphabetic writing.

Lastly there was the invasion by the Dorians who, sometime around 1100BC, arrived from the northwest and north-central mainland into the south of Greece — the area of the Peloponnese mountains — and brought with them still more new cultural ideas. Of these the most significant was a great sense of symmetry and feeling for shape, which is evident in their pottery and sculpture. This was to play a vital part in the development of Greek astronomy and mathematics.

The earliest specifically Greek view of the universe is found in the epic poems attributed to Homer; this view depicts the earth as a flattish disc floating on water, the water and the earth being encased in a sphere. Clearly, this owes something to Mesopotamian ideas — the earth with water around it — but the concept of a dome, a hemisphere, has been replaced by a sphere. Why did the Greeks do this? They could not know from experience that the starry skies would appear like a dome even from underneath the earth. It seems certain that the real reason for the change was aesthetic. A sphere is more elegant than a hemisphere, and an earth fixed in the centre of this sphere would have appealed more to a sophisticated, architectural Dorian cast of mind than would an earth stuck to the bottom of a dome.

The next development was instigated by Pythagoras, who in the fifth century BC, some three and a half centuries after Homer, continued with the spherical universe but turned the earth from a flattish disc into a sphere. This again was probably partly for aesthetic reasons, but it was tempered by observations of the curved shadow cast by the earth on the moon during a lunar eclipse. Pythagoras also suggested that the sun, moon and planets move inside the sphere of the heavens in circles; this was to lead to the next development of the Greek cosmos,

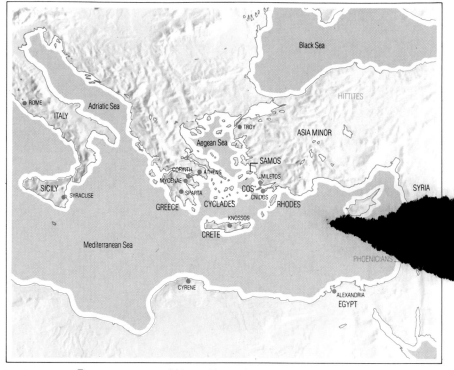

THE GREEK WORLD The civilization of Ancient Greece had a lasting influence on the development of Western thought, in the sciences as well as the arts. The great intellectual centres of Athens and Alexandria saw important contributions made in every branch of learning, from astronomy, to biology and medicine (above). Aristotle developed a geocentric view of the universe (below), in which four elements — earth, water, air and fire — were surrounded by the sphere of the fixed stars and the sphere of the planets. These spheres were composed of a fifth element — 'aether'

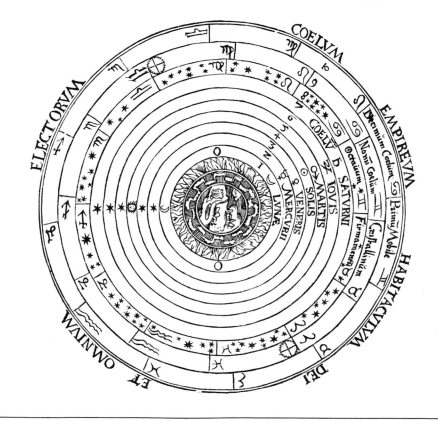

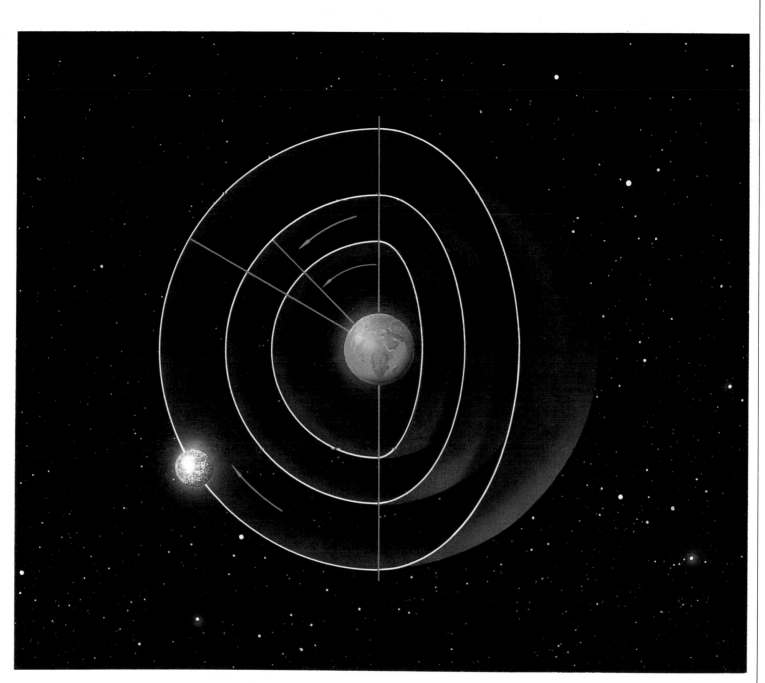

which was proposed sometime about 360BC by Eudoxos.

Eudoxos devised a scheme of concentric spheres, similar to the nests of ivory balls within balls carved by the Chinese. At the centre of the spheres lay the earth, while the outermost sphere represented the spherical universe. The ingenuity of the scheme was that the spheres were pivoted at various angles to one another to account more accurately for all the observed motions of sun, moon and planets.

Eudoxos probably looked on his spheres as a mathematical description, not having any real existence, but this was not the view of his successor Aristotle (384-322BC), who seems to have thought of them as real. However, Aristo-

tle's greatest contribution to the Greek conception of the universe was not his solidification of Eudoxos' spheres, but his welding of the four elements — earth, air, fire, and water — into one vast scheme of astronomy and physics. In a spherical universe with the sun fixed at the centre — Pythagoras' idea — he suggested that change was confined to things on the earth and in the air surrounding it. The heavens were changeless, which was reasonable enough since they always appeared the same and had done so for countless generations. He believed them to be composed of an unalterable fifth essence. And it was, he thought, their nature to rotate ceaselessly at a regular rate as Pythagoras had originally proposed.

THE MOVING MOON Eudoxos of Cnidos devised an elaborate theoretical system of spheres to account for the moon's motion (above). The spheres are pivoted at angles to each other to account for the movements he observed over one month (inner arrow), 18 years (centre arrow) and a day (outer arrow). Eudoxos went on to apply the same system to the movements of the planets.

Discovery of the Planets

PLANETARY MOVEMENTS The Mesopotamians were the first race to attempt to express their observations of the movements of the sun, moon and visible planets — notably Venus — in mathematical form. By relating the specific position in the sky to the time of a specific observation, a characteristic zigzag line can be plotted (above), indicating how quickly the object under observation reaches its extreme positions.

Jupiter (16 moons)

We do not know how early the planets, which at first included the sun and moon, were discovered. To the most primitive observers of the sky,the moon could readily be seen to weave a monthly course among the stars, and the Egyptians were aware of the motion of the sun among the stars. It was the Mesopotamians who first began to study these motions scientifically, applying mathematics to express the results of their observations, although they did not, as far as we know, commit themselves to any particular planetary theory as the Greeks were later to do.

This early Mesopotamian work has been discovered partly by examining the tens of thousands of early cuneiform clay tablets. These date from about the first half of the third millenium BC, and most are collected in the vast library at Nippur. Others are from the later Mesopotamian library of King Ashurbanipal, who, in the seventh century BC, collected some 25,000 tablets at his palace at Nineveh. From these we find they observed the sun, moon and all the brighter planets, particularly Venus which, at times, is the brightest object in the night sky after the moon. At regular intervals the Mesopotamians noted their positions in the sky and their rate of motion. If these observations are plotted on a graph, zigzag lines result, thus indicating the rates at which these bodies reach their extreme positions, and it is clearly evident that the Mesopotamians were making a mathematical analysis of celestial movements.

The Mesopotamian discoveries found their way to Greece, where they were used to construct mathematical 'models' to account for the observed motions. However, all the Greek models adopted from Pythagoras the basic concept that the planets — heavenly bodies — had circular, or heavenly, motions and travelled at an unvarying speed, despite observations that showed this was not the case. According to observation, no planet moved at an unvarying rate across the sky; some, like Mars, Jupiter and Saturn, perform loops in the sky, sometimes moving forwards, sometimes backwards. Thus the problem facing Greek and later astronomers was, in the medieval phrase, to 'save the phenomena', in other words to account by some mathematical means for the observed motions using only regular motion in a circle. The form of mathematics the Greeks used to achieve this was geometry, based on the *Elements* laid down by Euclid, at which they excelled.

The concentric spheres theory suggested by Eudoxos was one way of 'saving the phenomena', but another method, due originally to the mathematician Apollonios of Perga who proposed it towards the end of the third century BC, used the 'epicycle' and 'deferent'. The epicycle was the smaller of the two circles, carrying

Pluto

Neptune (2 moons)

Saturn (17 moons)

Uranus (5 moons)

the planet on its circumference; the deferent was larger, with the centre of the epicycle moving round on its circumference. The earth was put at the centre of the deferent. Although the epicycle and deferent moved at a regular rate, the theory still accounted for the loops and irregularities observed in planetary motions.

The great Hellenistic astronomer Ptolomy of Alexandria used this system in the second century AD but, to account better for the observed motions, he had to offset the centre of all deferents slightly from the centre of the earth. Astronomers seem to have accepted this without objection, probably because Ptolemy's *Almagest*, which contained his scheme, was a masterpiece of clear explanation. However, in

the Renaissance, objections were soon raised. Copernicus (1473-1543) disliked the number of epicycles then deemed necessary to account for the observations, and also thought Ptolemy had gone against the principle of regular motion. His way of 'saving the phenomenon' was to put the sun at the centre of the deferents.

Yet some 80 years after Copernicus' *De Revolutionibus* (1543) appeared, the German astronomer Johannes Kepler (1571-1630), using the very accurate observations of Tycho Brahe, showed that everyone had been mistaken. The planets move round the sun in ellipses, not in circles, and at a continually varying rate. This behaviour was not explained until Newton and his new laws about motion.

THE SOLAR SYSTEM The nine known planets which make up our solar system are shown *(above)*. Their sizes in the illustration are related to their actual masses. In addition, the system includes the sun, the various moons orbiting the planets, comets, asteroids and meteoroids. Pluto, the outermost planet, is 39 Astronomical Units (3,660 million miles/5,900 million km) from the sun.

Charting the Skies

The earliest known charting of the skies is to be found in Egyptian tombs and in Mesopotamia. However, of the drawings of Egyptian constellations, only one can now be identified for certain; this is our constellation of the Plough or Dipper, which they showed as a bull. We do know that they considered the bright star Sirius (then known as Sothis) to be of particular significance because it appeared at the time of the annual inundation of the Nile, and that, in order to help in time-reckoning during the night, they divided the entire sky into 'decans' or tenths. However, since each decan covered an arc of 36 degrees, this was too large a division to permit the definition of stars' precise positions in the sky.

The Mesopotamian astronomers recognized constellations too, and we know that they had mapped out the equivalent of what we call Taurus (the Bull), Leo (the Lion) and Scorpio (the Scorpion). By 700BC at the latest, they were able to specify the positions of the separate stars in each constellation, and they also recognized

that the sun, moon and planets all move within a certain narrow band of sky. This band later became known as the 'zodiac'. The signs of the zodiac are still a feature of astronomy today .

Of Greek astronomers, the first to compile a catalogue of star positions was Hipparchos of Rhodes, who did so some time about 120BC, though many observations of position had been made a century earlier by two astronomers, Aristyllus and Timocharis. To specify star positions in any detail, other than by description (for example, 'the star at the tip of the tail of the Little Bear — Ursa Minor' or 'the star in the right shoulder of Perseus') it is necessary to quote the angles at which a star is observed. This is because all measurement of the distances between stars on the celestial sphere is in angles. (Even today, the celestial sphere is a convenient way to describe the sky when it comes to positional measurement.)

The Greeks specified star positions by measuring their celestial longitude and celestial latitude; these are coordinates which

north celestial pole

north pole of the ecliptic

autumnal equinox

N

earth

celestial equator

S

first point of Aries or spring equinox

ecliptic or apparent path of the sun

south pole of the ecliptic

south celestial pole

CELESTIAL SPHERE To chart the skies, astronomers still find it convenient to imagine the stars fixed on the inside of a sphere. The drawing shows how the sun moves to its

highest point in the sky and then moves down again. This is the summer solstice. Winter solstice is when the sun is at its lowest point. The picture illustrates how summer

solstice for people in the northern hemisphere must be the winter solstice for those in the southern hemisphere, and vice versa.

CHINESE STAR CHART The Chinese Tunhuang star map of AD940 is, despite its age, a Mercator projection. On the left is the Plough or Dipper and comparing this with a modern star chart or planisphere will allow other constellations to be recognized.

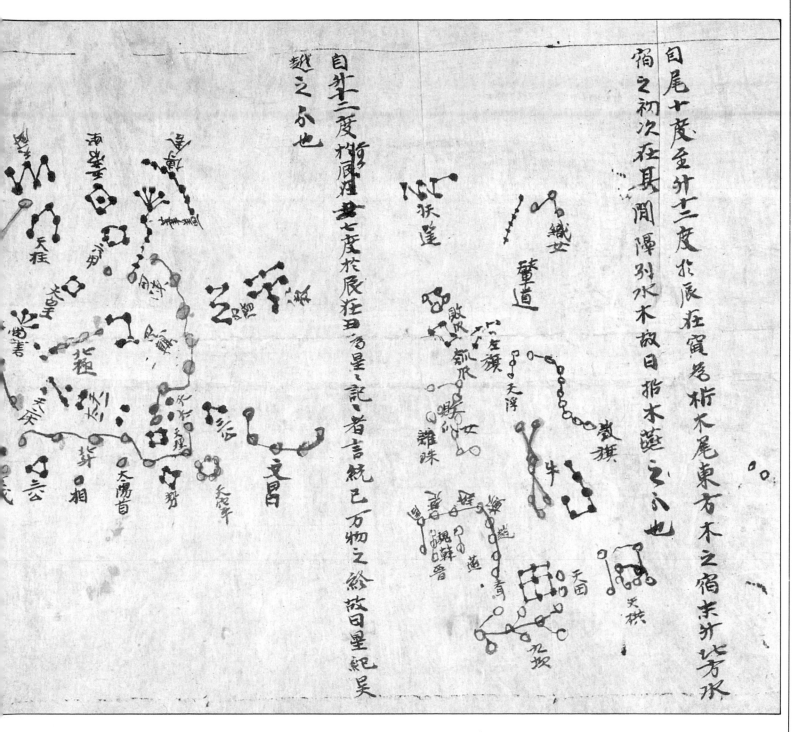

lie along the ecliptic (the apparent path of the sun in the sky) and northwards and southwards from it. But these coordinates are not unique. For instance, Chinese astronomers were much concerned with the north celestial pole — the point in the sky about which the whole celestial sphere seems to pivot due to the earth's daily rotation. Because of this, they measured star positions northwards and southwards from the celestial pole, and eastwards and westwards along the celestial equator, which is 90 degrees from the celestial pole and so the equivalent on

the celestial sphere of the earth's equator. They did not use the ecliptic. The Chinese system is similar to the one used today; since the end of the sixteenth century astronomers in the West have given star positions in coordinates along the celestial equator and northwards and southwards from it. These coordinates are now called 'right ascension' and 'declination', rather than celestial longitude and latitude.

The point from which right ascension starts is the point where the sun, moving from south to north, goes across the celestial equator. This

CHANGING VIEW OF THE SKIES A star chart from Flamsteed's star atlas *Historia Coelestis Britannica* (1725) *(top)* and Edmond Halley's chart of the southern stars made in 1678 from his observations on the island of St Helena *(above)* is worth comparing with a twentieth-century version. The photographic chart *(above right)* is a part of Franklin Adams' photographic compilation made in 1910. Such a chart shows the sky as it appears — there are no constellation figures and no errors of draughtsmanship. It also shows far more stars than the old hand-drawn type of mapping.

crossing of the ecliptic and celestial equator is known as the vernal or spring equinox, because the sun reaches it on about 21 March, at which time day and night are equal in length. But the vernal equinox is not fixed in space; it moves backwards (westwards) very slowly — only about 1.3 degrees per century. This astonishing result of precise measurement was discovered by Hipparchos, and we now know that it is caused by a movement of the earth's axis in space.

The Chinese seem to have been the first to prepare star atlases, and to show the stars as dots connected by thin lines, for describing the constellations. Moreover, the great star map drawn at Tunhuang in northwest China in the tenth century AD displays the heavens on a flat sheet in what is now known as the 'Mercator projection', after the Belgian cartographer who devised the same system five centuries later. Star atlases did not appear in the West until after the Renaissance; then they used coor-

dinates of the stars and dots of various sizes to indicate differences in brightness. These were based on a system also devised by Hipparchos.

The most important of the early Western star atlases was that by Johann Bayer. Published in 1603, it showed the constellations of the southern hemisphere skies as well as the northern and, most importantly, introduced a new way of designating stars, using the letters of the Greek alphabet. The brightest star of each constellation was alpha, the next brightest beta, and so on. In Orion, for example, Betelgeuse was also called alpha Orionis, Rigel was beta Orionis, and so on down the scale. Later on, in other atlases, stars were given Roman letters or numbers after the letters of the Greek alphabet were exhausted, and some objects like nebulae were known by numbers associated with their appearance in special catalogues.

Catalogues and atlases continued to improve as accuracy in observing increased. In the seventeenth century, the use of the telescope

SHAPES OF CONSTELLATIONS This illustration of the celestial sphere shows some of the figures associated in the West with the constellations, including Cancer and Leo. It describes the celestial sphere as seen from outside, but because the earth is generally considered by astrologers to be at the centre of this sphere, we as earth-bound observers would not have such a perception of the skies.

ushered in further progress in precision observing; positions could be determined with at least 10 times the accuracy previously obtainable. Then, over the years, improvements in the optical quality and size of telescopes made it possible to chart still dimmer objects and to do so more precisely than before. In 1885, Paul and Prosper Henry in Paris began to apply the newly invented art of photography to charting the sky; they were so successful that an international photographic sky chart — the *Carte du Ciel* — was proposed and many observatories agreed to help in compiling it though, unfortunately, not all completed their work. Later, in the 1930s, the Estonian optician, Bernhard Schmidt (1879-1935), invented a new kind of telescope which could photograph areas of the sky 25 times larger than was possible previously, and this extended the power of photographic charting. In the 1950s, a large Schmidt telescope at Palomar Observatory, California, made a photographic chart of the whole sky visible from the observatory; this has proved to be of immense significance to astronomers.

The importance of photography in charting the skies is two-fold. On the one hand, a photographic plate does not miss any ordinarily visible stars and allows dim objects to be detected because their images can be built up by a long exposure. This is something the eye cannot do. Again, a photographic plate can be examined under a microscope and positions of stars measured with a degree of precision impossible for an observer to achieve at the telescope. In the 1970s, computerized equipment was employed to measure the thousands of images on a celestial photograph automatically; it is now generally used for this time-consuming task, so releasing astronomers for other work. The most advanced project of this kind is at the Institute of Astronomy at Cambridge University. Here, plates are examined, positions measured and charts automatically drawn up of selected celestial objects.

Distances in Space

Measuring the distances of the sun, moon and stars from earth has always been an aim of astronomers, but it is difficult to achieve because there are no direct methods. Estimates were made; the early Chinese, for example, who adopted the Mesopotamian system of the universe, considered the dome of heaven to be some 25,000 miles (40,000km) away. This echoes the view that celestial bodies were a long but not infinite distance away.

The first to try to measure distances by observation were the Greeks. Some time during the third century BC, Aristarchos of Samos (310-230BC), the astronomer who, as Copernicus knew, had suggested that the earth orbited the sun, tried to find the distances and sizes of both the sun and moon. By applying his considerable knowledge of geometry, his idea was to measure the observed angle between the moon and the sun (the angle MES) when the

moon reached its first quarter and when, therefore, the angle EMS is a right-angle. Unfortunately, the exact moment of first quarter is difficult to judge and the angle MES, which is itself close to a right-angle is difficult to determine precisely. Aristarchos' results were inaccurate because of this and other reasons. He found, therefore, that the sun was between 18 and 20 times further off than the moon, whereas the correct value is closer to 340; but at least he made an attempt at the measurement.

Hipparchos, a century later, was more successful. He again treated the problem mathematically, but his method was more practical than that of Aristarchos. First of all he obtained the moon's distance by studying the observations of a total eclipse of the sun. At Alexandria only part of the sun's disc was hidden though it was totally obscured to observers in the northwest of Turkey. From this, he was able

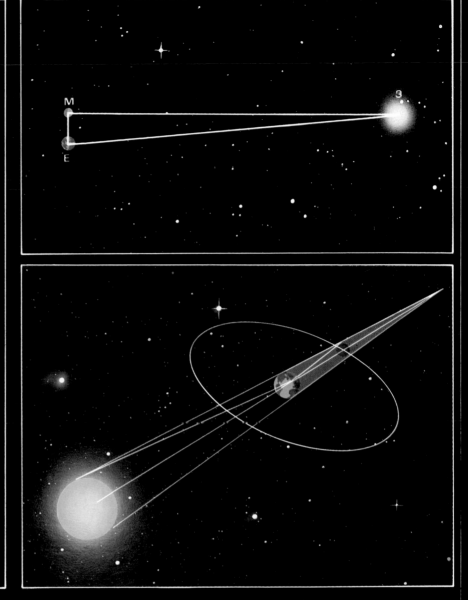

to find the distance of the moon expressed in terms of the size of the earth: he found it to be at least 29½ times and not more than 33½ times the earth's diameter. The modern estimation is that it is 30 times. Hipparchos next attempted to discover the distance between the earth and the sun from the shadows cast during a solar eclipse. Because the sun is so very much further away the angles involved are tiny, and the problem was much more difficult. This may be judged from the fact that Hipparchos was only able to prove that the sun was at a minimum distance of 245 times the earth's diameter and a maximum of 1,250 times. The correct value is 390 times, but all the same Hipparchos was nearer the mark than Aristarchos. Indeed, his researches proved that he was the first astronomer to work in a systematic fashion and his conclusion, provided much of the basis for the geocentric view of the universe Ptolemy devised.

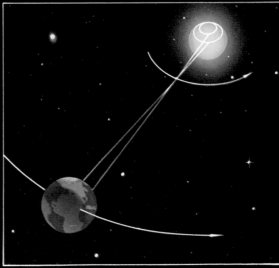

MEASURING DISTANCES
Aristarchos' attempt to measure the distances of the sun (S) and the moon (M) from earth (E) were based on geometry (top). He measured the observed angle between the sun and moon (angle MES) when the angle EMS was a right-angle. Hipparchos used eclipses to determine these distances. In this diagram (above) the moon is eclipsed by the earth and the distance of the moon can be calculated by how much time it takes to pass through the earth's shadow. Halley's idea was to use the transit of Venus to calculate the sun's distance (left).

No real improvement was made for over 1,800 years until new discoveries about planetary orbits by Johannes Kepler (1571-1630) led to more efficient methods of determining the sun's distance. What Kepler found was that the planets orbit the sun in ellipses, and that the average distance from the sun of each planet was proportional to the time the planet took to complete an orbit. With this in mind, if the distance of the earth from some other planet could be determined, and if it were also known how long each took to orbit the sun, their distances from the sun could be discovered. The first to try to do this was Jean Dominique Cassini at the Paris Observatory. In 1672 he measured the distance to Mars using a telescope to determine the small angles. He obtained a value of about 86 million miles (139 million km) which is very close to the modern value of almost 93 million miles (150 million km).

The astronomer English Edmond Halley (1656-1742), who is known mainly for the comet named after him, pointed out that Venus comes closer to the earth than Mars and should, therefore, give an improved value for the distance. However, when Venus is at its closest it lies between the earth and the sun, so it can only be observed on those rare occasions when it is seen to cross or transit the sun's disc. Halley first made his suggestions about Venus in 1691,

but it was not until 1761 and 1769 that such transits occurred. Halley was not alive by then to record the observations, but the astronomers of the time made the necessary observations and when these were collected and examined in 1824 they gave a value of 96 million miles (155 million km).

In the years that followed other methods were developed, and by the 1930s the last extensive optical methods were used on the close approach to the earth of the minor planet Eros. The results took years to analyze but by 1941 Spencer Jones was able to give a value of 93 million miles (150 million km). More recent measurements, using the radar technique of emitting radio pulses to be reflected back by a nearby planet and timing their return journey, have confirmed this value.

The question of determining the distances of the stars has been a great puzzle to astronomers for a long time. Attempts made in antiquity or after the Renaissance all failed. We now know this is because the angles to be observed are so extremely minute — at least some 26 times smaller than the angle to be measured for determining the sun's distances. When the Pole, Nicolaus Copernicus (1473-1543) revived the idea that the planets orbit around the sun, one of the scientific arguments against his theory was that no annual change in star positions was observed. If the earth really were orbiting the sun, then its distance from different stars on the celestial sphere would change as the year passed, yet no such change could be detected. Copernicus claiméd this was because the stars were so far away that the change was too small to see. He was correct, though he could not prove his point. Later, in 1576, Thomas Digges published his view that the universe of stars was not really confined inside a sphere but extended infinitely out into space; however, this did not alter the principles involved, and attempts continued to be made throughout the seventeenth and eighteenth centuries to detect the tiny angles.

The principle of detection was based on the idea of triangulation, which was used first in the ancient world by surveyors, particularly in determining the distance of objects they could not conveniently reach. The method essentially consists of observing the distant object from two separate positions which are at a known distance apart. Once the distance from the earth to the sun was known, astronomers began to make measurements to try to detect the expected 'parallactic shift' of stars, observing the same stars at six-monthly intervals. In this way they could use the diameter of the earths' orbit as their baseline, that is the distance between their observing positions.

Some careful observations along these lines were carried out during the late 1720s by James Bradley (1693-1762) and William Molyneux at Kew near London, and then by Bradley on his own, at Wanstead, which is also near London.

MEASURING DISTANCES One of the fundamental tasks of astronomy over the centuries has been the accurate determination of the distances of the sun, moon, planets and stars from the earth. The Greeks were the first to attempt this in a scientific way but it was not until 1,800 years later that Kepler's theory about planetary orbits led to more efficient methods of determining the sun's distance. In a similar way, attempts to measure the distance of stars failed until observing equipment was improved. The first successful determination of a star's distance was made by Bessel in 1839.

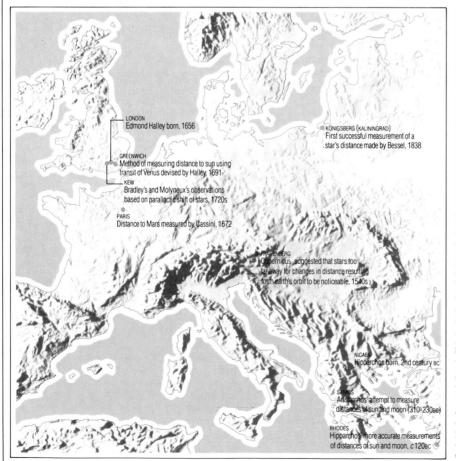

LONDON
Edmond Halley born, 1656

KÖNIGSBERG (KALININGRAD)
First successful measurement of a star's distance made by Bessel, 1838

GREENWICH
Method of measuring distance to sun using transit of Venus devised by Halley, 1691

KEW
Bradley's and Molyneux's observations based on parallactic shift of stars, 1720s

PARIS
Distance to Mars measured by Cassini, 1672

FRAUENBERG
Copernicus suggested that stars too far away for changes in distance resulting forth earth's orbit to be noticeable, 1540s

NICAEA
Hipparchos born, 2nd century BC

SAMOS
Aristarchos' attempt to measure distances of sun and moon (310-230BC)

RHODES
Hipparchos' more accurate measurements of distances of sun and moon, c 120BC

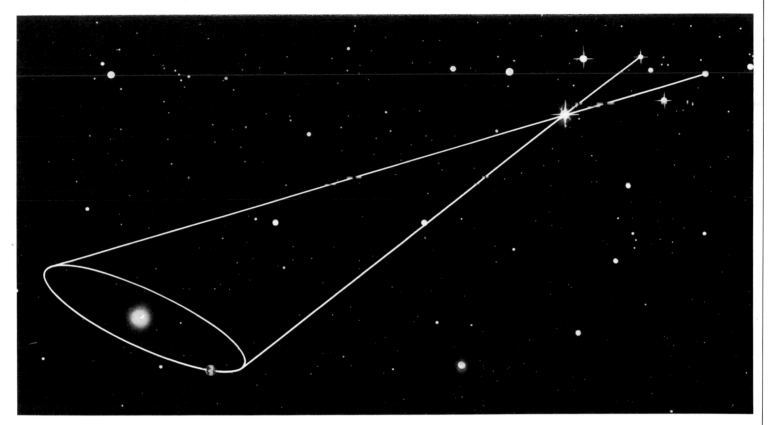

Bradley did observe a shift in position of a particular star, gamma Draconis, which appeared almost overhead and so was ideal for such observations, but the shift was in the wrong direction. Other stars showed this too, and in 1729 he was able to detect the cause: a combination of the motion of the earth through space and the speed at which light travels. These observations were, in fact, the first observational proof that the earth does move in space; every astronomer since Copernicus had taken this on trust, but now there was real evidence for it. However, the true parallactic shift of the stars eluded even Bradley's precise measurements.

The first successful determination of a star's distance was not made until 1839 when Friedrich Bessel (1784-1846) at Konigsberg, (Kaliningrad) achieved success. He used a new, vastly improved refracting telescope, pivoted so that it could readily follow the curved path of the stars across the sky, and with its front lens split into two halves that could move relative to each other and thus provide extremely accurate measurements. With this, Bessel was able to detect the minute angles, which are equivalent to the thickness of a human hair at a distance of 98ft (30m). He found that the star 61 Cygni was at a distance of almost 58 million million miles (some 93 million million km) or 620,000 times as far away as the sun. A year later Thomas Henderson, who from 1823 to 1833 in South Africa had observed the star alpha Centauri, was able to announce its distance from earth as 177,000 times the sun's distance. The values for both stars were underestimates, but they were of the correct order of magnitude. Once these successes had been achieved, others followed. More measurements were made and when photography became available as an aid in the 1880s, still greater precision was available and the distances of many stars could be measured.

Direct measurements of this kind, known technically as measurements of 'trigonometrical parallax', can only take astronomers to distances of some 18 million times the distance to the sun or some 300 light-years. A light-year is a distance, not a period of time; it is more convenient than a mile or a kilometre which are too small to be used to describe astronomical distances. One light-year is 5,800,000 million miles (9,500,000 million km) — the distance light travels in a year at 186,000 miles per second (299,330 km per second). Distances over 100 light-years require methods other than trigonometry. One of these is to use a class of star called a Cepheid, which varies in brightness and whose observed variation of brilliance — the way it 'winks' — is directly linked to its intrinsic luminosity. As the trigonometrical parallax of some Cepheids has been measured, and since the way brightness drops off with distance is also known, Cepheids can be used as standard lighthouses in space. They can take astronomers out some 13 million light-years into space, but for distances greater than this, other methods need to be used.

TRIANGULATION First used by astronomers in ancient times, triangulation can be used to calculate the distances of an inaccessible object. The method consists of observing the object, for example a star, from two different positions that are a known distance apart. When the distance between the earth and the sun was realized astronomers used the diameter of the earth's orbit as the baseline to attempt to detect the 'parallactic shift' of stars, observing the same star at six-monthly intervals.

New Stars

From time to time a bright star appears in the sky in a position where no star has previously been seen. Events of this kind seem to have passed unnoticed by the Egyptians, and such Mesopotamian records as we have do not record any such appearances. There are no records of such 'new' stars in Greek observations either, but this is predictable because the Greeks believed the heavens to be immutable, subject to no change whatsoever. Aristotle in fact laid this down as part of his detailed description of the universe. If such an event had been seen, then it would have been put down to some transitory happening below the sphere of the moon, meteorological not astronomical. The Greek attitude was accepted by medieval Europe and by the Islamic world. A new star was recorded in AD1006 but it was not recognized by the astronomers for what it was.

China is the one independent civilization whose records exist from early enough to act as a check, and as early as 1300BC there is a record of the appearance of a 'guest star'. This, like many of the earliest Chinese records, was made on pieces of bone from the shoulder-blades of animals like oxen or on the shells of turtles used for divination. The Chinese, with meticulous thoroughness, recorded not only prophecies but also subsequent events, among which are astronomical and meteorological occurrences. Thus they recorded the appearance of a 'new' star in AD1054, in a position in the sky which coincides with what we call the Crab nebula. It was not recorded in the West.

The first record in the Western world of a new star being recognized as such was made by the Danish astronomer Tycho Brahe (1546-1601) in 1572. This sudden appearance of a 'new' celestial body was in fact the stimulus for his work in cataloguing the positions of stars and planets which he did with great precision. These catalogues were to assume immense importance in the hands of his assistant Johannes Kepler, who himself observed a new star in 1604. In 1596 David Fabricius observed a star flaring and subsequently fading, but it was not

METHODS OF RECORDING STARS
The Chinese used oracle bones *(above)* to record occurrences in the sky. These bones bear carved inscriptions from about 1300BC, that describe astronomical and other events of the time. Much later, in the sixteenth century, the Danish astronomer, Tycho Brahe, recognized and recorded a 'new' star on this chart *(right)*. This was the first record in the West of such a phenomenon.

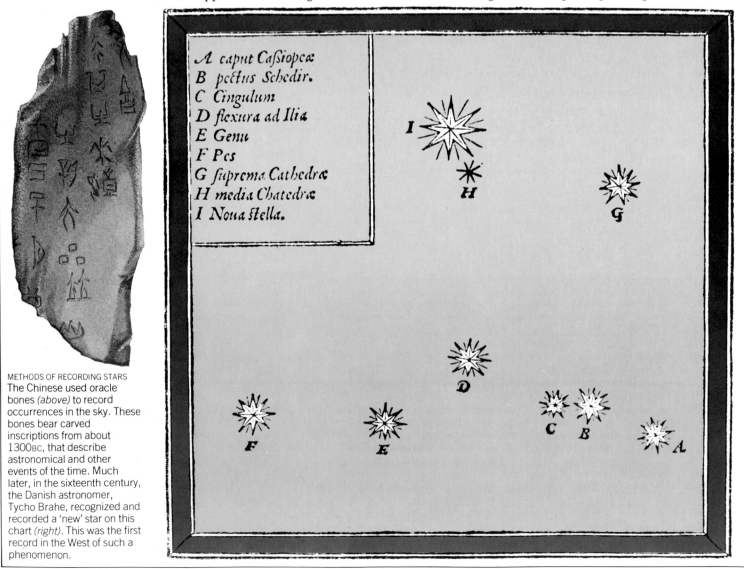

A caput Cassiopeæ
B pectus Schedir.
C Cingulum
D flexura ad Ilia
E Genu
F Pes
G suprema Cathedræ
H media Chatedræ
I Noua stella.

as bright as Kepler's or Brahe's stars.

The true nature of the very bright stars or 'supernovae' only became clear during the 1960s but by the late 1920s it was realized that 20 or 30 novae, like the one Fabricius observed, flared brightly each century, and some others brightened very intensely. In 1933, these brighter ones were called 'supernovae' by Walter Baade and Fritz Zwicky in the United States. They are exploding stars which leave a small but very dense star behind, together with a cloud of gas. The Crab nebula is such a remnant of the 1054 supernova observed by the Chinese. Further research has shown that there are two types of supernova: one reaches some 500 million times the brightness of the sun, the other some 3,000 million times. Because their true brightness is known, they are useful to astronomers for determining distances of millions of light-years and more away in space. Both types of supernova are rare, however, and may only appear centuries or even thousands of years apart in our region of space.

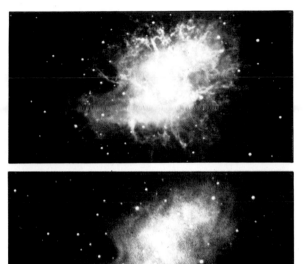

CRAB NEBULA The Chinese observed what is now known as a 'supernova' in 1054; this exploding star in Taurus left a small but very dense star behind, together with a cloud of gas, which is called the Crab nebula. It is about 6,000 light-years distant. These three views show the nebula at different wavelengths: infrared *(left above)*, yellow *(left)* and red *(below)*.

The Stellar Universe

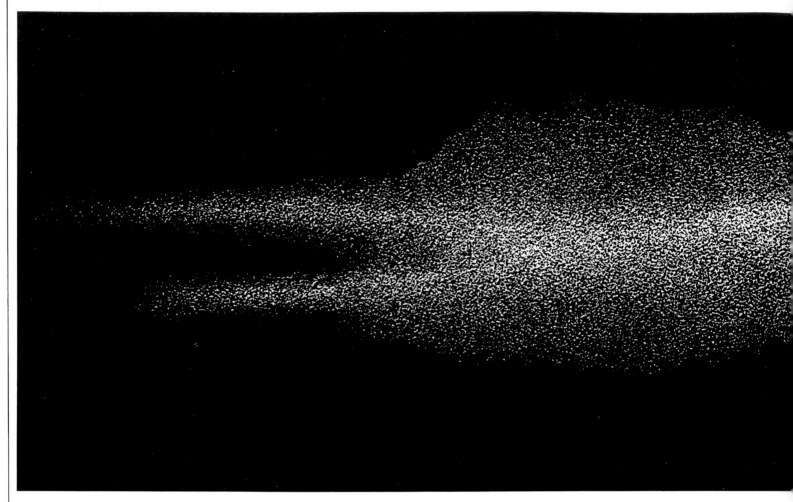

From primitive times, astronomers were primarily concerned with the sun, moon and planets. This was indeed the rationale of early astronomy, but when Newton published his explanation of planetary motion in 1687, it had clearly become time for astronomers to broaden their horizons. Professional astronomers were, in fact, spending their time on a new problem, but this was a practical one — determining longitude at sea.

In the seventeenth century, expanding maritime nations were vitally interested in this question; stars became practically important. It was a problem, essentially, of accurate timekeeping at sea and because no suitable clocks were available at that time, it became evident that the most practicable way was to use the moon's position among the stars as a time indicator. But this required more precise determination of the positions of the moon and stars than existed, and led to the establishment of national observatories at Paris in 1667 and Greenwich in 1675.

Although professional astronomers had their official preoccupations, Newton's colleague Edmond Halley (1656-1742), Astronomer Royal and Director of Greenwich Observatory, managed to do a little stellar astronomy

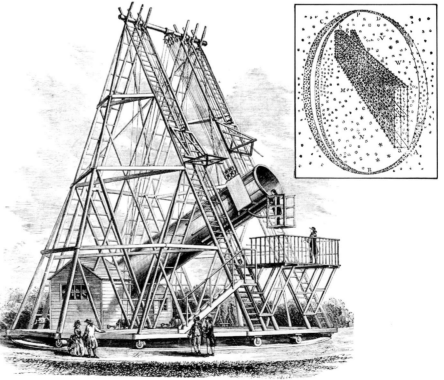

NINETEENTH-CENTURY TELESCOPE
Joseph von Fraunhofer's telescope was fitted with a heliometer — a split front lens designed to measure the diameter of the sun. Bessel also used it to make the first correct measurements of a star's distance.

HERSCHEL'S WORK William Herschel, sometimes known as the 'father of stellar astronomy', worked inexhaustibly to count and catalogue the bodies of the heavens. It may be seen from the illustration *(above)* from c 1785, that he considered the system of stars to form a giant island in space. His scheme of the Milky Way, our Galaxy, may also be understood by this diagram from *Encyclopaedia Londinensis* (c 1807)*(inset)*. A, B, C and D are areas of sky lying in the Milky Way that he had observed. M, N, V and W are also areas of observed sky. Herschel concluded that the Milky Way was box-shaped, but divided at 'g'. He was able to observe and catalogue the universe partly because he had a unique flair for building efficient and powerful telescopes, such as this 40ft (12m) long reflecting telescope*(left)*.

besides merely charting the stars. In 1715 he wrote about the appearance of new stars and about cloud-like objects or 'nebulae' in space, and in 1717 he made the important discovery that the stars are not fixed in space but actually have motions of their own. In Paris his contemporary Jacques Cassini made a valiant attempt to measure a stellar distance.

Halley's pioneering work was not followed up until the latter part of the eighteenth century. Then William Herschel (1738-1822), a professional musician from Hanover who had settled in England and was becoming well known musically in the fashionable resort of Bath, took up astronomy as a hobby. Dissatisfied with such telescopes as he could hire or buy, he began to make his own and proved to have a flair for this. It was with one of his own telescopes that he discovered the planet Uranus in 1781, the first new planet to be found since before the days of written history. This brought him fame, and led to his receiving a royal pension so he could devote his life to astronomy.

From the late 1770s, Herschel observed the skies, charting the stars and nebulae, for his interest was almost solely in stellar astronomy. The most indefatigable observer of all time, he counted the stars in 3,400 small areas of the sky,

discovered the existence of many pairs of stars orbiting each other, and catalogued the positions of no less than 2,500 nebulae. His star counts led him to suggest that the sun and all the other stars formed a giant island in space, the edges of which we see as the hazy band of light called the 'Milky Way', stretching right round the sky in the northern and southern hemispheres.

Towards the end of the time Herschel was observing, Joseph von Fraunhofer (1787-1826) followed up results obtained by William Wollaston, who had been studying the spectrum of the sun. In order to try to separate the colours of the spectrum, Wollaston had passed sunlight first through a slit before reaching a prism which transformed the beam into a coloured band. Wollaston could not separate the colours but found that the spectrum was crossed by numerous dark lines. He did not pursue matters further, but von Fraunhofer, who had built an efficient spectroscope for viewing the spectrum, set about studying the solar spectrum in detail. He mapped the positions of 324 dark lines and, as it turned out later in the nineteenth century, this proved to be work of great importance in gaining a true understanding of the nature of the stars themselves.

The Nature of the Stars

It was in 1844 that the famous philosopher Auguste Comte (1798-1857) stated that man would never learn of what the stars were made because he could never reach them to find out. Yet, astonishingly, within only two years of Comte's death, evidence was to hand to prove him utterly mistaken.

As early as 1752, Thomas Melvill' had discovered that the chemical sodium emitted a yellow light when heated until it glowed, which bent or refracted by a specific amount when passed through a prism. This discovery had stimulated the research by Wollaston, von Fraunhofer and others but the trouble was that while the dark lines lettered D by von Fraunhofer coincided with Melvill's yellow light, they were also present when other substances were heated in a flame and their light examined with a spectroscope. Only in 1856 did William Swan, a chemist, manage to prove they were indeed due to sodium; they had appeared so frequently because the other substances used were impure and contaminated with sodium. Next, William Miller discovered that when he passed an electric current across two pieces of metal and obtained a spark, the lines in the spectrum given by the spark were from different metals.

Finally, in 1859, it was Gustav Kirchhoff (1824-87) and Robert Bunsen (1811-99) in Heidelberg who were able to put all these facts together and confirm from their own experiments that every chemical element displays its own particular lines and no others. The pattern of lines can be said to be an element's fingerprint. They also found that while a heated gas gives bright lines on a dark background, a very dense gas, a solid or a liquid heated until it glows, emits a continuous coloured spectrum. Moreover, should there be cooler gas lying between the observer and the glowing solid or liquid body, or between the observer and a very dense gas, then the continuous spectrum will be crossed by dark lines,

RELATIVE SIZE This illustration shows the sun and earth to the same scale. Only a small section of the sun can be shown — its diameter is over 109 times that of earth.

and these lines are characteristic of the chemical elements present in the cooler gas.

Now, at last, it was possible to discover some of the chemical substances present on the sun. The continuous spectrum did not indicate the composition of the main body of gas which lay underneath but the cooler outside gases. Nevertheless, this was a great step forward, and it was evident from the solar spectrum that allowed William Ramsay in London to isolate a new chemical element in the laboratory in 1895; he named it 'helium' from the Greek *helios*, sun. This discovery proved that the theories of Kirchhoff and Bunsen about the spectrum of the sun and spectra produced in the laboratory were correct. More important, it was an additional proof that the same physical and chemical laws which operated on earth, also operated in space. Newton's work had shown that the ordinary laws of motion could be applied to the motion of the planets, and Herschel's discovery of double stars showed that they worked deeper in space; now this principle was extended further. Before Ramsay's discovery, this basic principle had been

STRUCTURE OF THE SUN A total eclipse of the sun by the moon *(left)* enables astronomers to view the solar 'atmosphere' or corona. Prominences (flame-like structures) can be seen erupting above the photosphere (ie the apparent surface of the sun), though ordinarily obscured by the glare. This eclipse was photographed by Don Trombino. A section through the sun *(below)* shows the central regions where thermonuclear reactions are taking place to generate the sun's energy. The sun's enormous substance is slowly being destroyed by the nuclear fusion of hydrogen into helium atoms. The outer layer describes the way energy escapes through convection currents of very hot gas.

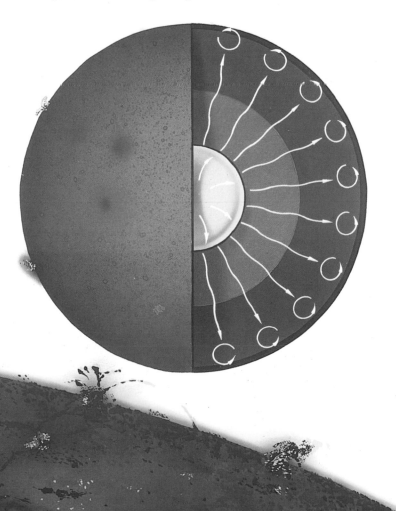

predicted, and in 1890 a new word, 'astrophysics', had been coined to describe the study of the physical and chemical nature of the stars.

Increasing attention was paid to the stars as physical bodies in their own right after this discovery, and spectra began to be classified according to the presence of various lines. Angelo Secchi had attempted such a classification as early as 1867, and seven years later Hermann Vogel added more detail. But, finally, it was research at Harvard University Observatory, especially that undertaken by Annie Cannon in 1890 and modified between 1918 and 1924 due to further information, that formed the basis for all subsequent classification. Annie Cannon's first arrangement of stars, which was indicated by alphabetical letters, was modified to give a new arrangement, O, B, A, F, G, K, M.

The Danish astronomer Ejnar Hertzsprung, who was concerned with determining stellar distances, wanted to find the true brightness of stars of the different classes; once these were known, the spectrum would give an indication

of true brightness that could be compared with apparent brightness to give a measure of distance. Henry Norris Russell, an American, was interested in trying to determine how stars change with age, and both he and Hertzsprung quite independently plotted the spectral class of a star against its true brightness. This led in 1914 to a most productive diagram — the H-R or Hertzsprung-Russel diagram — which has been used as a basis for much later discussion. It indicates that the different classes O through to M are a measure of temperature, and also gives hints about an evolutionary sequence.

Russell thought that stars began as very hot bright bodies and then cooled down, but in the 1920s this view was challenged and overthrown, notably by Arthur Eddington at Cambridge University. Eddington realized that nuclear energy was what kept stars shining, and that they began as dim cool bodies which subsequently heated up. The atomic reactions involved were studied by Robert Atkinson and Carl von Weizsacker and, most notably in 1938, by Hans Bethe.

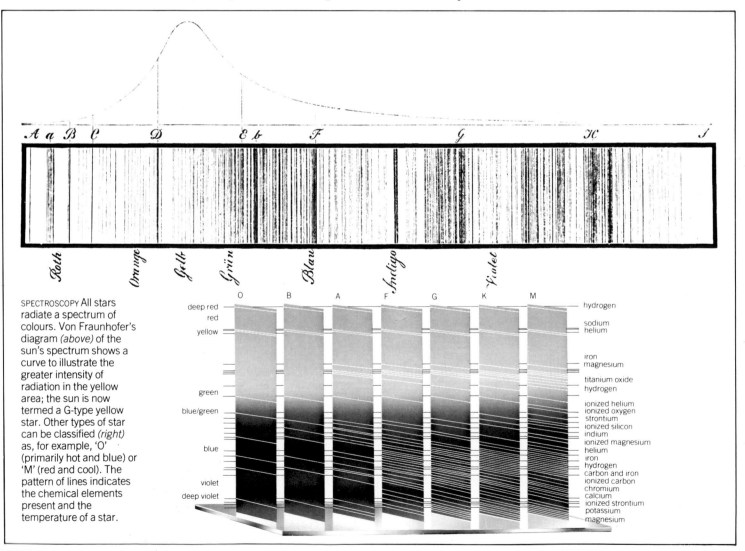

SPECTROSCOPY All stars radiate a spectrum of colours. Von Fraunhofer's diagram (above) of the sun's spectrum shows a curve to illustrate the greater intensity of radiation in the yellow area; the sun is now termed a G-type yellow star. Other types of star can be classified (right) as, for example, 'O' (primarily hot and blue) or 'M' (red and cool). The pattern of lines indicates the chemical elements present and the temperature of a star.

Since the Second World War, nuclear physics has developed immensely and so has astrophysics, leading to new realizations about stellar types and stellar evolution. Observations have been extended: total eclipses of the sun have been examined to provide evidence of the sun's outer envelope of gases, while, since the 1970s, spacecraft have brought new evidence not only about the sun but also about the stars. Yet as early as 1924, Eddington's theoretical research had shown that atoms could be unusually tightly packed together to give a superdense star which would shine with a white light. Such a star was in fact discovered by Walter Adams using the huge 100in (2.5m) telescope at Mount Wilson in California. Called a 'white dwarf', which is a star towards the end of its life, it is so dense that one teaspoonful would weigh about 5 tonnes.

In 1941, George Gamow and Mario Schönberg showed that, in theory, more massive stars would not collapse to become white dwarfs but 'neutron' stars, where one teaspoonful would weigh a thousand million tonnes. Such stars would be difficult to observe, but in 1967 Jocelyn Bell Burnell and Anthony Hewish discovered the first neutron star — also called a 'pulsar' — by using a novel radiotelescope at Cambridge University.

The neutron star is not the densest state a star can reach. Previously, in 1798, Pierre Laplace (1749-1827) had applied Newton's theory of gravitation to a new theory that some stars might be so small and dense that no light could escape from them. However, after the arrival of the theory of relativity in 1915, and a demonstration in 1916 by Karl Schwarzschild that great densities would give rise to non-radiating bodies or 'black holes', the subject needed reviewing. In 1931 and 1932 Subrahmanyan Chandrasekhar and Lev Landau separately tackled the question and concluded that dark concentrations of material could form and would attract everything that came too near them. In the 1970s possible observational evidence of such black holes was found; these may be the graveyards of stars that were once very much larger than our sun.

H-R DIAGRAM These diagrams both show the relationship between spectral class and absolute luminosity or true brightness for individual bright stars whose distances have been measured. The spectral class (B, A, F, G, K, M or N) appears as the horizontal coordinate, while the true brightness appears as the vertical. The black dots and little circles (below left) denote stars whose parallaxes have been measured. A similar diagram (below) has dots, circles and triangles which refer to moving clusters of stars, of which the Hyades is one. From these diagrams, conclusions can be made about the comparative brightness of stars of different classes, and about temperature.

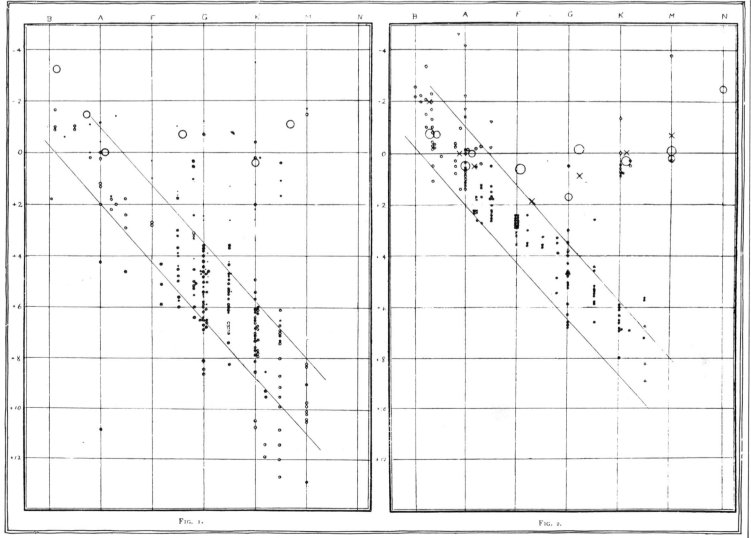

FIG. 1.   FIG. 2.

The Nebulae

ORION NEBULA At the centre of the attempt by Galileo, Halley, Herschel, Rosse and Huggins, among others, to resolve the nature of nebulae, the great nebula in Orion is a magnificent sight. Using a **spectroscope to view a nebula, Huggins saw a** 'single bright line only!' and the problem was solved: nebulae consist of luminous gas. This photograph of the nebula in Orion — still recognized by its Messier number, 42 — was taken with the Anglo-Australian wide-angle Schmidt telescope at Siding Spring Observatory in Australia. There is now firm evidence that within this nebula — known to be at a distance of 1,300 light-years — stars are being born.

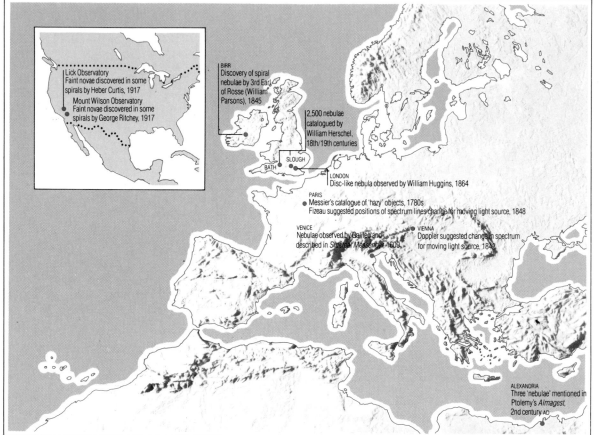

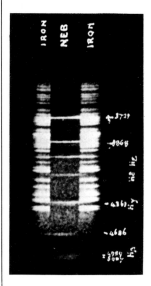

Inset map labels:

Lick Observatory
Faint novae discovered in some spirals by Heber Curtis, 1917

Mount Wilson Observatory
Faint novae discovered in some spirals by George Ritchey, 1917

BIRR
Discovery of spiral nebulae by 3rd Earl of Rosse (William Parsons), 1845

2,500 nebulae catalogued by William Herschel, 18th/19th centuries

SLOUGH

BATH

LONDON
Disc-like nebula observed by William Huggins, 1864

PARIS
Messier's catalogue of 'hazy' objects, 1780s
Fizeau suggested positions of spectrum lines change for moving light source, 1848

VENICE
Nebulae observed by Galileo and described in Sidereal Messenger, 1609

VIENNA
Doppler suggested change in spectrum for moving light source, 1842

ALEXANDRIA
Three 'nebulae' mentioned in Ptolemy's Almagest, 2nd century AD

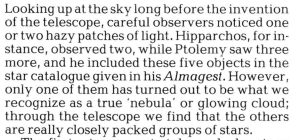

INTEREST IN NEBULAE Some observations of the positions of nebulae were made in Greece *(above right)*. Galileo, in Venice, was the first to examine nebulae with the telescope. He thought they were groups of stars, but other astronomers, including Halley, disagreed. Messier in Paris and especially Herschel in England achieved some efficient cataloguing, then Huggins made his important discovery that prompted the later understanding of the true nature of nebulae. The illustration *(above)* shows the spectrum of the Dumb-bell nebula in Vulpecula, with comparison spectra on the left and right. A picture of this nebula *(opposite page, below)* shows it consists of enormous clouds of luminous gas. Lord Rosses's drawing *(opposite page, above)* of the nebula he observed in the constellation Cares Venatici shows it has a spiral structure. This was to prove a very important discovery.

Looking up at the sky long before the invention of the telescope, careful observers noticed one or two hazy patches of light. Hipparchos, for instance, observed two, while Ptolemy saw three more, and he included these five objects in the star catalogue given in his *Almagest*. However, only one of them has turned out to be what we recognize as a true 'nebula' or glowing cloud; through the telescope we find that the others are really closely packed groups of stars.

The first astronomer to take real advantage of the new invention for examining the stars was Galileo (1564-1642), who, in 1609, turned his telescope to various nebulae. In his book *The Sidereal Messenger*, describing these first observations, he wrote '... the stars which have been called by every one of the astronomers up to this day *nebulous*, are groups of small stars set thick together in a wonderful way ...' As time passed, however, telescopes improved and more observers began to use them; Galileo's view that nebulae were nothing more than stars clustered together was challenged. Although some hazy patches appeared to consist of stars, others appeared as nothing more than glowing clouds. To a few astronomers, they were evidence of holes in the sky through which light from the eternal reaches of heaven could be seen, but most took a more scientific view, assuming them to be objects situated in an infinite universe, as observed by Thomas Digges.

The foremost of these was the English astronomer, Edmond Halley (1656-1742). In 1715, he wrote that the nebulae '... are nothing else but the Light coming from an extraordinary great Space in the Ether, ie covering great areas of space, through which a lucid *Medium* is diffused, that shines with its own proper Lustre'. In other words, the nebulae were huge clouds of material shining on their own account. Of what the clouds were made Halley did not conjecture; physics was not then at sufficiently advanced a stage to begin to furnish an explanation. Halley's and Galileo's views were in opposition, and for the next two and a half centuries astronomers were undecided as to which was correct.

During 1771 and 1784, Charles Messier (1730-1817), a French astronomer, prepared two catalogues of all hazy objects then detected. The second contained no less than 104 items, and was to prove of permanent value — many nebulae are still referred to by their Messier number — yet Messier's purpose in drawing it up was not to help solve the problem of the nature of the nebulae, but rather to help him in his study of comets. When comets are not close to the sun, they glow dimly and show no tail, and can readily be confused with nebulae; it was the avoidance of such confusion that motivated Messier. Yet at the same time as he was still cataloguing, William Herschel (1738-1822)

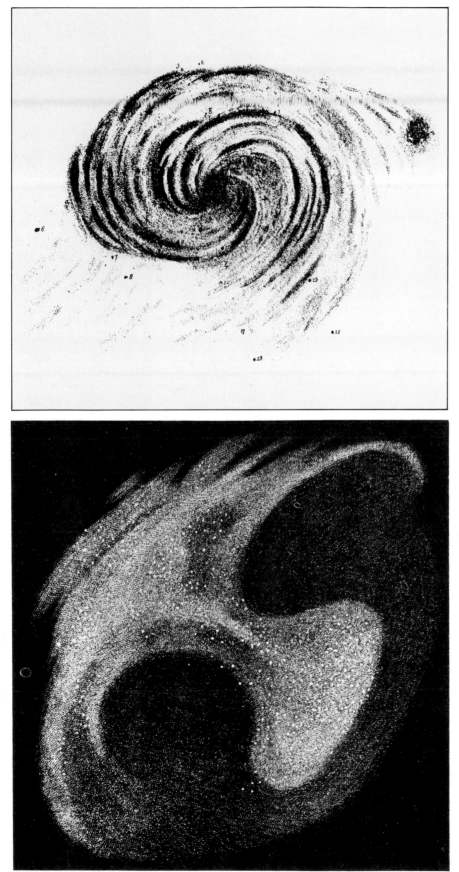

began to investigate nebulae in detail.

Herschel catalogued some 2,500 nebulae, and as his telescopes grew in size, the observable detail increased. To begin with, Herschel took Galileo's view; he thought that nebulae were really stars clustered very close together. Larger telescopes should, therefore, have enabled him to resolve the hazy objects into separate stars. Yet Herschel then came upon a new problem: by comparing his own observations of the great nebula in Orion with those made a few decades earlier, he thought he had detected a change. If such a change was real, Herschel argued, it must mean that the nebula was fairly small, otherwise no alteration would have been noticeable over so comparatively short a time. And if it were a small object, then it could not contain stars which, he correctly believed, needed some large space in which to exist, even if they were clustered together.

Herschel's observations, made after he became a professional astronomer, led him to study the distribution of nebulae across the sky and, in the end, to conclude that the existence of true nebulae seemed likely, as well as the existence of compact clusters of stars. Not everyone agreed, however, and William Parsons, the 3rd Earl of Rosse (1800-67), constructed, in 1845, a giant telescope — with one and a half times the aperture of Herschel's largest — and hoped to settle the problem using it. Yet his observations, exciting though they were, did not bring about a solution to the question. Certainly Rosse's telescope enabled him to resolve into separate stars nebulae that had still appeared hazy to Herschel, but the Orion nebula continued to be a hazy mass, rather than separate stars. Moreover, Rosse discovered that some nebulae have a spiral shape, looking like giant 'catherine wheels' or 'pin-wheels'. Yet his view remained unchanged: all nebulae would be resolved into stars if only telescopes powerful enough could be constructed.

Others who also looked at the nebulae became convinced of changes, difficult though these were to detect in such objects as dim, diffuse nebulae. They did not agree with Rosse's opinion. It was not until 1864 that the answer was found, and then not by using a vast aperture but a spectroscope. In that year, another well-to-do amateur astronomer, William Higgins, wrote of a disc-like type of nebula: 'On the evening of the 29th August 1864, I directed the telescope for the first time to a planetary nebula in Draco. I looked into the spectroscope. No such spectrum as I had expected! A single bright line only!... The riddle of the nebulae was solved. The answer, which had come to us in the light itself, read: Not an aggregation of stars, but a luminous gas.' The research of Kirchhoff and Bunsen on spectra had made it clear that bright lines on a dark background could only be generated by a diffuse mass of gas. Halley's surmise had been correct; space was populated not only by stars but also glowing gas.

The Galaxies

The discovery that space contains clouds of gas as well as stars emphasized the usefulness of spectroscopy in determining the nature of celestial bodies by analyzing their light. But there were other kinds of observation that had also to be taken into account when considering the nature of the universe. One of these was the way the nebulae were distributed in space. Since Herschel's time, it had become clear that spiral nebulae avoided the area of the Milky Way. If Herschel's idea were true — that our star, the sun, is a member of an island of many stars — then perhaps nebulae of this kind were in fact other more distant star islands.

William Herschel's son, John, who had taken one of his father's large telescopes to South Africa in the 1830s to observe the southern skies, believed he had seen far beyond our own Milky Way and out into the depths of a much larger universe. But by the end of the nineteenth century, opinion was again hardening in favour of the view that the Milky Way was the only star island in existence. This was partly due to the fact that if other star islands existed in space there seemed to be no reason why they should avoid the Milky Way region of the sky, and partly to a new discovery made in 1885. In that year, a bright star had flared up in the spiral nebula in Andromeda; indeed, it was so intense that it was one-tenth as bright as the spiral. We now know that it was a supernova but at that time the phenomenon was not known, and it seemed impossible that a single star could exceed in brightness a million normal stars, which is what would be necessary if the Andromeda spiral were a distant island universe. In consequence, the nebula must surely lie within our own star island.

As the twentieth century dawned, James Keeler at Lick Observatory in the United States had taken photographs of spiral nebulae making it clear that there were hundreds of thousands of such objects, but still the general view was that they would evolve in star clusters or even into single stars. Indeed, when, in 1912, it became possible to examine the spectra of nebulae, this view seemed to be confirmed because they were all found to display primarily the continuous background and dark lines typical of stars. Then, a year later, Melvin Slipher of the Lowell Observatory in Arizona produced some puzzling evidence. He discovered a shift of the spectral lines in the spectrum of the Andromeda nebula. Such a change in a spectrum had first been suggested by Christian Doppler (1803-53) and Hippolyte Fizeau (1819-96). In 1842, Doppler claimed that if a body that was emitting light moved towards an observer, its light would become bluer, but if it were moving away, a reddening would take place. Six years later Fizeau pointed out that the position of the spectral lines would change: there would be a shift towards the blue if an object were approaching, and a shift towards the red if it were receding from the observer. Today, this shift of the lines is known to astronomers as the 'Doppler shift'.

The Doppler shift is important because it is the sole means we have of determining motion in the line-of-sight, ie motion directly towards or away from us. This is because the distances of stars and nebulae from earth are so great that no noticeable change of size occurs while they are moving in this way. Slipher was the first to detect such a shift in the spectral lines of a nebula, and the result he obtained was staggering: the Andromeda nebula appeared to be rushing towards us at more than 670,000 miles per hour (some 300km per second). Further observations made subsequently at the Lowell Observatory showed similarly immense velocities for other spirals, and many astronomers began to favour the view that such objects must be separate island universes. This view was quite in keeping with their star-like spectra.

The island universe interpretation was again strengthened in 1917 when two more American astronomers, Heber Curtis at Lick Observatory and George Ritchey at Mount Wilson, both discovered faint novae in some spirals. Old photographs were examined for further evidence and Curtis became convinced that the Andromeda nova really had been of abnormal brightness. However, Harlow Shapley at Mount Wilson did not agree with the idea that spirals were distant and separate star systems. Working on the size of the Milky Way system or 'Galaxy', he had measured the distances of many globular clusters, ie compact, spherically shaped clusters each containing thousands of stars. Measuring the distances to these by Cepheid variables observed in them, he arrived at a huge figure for the size of the Galaxy. It had, he claimed, a diameter of no less than 300,000 light-years. This meant that if the spiral nebulae really were island universes, they must be extremely distant.

Another line of research at Mount Wilson made this seem virtually impossible. Adriaan van Maanen believed he had measured a rotational movement in some spirals. If the spirals really were very distant island universes then the velocities of the stars in their outermost regions would exceed the speed of light. This was totally unacceptable. The situation seemed now to have reached an impasse, though many astronomers expressed grave doubts about the reality of the motions van Maanen had observed and certainly their consequences.

The riddle was solved quite suddenly during 1923 and 1924 by Edwin Hubble (1889-1953), using the very large telescopes at Mount Wilson. With the giant 100in (2.5m) reflector, he discovered a Cepheid variable in the Andromeda spiral, which gave him an unequivocal distance of over one million light-years. The universe was therefore larger than anyone had previously believed, and composed not only of our Galaxy but also of hundreds of thousands of other separate star islands or galaxies.

NEAR GALAXIES The great galaxy in Andromeda (M31) is one of the Local Group of galaxies which includes our own Galaxy. Although it is 2.3 million light-years distant, it is visible to the naked eye as a faint, moon-sized patch of brightness. This light left the galaxy 2.3 million years ago. The photograph *(left)* was taken using the 48in (1.2m) wide-angle Schmidt telescope at Palomar Observatory. Two other galaxies visible to the naked eye are the Magellanic Clouds, although only from the southern hemisphere. The large one, 160,000 light-years away, is illustrated here *(inset)*, photographed with the Anglo-Australian Schmidt telescope.

Mapping the Moon

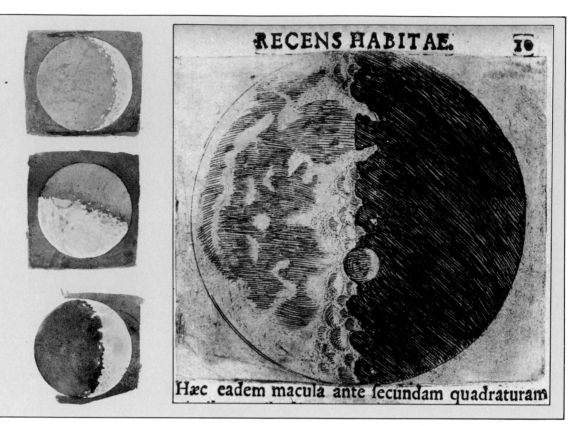

GALILEO AND THE MOON
Galileo used his newly invented telescope to make the first thorough studies of the heavens from 1610 onwards. His remarkable drawings of the phases and surface of the moon *(right)* recorded the presence of craters, 'spots' and dark areas, which, later, were incorrectly thought of as seas. Among his other discoveries were the four largest satellites of Jupiter, the phases of Venus and sunspots. His observations led him to support the Copernican belief that the earth, rather than being fixed at the centre of the universe, revolved around the sun. However, his support raised a storm of protest in Roman Catholic Italy.

RECENS HABITAE.

Hæc eadem macula ante secundam quadraturam

The moon may have been one of the first celestial bodies to be observed by mankind, and at first interest centred on its movements, its phases and eclipses. Its surface was not seriously studied. Anyone looking up at it could see there were light and dark patches, which could be imagined as the face of the 'man in the moon', when the moon was full. However, Greek astronomers after Aristotle entertained the general idea that celestial bodies were changeless and without blemish, and this led to explanations of its appearance which had nothing to do with the physical nature of the moon itself. The moon did not seem amenable to scientific study, being made of an incorruptible element. Physical study of the moon did not begin until well into the Renaissance, when William Gilbert, the court physician to Queen Elizabeth I and a pioneer investigator into the earth's magnetism, drew a map of the moon. Precisely when he did so is unknown, but it must have been sometime before 1603, the year of his death. However, the map was not published for almost half a century, and by then it had been superseded by maps prepared from observations with the telescope.

The first such map was prepared by Thomas Harriot, probably in July 1609, and in the following winter Galileo made some drawings at the telescope. He observed 'spots', craters and dark areas which came to be called 'maria' or seas, though in fact we now know them to be vast plains. But Galileo's most important activity was his attempt to measure the height of the mountains observed there. This he managed to do by measuring the lengths of the shadows they cast across the moon's surface and then, knowing the angle of the sun above the lunar surface at the time he was observing, he was able to calculate the heights. His results were large, but that is not significant. What is important is that he appreciated the moon as an earth-like body, with mountains, valleys, craters and other surface features.

During the rest of the seventeenth century, many moon maps were drawn. Of the people who prepared them, perhaps the most notable were the Polish brewer Johannes Hevelius (1611-87) and the Italian priest Giovanni Riccioli. Hevelius drew a series of maps, which were published in his *Selenographia* (atlas of the moon) of 1647, and gave the various lunar features terrestrial names. His maps were detailed and also showed the areas of the moon's 'librations'. These are areas near the edge of the disc of the moon which are only sometimes visible, this oscillation being caused by the rotation of the moon on its axis as it orbits the earth. As a general rule, the moon rotates once on its axis each time it completes one orbit of the earth; it is for this reason that we never see the far side of the moon. However, because the moon's orbit is an ellipse and not a circle, the moon's velocity is continually changing, and sometimes the rotation of the moon and its orbital position get a little out of step; the librations are the result of this.

Riccioli published his map three years after

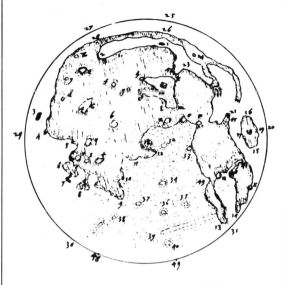

MAPPING THE MOON The first known moon map based on telescopic observations *(above)* was drawn by Thomas Harriot, an English astronomer who was tutor to Sir Walter Raleigh in the sixteenth century. The first complete atlas of the moon was compiled by Johannes Hevelius, who published his *Selenographia (left)* in 1647. Many of the names he gave to the various features he charted are, in the main, still in use today.

the *Selenographia;* it was based to a great extent on observations made by Francesco Grimaldi, one of his most able pupils at Bologna University. The map was good but more important for us is that its system of nomenclature was adopted by all later astronomers. Riccioli did not by and large use terrestrial names, but he invented new ones. The large dark areas received dramatic titles, like *Mare Tranquilitatis* or Sea of Tranquility and *Mare Nectris* or Sea of Nectar. Craters were named after famous astronomers, Ptolemy being honoured by a huge walled plain near the centre of the disc, and Tycho Brahe by the most prominent crater of all, which is to be found in the south-southwest quadrant. The system has, of course, received additional names since Riccioli's time as more features are discerned, and it is because of its flexibility that it has lasted.

In the eighteenth century still more maps appeared, notably one by the German Tobias Mayer, which was published posthumously in 1775. This contained a system of selenographic coordinates. Lunar studies entered a more detailed phase in the nineteenth century, especially due to the painstaking observations of Johann Schröter and later Johann Mädler whose full description of the lunar surface, the fruit of his collaboration with Wilhelm Beer, was the *Mappa Selenographia (Map of the Moon)* in four volumes (1834-6) and *Der Mond... Selenographie (The World...of the Moon)* which was first published in 1837.

After the Beer and Mädler work, still more observations were made and by the 1850s it had become clear that the moon is a lifeless world, without an atmosphere and subject to some extremes of temperature. In the late 1950s, it was found that there occurred what have been termed 'transient lunar phenomena' (TLPs) which appear to be due to the sporadic release of subsurface gas. However, the greatest strides forward in the twentieth century have been due to the developments of rocket technology which have led to the space age, the launching of artificial satellites, moon orbiting probes and, in 1969, the first landing of human beings on the lunar surface.

Space technology has so far led to a number of important results. In the first place, a moon-orbiting Russian probe photographed the rear face of the moon in 1959, giving the first glimpse of a surface never before observed. Improved technology has now allowed this entire face to be mapped in detail. Secondly, manned landings on the moon have made it possible to bring samples of lunar rock back to earth for analysis, and it is clear that the material of which the moon is made is not dissimilar to the material composing the earth, thus confirming the belief that both were formed at the same time, probably some 4,500 million years ago or so. Thirdly, it has been possible to leave experimental equipment on the moon to monitor 'moonquakes' and to reflect laser beams, so that it is now possible to determine the moon's distance to within a few centimetres, a precision never before possible.

OUTWARDS AND ONWARDS When the American astronauts Neil Armstrong and Edwin 'Buzz' Aldrin left their *Apollo 11* spacecraft on 20 July 1969 to take man's first steps onto the moon's *(far right)*, the event was the climax of perhaps the biggest technological programme in human history. A total of 17 *Apollo* missions were launched and six lunar landings made, the last being that of *Apollo 17* in December 1972. As well as bringing back 900lb (400kg) of lunar rock, the *Apollo* programme greatly enhanced man's knowledge of the moon's early history, magnetic field, heat flow, volcanism and seismic activity. To date, however, exploration of the planets has been left to unmanned probes. The three photographs *(right)* are views of the moon taken by the *Apollo* astronauts.

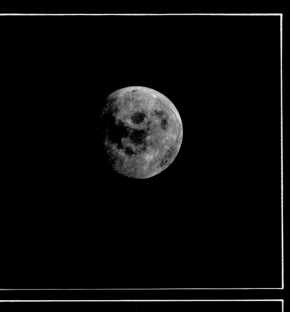

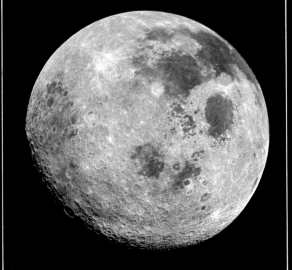

The Origin and Nature of the Planets

Although early civilizations speculated on the beginning of the world and the creation of the universe, they could do little more than exercise their imagination. They had few facts to work on, and their understanding of physical laws was too rudimentary for any truly scientific speculation. In the Greek era, some philosophers spoke of a primeval substance — usually water — from which everything was formed, but once the concept of five elements arrived, no further progress was made. Because the 'fifth essence' was incorruptible, it did not obey physical laws; the creation of the earth and of the universe had, in a sense, been placed outside scientific study.

It was not until the coming of the Renaissance in the West, and the subsequent growth of scientific questioning in its modern form, that anything approaching an explanation could be made. The first to attempt this was the French mathematician, physicist and philosopher René Descartes (1596-1650), who in 1644 published his *Principia Philosophiae (Principles of Philosophy)*. Descartes' ideas covered, he thought, the whole universe yet, looking back on them now we see them to be concerned primarily with the planetary system. In the mid-seventeenth century the implications of an infinite universe were not fully appreciated and astronomy's main concern was to explain planetary motion.

Descartes conceived of a universe that was a 'plenum' — full of matter — the particles of which jostled against one another. He did not, however, accept the idea of the atom as the smallest unit of matter because, he said, one could conceive of particles being subdivided again and again *ad infinitum*. Within his universe, Descartes thought everything was arranged like a collection of vortexes. At the centre of each vortex of whirling material was a star. As time passed, a skin grew over each star (he thought the appearance of spots on the sun was evidence for the beginning of such a process), and in due course the skin would stop the star shining. The vortex would then collapse, and the 'dead' star would move either from one vortex to another and so become a comet, or it would stay in another vortex moving in orbit around the star at its centre. The 'dead' star would then become a planet. Descartes' ideas are not acceptable today because we now know that stars, comets and planets could not behave in this way. But at the time it appeared a brilliant synthesis, for it was the first new self-consistent philosophical scheme of the universe using physical explanations since Aristotle.

It was Isaac Newton's mathematical analysis of planetary motion and concept of universal gravitation, which he published in 1687 that finally made Descartes' theory untenable. However, these ideas took time to be digested, and there was no more speculation until the eighteenth century. Then, in 1745, the French biologist, Le Comte de Buffon, proposed the first of what have since come to be called 'catastrophe theories' of planetary formation. Buffon suggested that a comet had struck the sun and splashed out solar material which then condensed to form the planets. Again, we now know that comets are not massive enough to do this, though in the mid-eighteenth century the masses of comets had not been determined.

A decade after Buffon's proposal, the German philosopher Immanuel Kant (1724-1804) put forward a quite different suggestion. In his *Universal Natural History and Theory of the Heavens*, Kant suggested a more uniform theory of planetary birth that made no use of catastrophic events. He claimed that the sun and its planets — the solar system — were part of a giant island which was only one among many such islands. In a brilliant piece of controlled imagination, he thought of the sun and planets as condensing from a basic primordial material. In 1796, which was 40 years on, the French mathematician Pierre Laplace proposed, quite independently, that the sun and planets had formed from a spinning mass of gas. He calculated that the spinning nebula would eject rings of material, each of which would condense into a planet. He called this a 'nebular hypothesis'.

After Laplace, opinion turned away from the Kant-Laplace nebular idea and returned to a catastrophe theory, though in recent years a form of the nebular hypothesis has re-emerged. Attacks on Laplace's ideas were made and, in the nineteenth century, a detailed mathematical analysis seemed to show that if such rings of gas formed, they would not condense into planets nor would they rotate as the planets are observed to do. In 1900, two Americans, Thomas Chamberlin and Forest Moulton, revived the catastrophe theory. The planets were formed, they suggested, when another star passed close to the sun, and material was drawn off from each; this condensed into large lumps and then into the planets. In England in 1916, the astronomer James Jeans examined this hypothesis in detail and modified it into a tidal theory. The close approach, he claimed, would give rise to tidal forces between the stars that would first cause them to elongate; only then, by definition, would material be drawn out to form the planets.

Other forms of catastrophe theory followed Jeans' tidal hypothesis. In 1935, an American, Henry Norris Russell, supposed that the sun had once been a member of a binary system (two stars in orbit around each other), and that the approach of a third star disrupted them, drawing the sun's companion star away with the result that material was drawn off to form planets. In 1941, Raymond Lyttleton at Cambridge University proved this could not happen with a passing star but might have been possible if the sun had been a member of a triple star system in the first place. Then in 1944, Fred Hoyle, also at Cambridge, developed both the

THE MYSTERY OF SATURN Galileo's sketches of what he called the 'triple nature' of Saturn *(above)* were made in 1612. Galileo discovered that the planet sometimes had an oval shape, but his telescope was not powerful enough to detect Saturn's rings.

Russell and Lyttleton theories by assuming a binary system of which the companion star to the sun was a supernova.

After the Second World War, however, and the discovery of thermonuclear energy generation inside stars, it became clear that hydrogen was the abundant element in the universe, and it proved possible to revive the nebular hypothesis. In 1945, Carl von Weizsacker, a German, found that if the nebula mainly consisted of hydrogen it would have formed into eddies which could have condensed into planets. Three years later, in 1948, the American Frank Whipple proposed a variation of the theory in which the sun condensed from a rotating dust cloud which captured another smaller cloud. But later theories have favoured the idea that the sun and planets condensed from the same material, a single cloud, and this remains a popular idea.

The discovery of the true nature of planets is comparatively recent. Not until the reorientation caused by Isaac Newton's theory of universal gravitation in 1687, which he and his successors thought extended throughout the entire universe, was it possible to cast away ideas that the planets were made of some unusual material. But with physical laws operating universally, it seemed likely that the laws of chemistry would do so too. Such an approach appeared to be borne out by observations with the telescope, and the fact that planets do not shine on their own account, but only reflect the light of the sun, was confirmed.

When Galileo observed Jupiter in 1609 and 1610 he found the planet to be accompanied by four orbiting moons. The discovery showed, he argued, that those who claimed the earth must be stationary because otherwise its moon would be left behind, were clearly mistaken. Yet his very argument showed that he assumed the planet Jupiter to be a physical body like the earth, without any evidence. In 1678, in *Lectures and Collections*, Robert Hooke gave a drawing of the planet which very clearly shows bands across the disc and the Great Red Spot, a feature familiar to present-day observers, and which he had first reported in 1665. It was William Herschel in the eighteenth century who took things a stage further and suggested that the bands were part of the planet's atmosphere.

Galileo also observed Saturn. He found it a puzzling object because at times he saw it looking as if it were a triple planet, and at others as if it were a single disc. Only improved telescope optics could solve the problem; the answer was given in 1655 by the Dutch scientist Christian Huygens (1629-95) who found that the planet possessed thin flat rings, and these varied in appearance as the planet orbited the sun. Two centuries later, the Scots physicist, James Clerk Maxwell (1831-79), proved mathematically that the rings could not be solid but must be composed of swarms of tiny particles, though it

was not until 1980 that the spacecraft *Voyager I* could confirm this at its close approach to the planet. The spectroscope and the *Pioneer* and *Voyager* spacecraft have confirmed what visual observation indicated: Jupiter and Saturn are physically and chemically similar.

Mars was also observed when the telescope came to be used regularly by astronomers, but because of the small disc it presents — it is only about one-eighth the apparent size of Jupiter — it is much more difficult to discern any detail. Nevertheless, in the seventeenth century, Gian Domenico Cassini, Felice Fontana, Robert

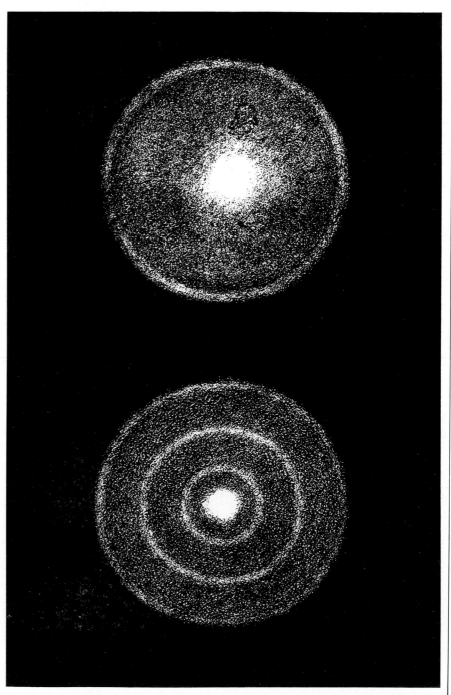

THE NEBULA THEORY The French mathematician Pierre Laplace argued that the sun and the planets had been formed from a spinning mass of gas *(below)*. This span off rings of matter, which gradually condensed to form the planets *(bottom)*.

RINGS OF SATURN In this photograph taken by one of the *Voyager* space probes far more of Saturn's rings are revealed than can be seen from earth. At their widest, the rings measure 169,000 miles (271,000 km) in diameter but are only 10 miles (16 km) thick. When edge-on to the earth, as they appear every 13¾ years, they disappear because they are so thin. They will appear at their widest again in 1987. Because we see Saturn from an angle, the rings look elliptical but they are, in fact, perfectly circular. They are composed of particles and contain ammonia ice.

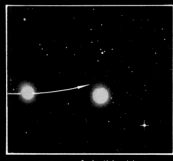

COLLISION THEORY 1. In this old hypothesis about the formation of planets, a star first approaches the sun.

2. The star and the sun collide.

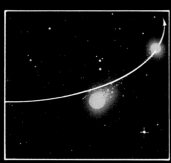

3. As a result of the collision, material is drawn out of both stars.

4. This material then forms into planets which go into orbit around the sun.

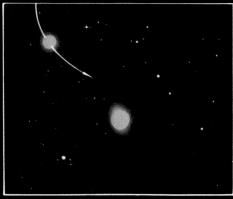

CLOSE APPROACH THEORY 1. A version of the collision theory, in this hypothesis a star approaches the sun.

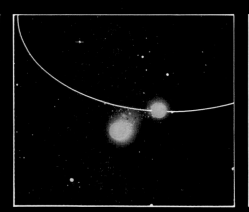

2. Instead of colliding, the star approaches the sun very closely, drawing out material from each.

3. This material then forms into planets which go into orbit around the sun.

MODERN HYPOTHESIS Present thinking about the origin of the solar system is a revival of a version of the nebular theory first proposed by Kant and Laplace in the eighteenth century. Kant imagined the solar system condensing from a basic primordial material; Laplace saw this as a spinning mass of gas. Rejecting 'catastrophe' theories, astronomers today, having established that hydrogen is the abundant element in the universe, are more inclined to believe in the version of the nebular hypothesis. In this theory, a cloud of gas (1) begins to condense in space (2). The densest condensation forms into a star — our sun — surrounded by smaller condensations or 'proto-planets' (3). The smaller condensations form into planets, asteroids or moons (4). The original material is in motion, so the sun and its eventual planet system are also in rotation.

MERCURY The first close-up pictures of Mercury taken by the space probe *Mariner 10* revealed for the first time a heavily cratered surface, strikingly similar to that of the moon. Like the moon, Mercury has no atmosphere, but it receives 10 times as much solar radiation. Mercury's craters are also smaller than the moon's because of the stronger gravitational force. The craters in both cases are thought to be the result of a meteoric bombardment in the past which affected the whole solar system.

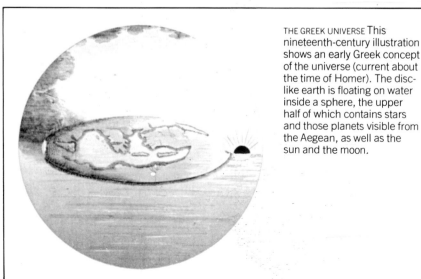

THE GREEK UNIVERSE This nineteenth-century illustration shows an early Greek concept of the universe (current about the time of Homer). The disc-like earth is floating on water inside a sphere, the upper half of which contains stars and those planets visible from the Aegean, as well as the sun and the moon.

Hooke and Giacomo Maraldi studied the planet and from the regular reappearance of dark spots found a rotation period of some 24 hours 40 minutes, correct to within two and a half minutes of today's accepted value. They also saw that the planet had two white polar caps. In the eighteenth century William Herschel made observations, and in the nineteenth the lunar observers Beer and Mädler studied the planet. But the most notable and controversial of all observers of Mars was the American business-man Percival Lowell (1855-1916) who founded the Lowell Observatory in Arizona and equip-ped it with some of the best types of telescopic equipment then available.

Lowell was a planetary observer who worked mainly in the first decades of the twentieth cen-tury. He became convinced that the surface of Mars did indeed carry a network of fine lines, first observed in 1877 by Giovanni Schiaparelli, and he felt certain there were artificial water-

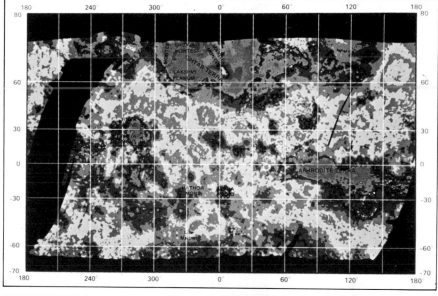

VENUS What Venus is really like remains something of a mystery. Heavy cloud covers its surface, masking it from view as shown in the photograph taken by Mariner 10 in 1974 (left). As the atmosphere is composed of a corrosive mixture of sulphuric, and other acids, some spacecraft have been destroyed before even attempting to land. Some photographs showing a rocky surface have, however, been taken by Russian probes. Radar equipment on orbiting spacecraft has managed to map the surface by probing beneath the clouds (above).

ways engineered by a Martian civilization. Only the close reconnaissance by the *Mariner* spacecraft from 1965 onwards finally proved what many astronomers suspected, that the presence of the canals was an optical illusion. The spacecrafts *Viking 1* and *Viking 2*, which soft-landed on the planet in 1976, made history by being the first probes to land on a planet and investigate the possible presence of life.

Being closer to the sun than the earth, the surface detail of the two planets Mercury and Venus is hard to observe, for when closest to us they present only a very thin crescent. Indeed, the surface features on Mercury and Venus (which is covered permanently with thick clouds) remained unknown until the close approach of the *Mariner 10* spacecraft in 1974 and the soft-landing of Russian *Venera* craft in 1975. And what is true of Mercury and Venus is true too of the physical nature of the outermost planets Uranus, Neptune (which was only

discovered in 1846 because of its gravitational disturbance of Uranus' orbit), and Pluto (discovered for similar reasons in 1930). Pluto's planetary status is now, however, in doubt; it may be a stray planetary satellite.

Satellites of the planets were not discovered until the invention of the telescope. Besides Galileo's pioneering discovery, satellites have been found to accompany Mars, Saturn, Uranus and Neptune; their discovery covers observations from the seventeenth to the twentieth centuries. Their nature, however, and the existence of some very small satellites orbiting Jupiter and Saturn, can only be determined by observations from spacecraft; these began in 1979. Although a watch is still kept on the planets themselves by terrestrial observers, it is now clear that the physical conditions of the planets and their satellites can only be fully studied in the future by orbiting spacecraft which may or may not land probes.

The Nature of Comets

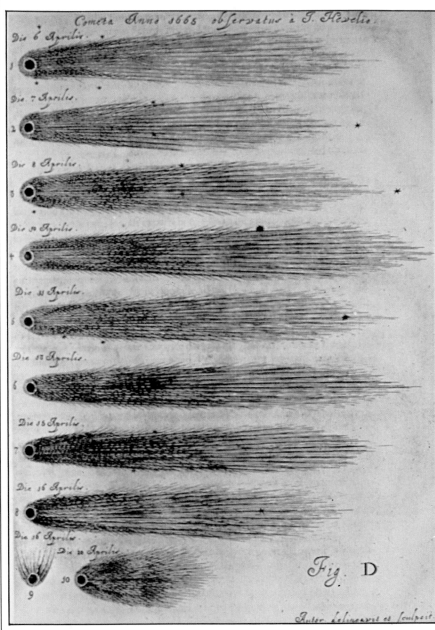

SPANNING THE SKY The passage of comets across the night sky has been a phenomenon which has fascinated man since earliest times. Their appearance was often seen as a sign of impending disaster *(far right)*. The sketches *(above)*, indicating clearly the shapes of individual comets, were made by the astronomer Hevelius, based on his telescopic observations. The photograph *(centre)* is of the comet Arend-Roland, which appeared in 1957. The 'spike' at the front is an effect created by perspective; in fact, it is an additional tail.

Comets are transitory, and the advent of bright ones visible without a telescope is infrequent; however, if an observer manages to spot one, a bright naked-eye comet is an awe-inspiring sight. With its bright head and long streaming tail, it is bound to attract attention, especially since it may appear in the night sky for weeks on end. Records of comets go back to antiquity — there is a Babylonian record of a bright one in 1140BC — and the Chinese records, which date from 613BC, are the most complete ancient records available. They have been a great help in tracing previous appearances of comets.

The periodic appearance of comets was not recognized at first and to the earliest astronomers they arrived without warning and slowly vanished, apparently to nothingness. But because bright comets vary remarkably in

appearance, the Greeks attempted to classify them. Their colour, their shape and the steadiness of their light were described but their true nature remained a mystery. Some of the followers of Pythagoras believed comets to be 'errant stars' but this view was not followed up. Perhaps the most astonishing of all the scientific opinions was the one that claimed comets were an optical illusion caused by reflected moonlight or starlight. The view that prevailed, however, was that comets were meteorological phenomena of the upper air. Once Eudoxos in the fourth century BC had propounded his theory of the universe as a nest of spheres, and Aristotle had elaborated this into a scheme whereby all change had to occur in the 'sub-lunary sphere' which contained the earth and the surrounding air, it became clear that comets, being transitory, could not be truly celestial bodies. It was suggested then by Aristotle in his *Meteorologia (Meteorology)* that comets and also meteors or 'shooting stars', which appear in the sky for seconds rather than for days and weeks, were due to vapours exhaled from the earth. These, he believed, collected in the sphere of air which lay just below the sphere of fire (a convenient sphere which 'explained' that flames always burned upwards because they were seeking their 'natural place'). Comets became visible, he thought, when they were ignited by the sphere of fire.

Aristotle's theory meant that comets possessed the qualities of dryness and heat, and being in the upper air they would affect terrestrial behaviour. Droughts and famines and even associated pestilences might well, therefore, be due to their appearance. Such a view

THE NAKED EYE To the unaided eye, only the luminous heads and tails of bright comets are clearly visible. Their luminosity is caused by their proximity to the sun. The examples here appeared in India *(above left)* and South Africa *(above right)*.

fitted with the general belief that the appearance of a comet presaged disaster of some kind, a view which has persisted among many people even up to the present. There was also an opinion, which again is still sometimes to be found, that comets are the souls of illustrious men being borne to heaven in triumph. The Romans, particularly, favoured this view and the bright comet of 43BC was widely held to be the soul of Julius Caesar.

The Greek and Roman views persisted in the West until well into the Renaissance. In China, however, comets were generally thought to be associated with the planets, each originating from a particular planet, although some Chinese philosophers believed them to be caused by a derangement of the two primary forces of nature, yin and yang. Additionally, in AD837, the Chinese first pointed out that a comet's tail always points away from the sun.

The next step in understanding came from Tycho Brahe (1546-1601) who observed the great comet of 1577 and collected and analyzed the observations of others, including Thomas Digges. Brahe found that with the evidence of observers in different places, he could attempt to measure the parallax, then the distance, of the comet from earth. In fact he was not able to determine the precise figure, but he did discern an important fact: the comet's parallax was far less than the parallax of the moon, in other words, the comet was further off than the moon. Comets were not, therefore, meteorological; they were truly celestial bodies. What is more, Brahe's observations led him to the conclusion that the comet had passed through at least one planetary sphere, and his belief in the reality of such spheres was shattered. This disenchantment with the celestial spheres as objects having a real existence soon became universal, especially when Kepler found from Brahe's own observations that the planets move round the sun in ellipses not circles.

The main question that faced astronomers after Brahe was to discover the true paths of comets. This may sound easy but it is not so.

Comets are only visible when they are comparatively close to the sun because only then do they shine; while visible, their paths curve strongly. The puzzle is, what does the comet do when it has ceased to be so close? Does it move away in a straight line or a curve, and if in a curve, is it an hyperbola or parabola (both of which are 'open ended' and do not close up on themselves) or a circle or ellipse? To answer these questions seemed to demand observations over a very great distance into space and, even with a telescope, comets ceased to shine too soon for accuracy.

When Newton published his *Principia* in 1687, he suggested that comets might move in a parabolic path (the kind of path followed by a projectile like an arrow or a bullet). Certainly they would, as celestial bodies, be subject to the law of universal gravitation. Appropriately, it was his contemporary Edmond Halley, without whose financial and editorial help the *Principia* would never have been published, who was the first to apply the laws to comets.

In 1682, a bright comet appeared and Halley noticed, after measuring its positions, that it seemed to have a path just like two other bright comets which had arrived in 1607 and 1531. He conjectured that the three comets were, in fact, all returns of the same body; if he were correct this meant that the body moved in an ellipse. He therefore applied Newton's laws of gravitation in order to calculate the disturbing effects on the comet's orbit of Jupiter and Saturn, and predicted that the comet would reappear in 1758. Halley died in 1742 but on Christmas Day, 1758, the comet did return and both Newton's law and Halley's prediction were justified.

Since 1758 many other periodic comets have been discovered and their paths calculated with considerable precision. Halley's is still of interest; its returns have been traced back as early as 87BC, and it is to be the subject of a spacecraft investigation on its next return in 1985 or 1986.

In the nineteenth century, it was discovered that there is a link between comets and the far

ISTI MIRANT STELLA

HAROLD

more transitory meteors, which are known to be rocky and metallic material burning up while travelling through the earth's atmosphere. Although meteors appear apparently at random at night and also by day, as Bernard Lovell, John Clegg and James Hey discovered using radio astronomical equipment in the late 1940s, they also appear in showers. The showers are repeated year after year, and it had been recognized in the 1880s by John Couch Adams (the co-discoverer with Jean Urbain Leverrier of Neptune) and Giovanni Schiaparelli, that meteor showers in August and November had orbits which seemed identical with those of two comets. By then some comets had been observed to undergo disruptions. For instance, at its appearance in 1845 and 1846, Biela's comet was seen to split into two and, at a calculated appearance in 1866 it never appeared, and has not done since. It was therefore recognized that the material of which a comet is composed may break apart and be dispersed along its orbit.

The nature and origin of comets have been well investigated during both the nineteenth and twentieth centuries. Forces that could have the effect of pushing, or pulling, particles to form a tail were studied first by Friedrich Bessel, John Herschel and Heinrich Olbers in the 1830s and 1840s, although the matter was not explain-ed in terms of radiation from the sun until the twentieth century. The spectroscope was used to study the composition of comets as early as 1864 by Giovanni Donati and then by William Huggins, who discovered that the complex molecules of hydrocarbons were present. Since that time further studies have been made, resulting in two models of a comet. One, proposed in 1953 by Raymond Lyttleton of Cambridge University, supposes comets to be collections of particles rather like sand-grains or gravel. The other and, at present, more widely accepted view is that comets are 'dirty snowballs' or collections of frozen gases with tiny meteoric particles embedded in them. This view was put forward in 1950 by Fred Whipple, and has since been elaborated.

As to the origin of comets, Lyttleton suggested, in 1950, that they come from dust and similar material scooped up by the sun as it travels through space, though most astronomers seem to prefer the theory proposed by Jan Oort in the same year. According to this theory, the solar system is supposed to be a vast spherical cloud of cometary material — rocks and lumps of frozen gas — around the solar system. Both this view and the nature of comets themselves may be confirmed by spacecraft, but this lies in the future.

HALLEY'S COMET The comet recorded by the Norman embroiderers of the Bayeux Tapestry as appearing in 1066 was named after the English astronomer Edmond Halley in the seventeenth century. Halley accurately predicted that the comet would appear at regular intervals, due to its elliptical orbit. By calculating back, it is possible to show that it had appeared in 1066.

Discovering Deep Space

NEW DISCOVERIES IN SPACE The development of radio telescopes has led to the discovery of new phenomena. Cygnus A, the brightest object in the sky at radio wavelengths, is now known to be two sources of radio emission close together, shown in this plot made from radio observations *(below)*. It is thought to be caused by material shot out from some explosive object lying between the two sources and visual observations show a single object there. Abell 1060 *(far right)* is located in a rich cluster of galaxies. Such galaxies appear however deep into space astronomers probe — isolated galaxies appear to be rarer. At an immense distance away — over 1,500 light-years — is the quasar 3C273, the brightest quasar in the northern skies *(below right)*. Probably the central region of a galaxy in the early stage of its development, the quasar is ejecting a mass of material.

The 1920s and 1930s saw the idea that the spiral nebulae are distant 'island universes' confirmed, but the discovery of the spirals by the American astronomer Edwin Hubble (1889-1953) was not the end of the story. These 'galaxies', as they came to be called in the 1950s, were found almost without exception to display a shift of their spectral lines towards the red end of the spectrum. True, Melvin Slipher had discovered that the Andromeda galaxy possessed a blueshift, but this proved to be an exception, for in 1917 he published a list of 25 galaxies of which no less than 21 had redshifts. When Hubble made his investigations, there was new evidence to show that far from being randomly distributed in space, the galaxies were to be found in clusters; all those with blueshifts turned out to be members of our own 'local group'. This is a collection of galaxies which includes the Andromeda galaxy, our own, and the Magellanic Clouds — two galaxies close to our own which appear like two pieces broken off from the Milky Way and are visible only to observers in the southern hemisphere. The outcome, then, was that distant galaxies all possess redshifts.

In addition, by 1929, Hubble had firm evidence for yet another factor of immense significance. This was a relationship between the distance of a galaxy and the speed at which it was receding, that is, between the redshift and the distance, as Carl Wirtz had suggested in 1921. But Wirtz had not had sufficient observational evidence before him to support his case, and this is what Hubble was able to supply. Indeed, by the early 1930s, he and his colleague Milton Humason were able to add still further

measurements and observe the relationships out not only to 7 million light-years (the limit for Hubble's 1929 announcement) but further than 100 million light-years.

One outcome of Hubble's work was that the increasing speed of recession with distance was just the kind of motion to be expected from the comparatively new theory of relativity, and the evidence helped in gaining an increased acceptance for it. The other significant effect was that it provided a new way of measuring distances into the far depths of space. The observations by Hubble and Humason gave an increase of velocity of almost 106 miles per second (170 km per second) every million light-years. In consequence, if a distant galaxy displayed a redshift velocity of 1,060 miles per second (1,700 km per second), this meant that it must lie at a distance of 10 million light-years.

In 1952, Walter Baade (1893-1960), the American, re-examined the evidence about the distances of galaxies determined from the brightness of Cepheid variables. Problems had arisen over the values previously obtained by Hubble because, in the first place, they made the galaxy seem far too large compared with other galaxies of the local group and, secondly, they suggested an age for the universe that seemed far too small. Thirdly, the figures made it seem that certain star clusters in the Andromeda galaxy were dimmer than their equivalents in our Galaxy. Baade proved that there were two 'populations' of stars, one old and one not so old. Each had Cepheid-type variables but the relationship between the rate of variation and the true brightness was not the same for both classes. The result of this was that

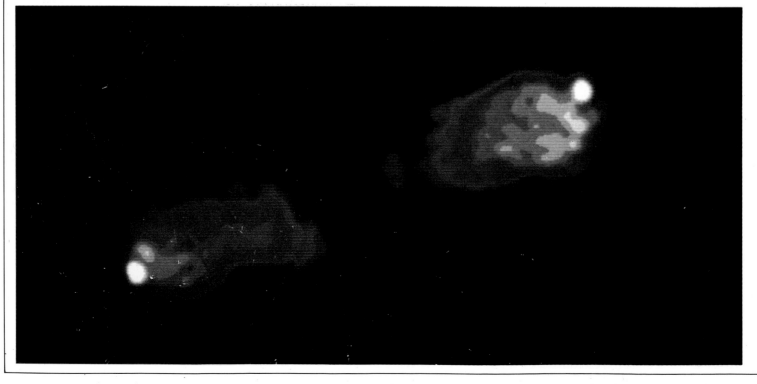

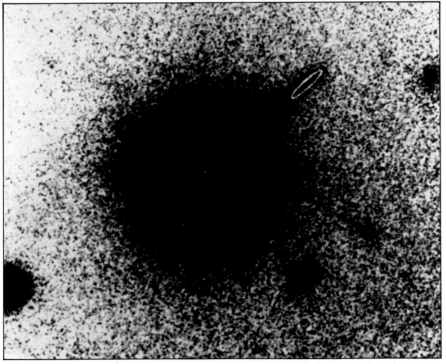

distances of galaxies had to be doubled, and the rate at which velocity changed with distance reduced.

The arrival of new telescopes, and particularly of radio telescopes, has brought about new discoveries in deep space. The first results from radio telescopes in the early 1950s indicated that 'radio stars' seemed to exist. However, in 1954, Baade and Rudolph Minkowski in the United States showed that a very strong radio source in the constellation Cygnus was a distant galaxy not a star, and later found evidence of an explosion. In 1960, Allan Sandage and Thomas Matthew identified objects known as 3C48 and 3C273 (from their catalogue numbers in radio source catalogues prepared by Martin Ryle and his colleagues at Cambridge University) with what appeared on photographs to be star-like bodies.

In 1962 Cyril Hazard and colleagues in Australia observed 3C273 as the moon passed in front of it. This confirmed its position with high accuracy and provided a clear estimate of apparent size. On this evidence, optical astronomers were able to confirm the star-like nature of the object and obtain its spectrum. The spectrum immediately presented a problem because it seemed to contain lines which could not be identified with any known chemical element. However, in 1963, Maarten Schmidt in the United States discussed the redshift and Jesse Greenstein and Thomas Matthews the similar spectrum of 3C48. Both gave evidence of immense redshifts, larger than anything previously observed. The identification of their lines had presented a problem only because it had not at first been realized that they had been shifted from the ultraviolet and normally invisible end of the spectrum into the visible region by so prodigious a redshift. The object 3C273, for instance, was found to have a velocity of recession of 29,450 miles per second (47,400 km per second). Assuming the law of the increase of redshift with distance, this meant that 3C273 was situated at over 1,600 million light-years.

The radiation emitted by these two objects is prodigious — something in the order of a hundred times that of an ordinary spiral galaxy — and because of this it seems obvious they cannot be stars. They therefore were given the name of 'quasi-stellar radio objects', abbreviated to 'quasars', although the term QSO was later used when similar objects were found that did not emit radio waves so intensely, if at all. Some astronomers, puzzled by how such objects could emit so much energy and by the detailed problems of interpretation of the spectra and their association with ordinary galaxies, have queried the redshift interpretation of distance. But in 1964, Greenstein and Schmidt countered some of these arguments with powerful evidence and more recent observations seem to confirm that QSOs are indeed at immense distances, and are probably galaxies in an early stage of development.

The Age and Origin of the Universe

People have often speculated about the beginning of the universe and have attempted to date its origin. Many of the ideas entertained over the centuries have had a religious background; people thought of their gods causing the actual creation and sustaining its continued existence. On the Indian subcontinent the picture was one of a cyclic universe which came into being and then, after a period of time, ended, only to be reborn again and again. The lengths of these cycles were measured in millions of years. In Western Christendom, the creation account that became accepted was that given at the beginning of the book of *Genesis,* and for some 1,600 years it was generally accepted as a correct description. The problem remained, however, to date it.

In the West, this question only came into prominence after the Renaissance, when there was a general tendency to define terms and explore ambiguities. This tendency was given expression by James Ussher (1581-1656), Archbishop of Armagh in Ireland, who devised a system of chronology for dating events in the Bible. By calculating the ages of the patriarchs, Ussher concluded that the Creation had occurred in 4004BC, a date which was for a time taken as the orthodox interpretation among Protestant scholars, and still has some adherents today.

Ussher's dating of Creation was a result of scholarly but not scientific research, and there were those who disagreed with it on scientific grounds when they came to consider other methods of determining the age of the earth. However, it was not until the nineteenth century that the problem was thrown into relief by theories of evolution and, in particular, Charles Darwin's famous book *On the Origin of Species* which apeared in 1859. This theory demanded a very long period for evolution, to be measured in hundreds of millions of years at least. If this were so, astronomers conjectured, then the universe itself must be two or three times older than that. This immediately raised a problem: how did the sun keep shining for so long?

This was an important question. Although in the mid-nineteenth century no one knew precisely how the sun generated its energy, it seemed clear that if it were just a giant body burning in space, it could not last for the kind of time evolutionists were demanding. Yet even before the arrival of Darwin's theory, evidence already pointed to millions of years, and in 1848 a German physician, Julius Mayer, made some proposals which he hoped would solve the problem. Recent research had shown that meteors and comets were related, while Mayer also knew that James Joule had recently found that heat could be generated by friction. Mayer therefore suggested that the sun's energy was continually being replenished by meteors which fell into it.

Mayer's idea was ingenious but when he calculated how much meteoric material was necessary, he was shocked to find that the sun would need twice the moon's weight in meteors each year. This was unbelievable. However, Mayer then suggested that the sun transformed its own material into energy, but at the time the idea seemed fantastic and unacceptable, although, with our knowledge of the existence of thermonuclear energy, where atoms are annihilated and turned into energy, we now know that this is the answer to the sun's radiative power.

In 1854, the German physicist Hermann Helmholtz suggested a new idea: the sun's energy came from its slow contraction under gravity, its central regions continually heating up as it shrank. This, Helmholtz calculated, would keep the sun shining for at least 22 million years, though others obtained a rather smaller figure. Both fell short of what geologists demanded even for the age of the earth. Different theories were refuted until, in 1887, the astronomer and physicist Norman Lockyer produced a new meteoric theory much broader in scope than Mayer's.

Lockyer said he could see no reason why meteoric material should not be distributed throughout the entire universe (this was, of course, before the discovery of galaxies) and be, in fact, its basic material. 'All self-luminous bodies in celestial space', he wrote, 'are composed either of swarms of meteorites or of masses of meteoric vapour produced by heat.' Ingenious though Lockyer's idea was, it did not find much support, even though he thought it would acount for the universe being about 2,000 million years old. Soon, however, it became evident that even the earth was older than this.

At the beginning of the twentieth century, it seemed that the only way of reaching a better estimate of the age of the universe was to discover how stars aged, yet this appeared difficult, if not impossible, to achieve. However, Jacobus Kapteyn, a Dutch astronomer, applied statistical methods to analyze stellar motions and, in 1904, showed that rather than travelling at random, they appeared to be moving in two streams. It was, in fact, the first evidence for the rotation of our Galaxy, although this was not recognized at the time.

James Jeans (1877-1946) used this result and studied the motions of open clusters of stars to attempt an analysis of the age of the universe. He realized that as such clusters move through space they would be affected by three things: firstly, the gravitational pull of all the other stars in the Galaxy; secondly, the gravitational pull of the other members of the cluster; thirdly, the effects of nearby stars not connected with the cluster. With Kapteyn's star-streaming evidence, Jeans was able to calculate how long clusters would take to disperse, and also how long binary stars (pairs of stars orbiting around each other) would take to break away from each other. By next examining the dispersion so far, he was able in 1928 to give a figure for the age of

THE AGE OF THE UNIVERSE The Andromeda galaxy *(above)* is 2.3 million light-years away from earth, which means we observe it now as it was 2.3 million years ago. It is comparatively near to our Galaxy. In astronomical terms it has similarities with our own Galaxy. Both are thought to be thousands of millions of years old. The Greek philosopher Thales developed the first scientific theory of creation *(right)*. He believed the flat earth rested on water, the air and fire above them completing the cycle of the four Greek elements. In this later Christian interpretation, God has been added, creating Adam.

the universe between 1 million million and 10 million million years. Many astronomers accepted this, but Arthur Eddington doubted some of Jean's arguments and settled for a figure a thousand times smaller. When the Hubble-Humason results for the recession of the galaxies were published in the 1930s, they also strongly suggested a much shorter time scale, probably some 2,000 million years. Clearly something was wrong and, as it turned out, both values were inaccurate.

Jeans' value was attacked in 1925 and 1927 when Jan Oort and Bertil Lindblad showed that the Galaxy did not rotate as Jeans had assumed, but that those clusters nearer the centre rotate more slowly than those nearer the edge. Thus stars in an open cluster would undergo more uneven gravitational effects and be dispersed sooner. In 1952, Baade showed that Hubble's distance measurements for the galaxies were too small; this increased the Hubble-Humason estimate of the age of the universe, but still brought it below the long time-scale of Jeans. A value of between 10,000 and 20,000 million years seemed probable.

When considering the recession of the

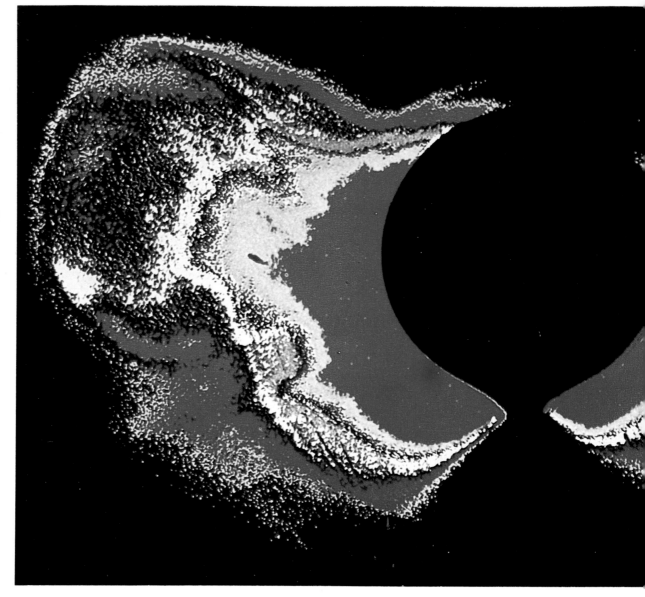

THE SUN'S CORONA Taken from *Skylab* at X-ray wavelengths, this photograph reveals the layers of thin gas trapped around the sun and the magnetic fields that hold them in place. From earth, the corona is only visible during an eclipse when it shows up as a faint haze; from space, however, away from the earth's atmosphere, it stands out clearly when the sun's disc is masked. During the *Skylab* operation the sun was studied in detail over a period of eight-and-a-half months, and revealed that the surface of the sun is far more complex than has previously been supposed. The sun is a fairly typical star; information about its composition and activity provides valuable clues to the nature of other stars in the universe.

galaxies – the 'expansion of the universe' – it becomes evident that if we go back in time, the galaxies themselves must have been closer to each other than they are now. Certainly there are different kinds of galaxy — not all are spirals, some seem to be elliptically shaped — but though Hubble had ideas about the evolution of such galaxies, this does not affect the idea of gradual change with time. After the 1930s it seemed likely that the universe began as a compact mass of material which began to expand; this is what has since come to be called the 'big bang' theory.

In 1933 and 1934, Georges Lemaître, a Belgian, had suggested just such a big bang beginning to the universe. He conceived of the universe as one huge superatom which, he thought, broke apart of its own accord, shooting out 'particles' like a radioactive substance just as radium does. These particles later formed galaxies, which still continued to move outwards. However, Lemaître did not believe that the galaxies would have carried on their recession due to this original ejection from the superatom, and invoked a 'cosmical repulsion' to explain the continuing expansion of the universe. The cosmical repulsion force, which took over from gravity at very large distances, was one of the concepts that could follow on from relativity theory.

In the late 1940s and early 1950s a modified form of Lemaiitre's theory was proposed in the United States by George Gamow and his colleagues Ralph Alpher, Robert Herman and Hans Bethe. They conceived of the initial explosion of the superatom at a very high temperature. This not only did away with the need to invoke cosmical repulsion, but also meant that the very earliest stages were amenable to study using the tools of nuclear physics. It has so far

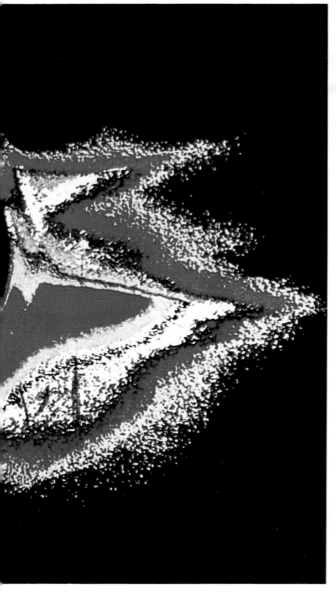

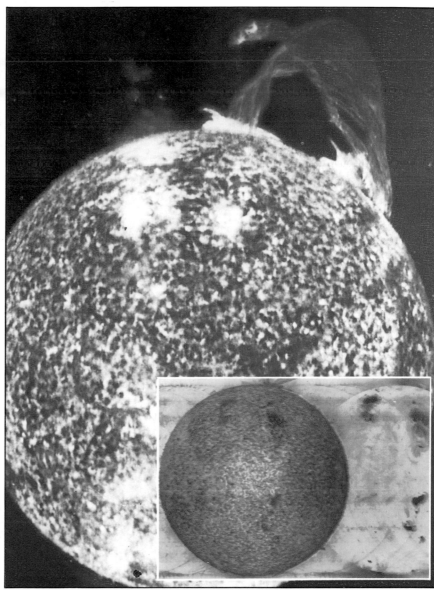

proved a highly successful theory and makes detailed discussion about the processes of the first fractions of a second after the initial explosion possible today.

The big bang theories do not answer the question of where the superatom came from in the first place, but this issue is neatly sidestepped in another class of theory — the 'steady state' theories — which seemed for a time to hold great promise. They were first suggested in 1948 in England by Hermann Bondi and Thomas Gold, who took as a basic principle that the universe must look the same not only from every point in space but also every point in time — the 'perfect cosmological principle' they called it. This they believed was necessary to conform fully with relativity theory. In such a universe, material moving away due to expansion is replaced by the continuous creation of atoms. The theory was modified by Fred Hoyle

in the same year, his steady state hypothesis containing an inbuilt, automatic balance between the rate of continuous creation and the expansion of the universe.

The introduction of the steady state theories came at a time of disagreements about the age of the universe, between the very long timescales and the very much shorter Hubble age. However, in 1965, Arno Penzias and Robert Wilson in the United States, using a radio telescope designed for other purposes, discovered a background radio radiation over the entire sky. This, it became realized, was radiation due to the original 'hot' big bang proposed by Gamow and his colleagues. With such evidence, as well as observations that indicate that the perfect cosmological principle does not hold everywhere in space, the almost universal opinion of astronomers is that the universe had a hot, big bang origin.

FLARES AND SUNSPOTS The bright surface or photosphere is in constant turmoil, with cyclic disturbances in the form of sunspots and giant flares arising out of disruptions in the magnetic field. Sunspots *(inset)* are the result of intense magnetism breaking up the surface to reveal cooler gases. Reactions between sunspots can cause massive loops or flares to balloon out into space. Such a flare photographed by *Skylab (above)* stretched 360,000 miles (576,000km) into space.

Relativity Theory

It was Galileo who, in his famous book *Dialogue on the Great World Systems* (1630) pointed out that the motion of bodies is relative. He cited the imaginary case of observers on board ship. Even though they might have fish swimming in a tank in the cabin, or birds flying about after being released from a cage, the observers could not tell whether the ship was stationary or moving across the seas. The motion of birds and fish would be the same in both cases. The situation was also appreciated by Descartes and by Newton, although Newton thought of absolute motion and absolute time, as most people still do today. However, as research progressed, it became increasingly clear that a stable point in the universe, from which everything could be measured, was hard to find. For instance, a body that is at rest on the earth is certainly not at rest with respect to the sun. When, in 1783, William Herschel had shown that the sun itself moves in space, it seemed that there was no fixed place. Subsequent research has shown that even the galaxies are not stationary. It is true that we can only measure the movement relative to us, but that does not mean that our Galaxy is stationary; it merely means that the redshifts we measure should be corrected by our own motion.

In 1889, the whole matter was very carefully examined by the French mathematician, Henri Poincaré, who came to the conclusion that since all the laws of physics are based on observations made on earth, they need a radical revision if there is no fixed place in the universe. Looking back on the strange results achieved from 1881 onwards in experiments conducted by the American physicist Albert Michelson, first alone and then with Edward Morley to measure the velocity of light, it is clear that some revision was necessary. At this time, it was generally believed that light travelled in something called the 'aether', which had neither weight nor any other measurable property, and what Michelson attempted was to measure the velocity of light in the aether in two directions at right-angles, one direction along the path in which the earth moves as it orbits the sun, and one perpendicular to it. It was presumed that there should be a difference between the two measurements: one would give the speed of light plus the velocity of the earth and the other just the speed of light.

The outcome of Michelson's own experiments and those he carried out with Morley was negative: the measurements showed no difference at all. Despite immense sensitivity, which should have enabled even a very small difference to be measured, they obtained a nil result. The velocity of light was the same in both directions. This seemed self-evident nonsense. Later research showed that the measurement at right-angles to the earth's motion should not give just the speed of light, but there should have been a measurable difference all the same. This was pointed out by Hendrik Lorentz, a

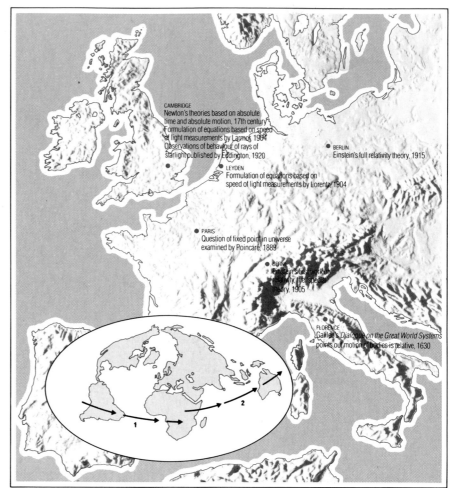

CAMBRIDGE
Newton's theories based on absolute time and absolute motion, 17th century
Formulation of equations based on speed of light measurements by Larmor, 1904
Observations of behaviour of rays of starlight published by Eddington, 1920

BERLIN
Einstein's full relativity theory, 1915

LEYDEN
Formulation of equations based on speed of light measurements by Lorentz, 1904

PARIS
Question of fixed point in universe examined by Poincaré, 1889

BERNE
Einstein's first work on relativity (the special theory), 1905

FLORENCE
Galileo's *Dialogue on the Great World Systems* points out motion of bodies is relative, 1630

Dutch physicist, who worked out the mathematical consequences of the experimental results, as also did a British physicist, Joseph Larmor. This research led to a series of mathematical equations linking the length, time and the massiveness of bodies with their velocity and also with the speed of light.

In 1905 Albert Einstein (1879-1955), a German physicist then working at the Patent Office in Berne, Switzerland, published his 'special theory' of relativity which considers bodies in uniform motion with respect to one another. This means that it does not consider acceleration or deceleration, in other words, the motion of bodies where the velocity is changing. This theory analyzes physical laws where there is no idea of a stationary point; it assumes that the speed of light is the maximum velocity which any body could achieve, and makes complete sense of the Michelson-Morley experiment. At the same time, Einstein also found that the mass of a body could, in theory, be turned into energy and that the speed of light is involved in that relationship too. This leads to the now famous equation $E = mc^2$ (when E is energy, m the mass of the body and c the velocity of light). In 1915, further research enabled him to publish his 'general theory' of relativity, which did con-

NEW IDEAS ABOUT SPACE AND TIME
Relativity theory was developed over a fairly short period of time but, although the key work was done by Einstein, other observations and research also contributed. Upsetting Newton's long-accepted notions of absolute motion and absolute time, relativity suggested that the universe was curved and added the fourth dimension of time to height, width and breadth. This revolutionary, although difficult, concept soon began to be confirmed by the results of observations made at the solar eclipses in 1919 and 1922 *(inset)*. In 1919 British astronomers observed along the path of the eclipse at Sobral in South America and Principe Island off the coast of Africa (1). Similar results were obtained when the 1922 eclipse was observed by American astronomers at Wallal in Australia (2).

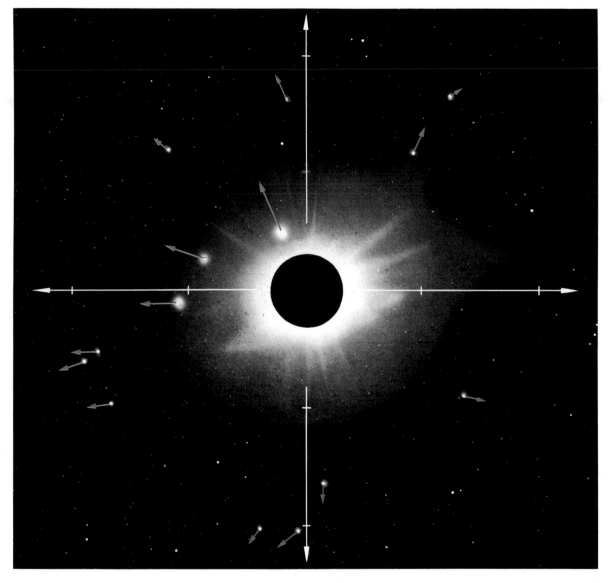

CONFIRMING RELATIVITY The strange predictions of Einstein's relativity theory were confirmed soon after its publication in 1915. According to the theory, rays of starlight would be bent when passing close to a massive body. The solar eclipse of 1919 provided an opportunity to test this and results published in 1920 by Eddington and his colleagues confirmed that the positions of stars shifted in apparent position as predicted. In 1922, another eclipse was observed by American astronomers, with the same results, as shown in the diagram (left). A series of experiments carried out at the end of the nineteenth century by Michelson and Morley came up with startling results that could only be fully understood in terms of relativity. They found that the speed of light did not vary with respect to an observer, however slow or fast that observer was moving. Extremely sensitive measurements of the velocity of light were made in two directions: one along the path of the earth's orbit and one perpendicular to it (below). The expected difference did not occur.

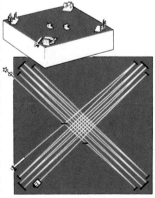

sider accelerated motion and showed that space and time are intimately connected. It is also a theory that indicates a close link between gravitation and space.

Since 1915, the general theory of relativity, which helped to bring about a revolution in our ideas of the physical universe, has been developed much further, especially by those astronomers concerned with the study of the universe as a whole. Like most scientific theories that upset many old ideas, and especially one with so many fundamental new concepts, relativity was at first viewed with grave suspicion by many scientists but, soon after Einstein had begun publishing his ideas, evidence supporting the theory appeared. Indeed, the first was pointed out by Einstein himself in 1915. He showed how the theory of relativity would account for an observed peculiarity in the motion of the orbit of the planet Mercury, a motion which could not be accounted for by Newton's theory of gravitation.

A second confirmation came in 1920 when Arthur Eddington and colleagues published the results of observations made at the total solar eclipse of the year before. Relativity predicted that rays of starlight would be bent when passing close to a massive body, partly due to the curvature of space itself. Since stars can be observed when the sun is totally eclipsed by the moon's disc passing in front of it, the eclipse offered an ideal opportunity to test this prediction. The result confirmed exactly the deflection calculated from general relativity. Additional confirmation using radio observations as well as light have since been made while, from the late 1970s on, other predictions, particularly those concerned with the mass of moving bodies and the distortion of time, have also been confirmed. There is now no doubt that relativity is another powerful theory in understanding the natural world, and one that has already had profound implications on the outlook in the relatively short time since it was devised.

New Universes

As will have become evident by now, our growing conception of the universe has been a continuous process of expanding frontiers and increasing knowledge of the kinds of objects that are to be found within its boundaries. To begin with, there was the basic idea of a dome, a hemisphere, then in Greek times, perhaps as early as the eighth century BC, an expansion to a sphere, later populated by earthly bodies composed of four basic elements and a fifth celestial, unchanging substance. Within the realm of celestial bodies were the sun, moon, planets and stars. Once Copernicus, in the late sixteenth century, had dethroned the earth from the centre and replaced it with the sun, the concept of an infinite universe arrived; this universe was still filled with the sun, planets and stars but the idea of boundless space was prevalent, as the Chinese had conceived 1,400 years before.

The infinite, sun-centred universe imagined by the West, however, had a new dimension compared with the old Chinese concept: its mathematical aspect. Newton had devised a universal mathematical law of gravitation that applied to all the planets and, he believed, the stars as well. When, in the 1780s onwards, William Herschel discovered stars orbiting around each other, there was proof that gravitation does operate far into space, and that mathematical analysis is valid into the very depths of space.

The next stage in understanding only came during this century after the arrival of the general theory of relativity. In 1922, the Russian mathematician Aleksandr Friedmann showed that one of the consequences of a relativistic universe in which there is motion, that is, in an expanding universe, is that space is curved. In other words, a body moving outwards will always travel in a curved path. The Russian's work remained unknown for a long time, but in 1927 and 1931 the concept of a curved universe closing round on itself but expanding in size, as the receding galaxies indicated, was also shown by Georges Lemaître to be a consequence of relativity. This meant that the universe was not infinite but it was unbounded: there is no limit to the motion of any body within curved space. The type of curvature being considered is extremely complex: the universe is not thought of simply as a sphere in infinite space, but as a sphere folded over on itself — a concept impossible to illustrate but one that can be expressed precisely in mathematical terms. This new universe of relativity may seem esoteric and even fanciful, yet research since the 1930s has shown it to be an apt description of reality and it has led to such exciting concepts as black holes.

As far back as 1798, the French astronomer and mathematician Pierre Laplace argued that there might be some stars which could emit no light even though they were shining. The basis of his case was Newtonian gravitation. Laplace

knew that the velocity a body needed to escape from a planet or star depended on how massive the star or planet might be. To give a modern example, a spacecraft needs to reach a velocity of 1.4 miles per second (2.3 km per second) to escape into space from the moon, but it requires a velocity of 7 miles per second (11.2 km per second) to escape from the heavier earth, and more than 385 miles per second (617 km per second) from the sun. Laplace calculated that there could be bodies which were so massive — his figure was 250 times the mass of the sun — from which particles of light as envisaged by Newton could not escape because they did not travel fast enough.

In 1916, Karl Schwarzschild, a German astronomer and mathematician, used relativity theory to discuss the behaviour of space around massive bodies. In 1931 and 1932, the Russian Lev Landau and the Pakistani mathematician Subrahmanyan Chandrasekhar then used Schwarzschild's results and discovered that if a body were more than one-and-a-half times the mass of the sun, its own force of gravity would

LEAVING THE EARTH The diagram illustrates Newton's theory about the different paths followed by a projectile ejected from the earth at different speeds. If ejected with sufficient speed, the body would go into orbit, as an artificial satellite actually does. Faster still and it would escape from the earth.

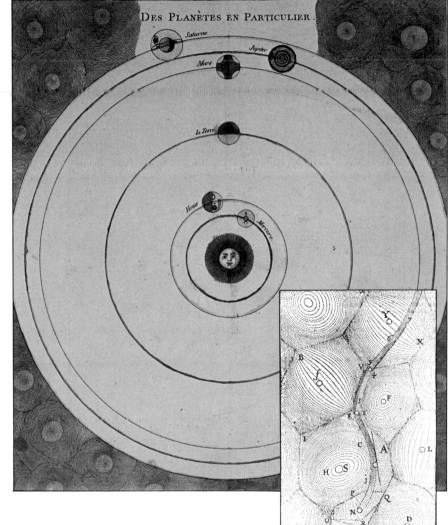

force it to collapse. Such a collapse was studied further by Chandrasekhar in 1934 and the Americans Robert Oppenheimer and Hartland Snyder in 1941; they realized that there could be very dense collapsed objects round which space would curve so strongly that neither light nor any other radiation could escape.

The research of this kind so far described was all theoretical, yet actual discovery of dense white dwarf stars from 1914 onwards made it clear that at least some stars did collapse at the end of their lives, and that their atoms could be crushed so that a teaspoonful of their material would weigh tonnes. Evidence for more compact stars did not come until 1967, when Jocelyn Bell Burnell and Anthony Hewish, using a new type of radio telescope at Cambridge University, discovered a pulsing radio source. This 'pulsar' was the first of a number of stars which are so compact that they weigh a million times more than a white dwarf, and are considered as 'neutron stars'.

If an immensely dense black hole — a star which collapses to virtually zero size with space so distorted around it that radiation cannot escape — exists, then the basic problem was to observe it. If such a star is a member of a binary system, it has been found that it would draw off material from its companion star. This material would circle round the black hole before falling in and would emit X-rays. Since the first launching in 1970 of satellites to observe X-rays, such X-ray binaries have been observed.

Finally, it may be that our picture of the finite but unbounded universe of the relativity theory is too restricted. Mathematically, it is possible to work out some detail of white holes, the converse of black holes. In these, matter, perhaps from black holes, streams out again somewhere else into space. Yet no firm evidence of this kind exists. All the same, looking back on the various universes imagined through history, each more comprehensively understood than its predecessor, it seems possible that new and broader conceptions may well be developed as our means of observing the universe grow and our powers to theorize and probe deeper into space expand.

MILKY WAY This is a view looking towards the centre of our Galaxy in the region of Sagittarius *(far left)*. Current research has led scientists to believe that a black hole probably lies at the Galaxy's centre.

THE CARTESIAN UNIVERSE Descartes saw the universe as being composed of vortices, as shown in this print of the solar system published in 1761 *(above)* These can be seen more clearly in the illustration *(inset)* showing his theory of how a comet moves from one vortex to another.

Observing the Skies

One obvious aspect of astronomy, as of every branch of natural science, is that much of its progress depends on observational techniques. Progress in theoretical research is important and will, more often than not, suggest new objects or possibilities for the observer to find or prove, while in astronomy the advent of new equipment has always had the most profound effect.

In the very earliest times before the great civilizations, observational techniques must have been very simple, and even Egyptian and Mesopotamian equipment, such as it was, would have been basic. The aim of these peoples was to observe the midday sun, the moon and the stars at sunrise and sunset. In more temperate latitudes, stone markers were used for similar purposes. However, we know that the Mesopotamian astronomers also observed the motions of the planets, and this must have involved a device for measuring angles. What precise devices they used we do not know, but it would appear probable that their methods were adopted by the Greeks, and their equipment was therefore similar in a number of cases.

Beside the gnomon — the vertical stake in the ground used to determine the length of the sun's shadow — the Greeks made use of the plinth, the armillary, and a device known as 'Ptolemy's rules' or 'Ptolemy's ruler'. The plinth was a narrow block of wood or stone with its narrowest side facing north and south and, carefully levelled, it indicated the height of the noonday sun. From it developed a 'meridional armillary', that is an armillary or ring placed vertically with its rim due north and south, again for measuring the sun's altitude. There was also an 'equational armillary', a ring set parallel to the celestial equator; with this, angles of a celestial body along the celestial equator could be measured. All these instruments were simple, with no moving parts.

The next stage in the development of such static instruments occurred in Islam, where large observing devices were made of stone, one of the most significant being a vast stone sextant — an instrument built in the form of the arc of a circle 60 degrees long and designed for measuring altitudes — with a scale of some 96 ft (30m) long. This sextant was constructed for the astronomer Ulugh Beg at Samarkland in Central America in the fifteenth century.

A different development in Greek times were instruments with moving parts. Ptolemy's ruler was one of these; it was a post with two arms which were linked together. The observer sighted along one arm and measured the angle from a scale on the other arm. During late medieval times other observing instruments were devised, the most famous being the astrolabe, developed in Islam, and the armillary sphere. This was a collection of metal rings depicting the circles of the celestial sphere which were used by astronomers to define the positions of celestial bodies. However, in thirteenth-century China, an instrument with one large circle and sights was built and mounted so that it could readily follow the stars as they pursued their curved paths in the sky. This novel device was the prototype of the 'equatorial mounting', which became universal in the West in the late nineteenth century for professional carrying telescopes.

In the 1570s the Danish astronomer Tycho Brahe designed and built new sighting instruments, mainly sextants and quadrants (these had scales of 90 degrees in length), which were constructed with a precision never achieved before. Moreover, he devised new

EARLY OBSERVATIONAL TECHNIQUES One of the earliest devices used for indicating the height of the sun or other celestial bodies was 'Ptolemy's ruler'. This early print shows astronomers observing the altitude of the sun *(below)*. Tycho Brahe measured the altitude of the sun using his large mural quadrant, situated at his island observatory at Hven (Uraniborg). The illustration *(below centre)* from Tycho Brahe's *Astronomiae Instauratae Mechanica*, 1598, shows Brahe and his assistant together with various instruments and Brahe's alchemical laboratory. More accurate observations were possible with the arrival of the telescope, shown here *(below right)* on Flamsteed's equatorial quadrant.

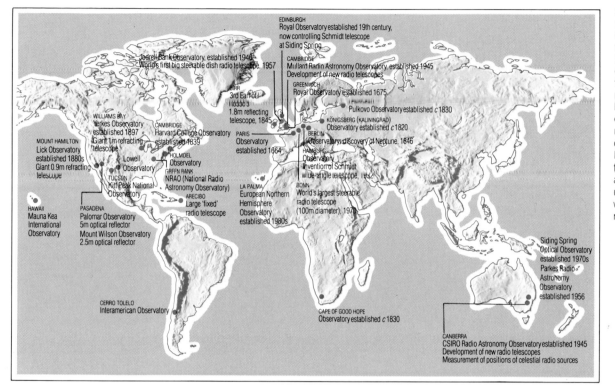

types of scale which could be read to a higher degree of accuracy, and devised a method of observing with these instruments which took into account the errors that even the most precisely built equipment will contain. A new age of precise and compact astronomical observation arrived.

While Brahe's instruments were still new, a revolutionary observing device arrived: the telescope. It is not known who invented it; the first patents were taken out in Holland in 1608, but there is evidence that the application was made by the constructors rather than the inventors of the device. Primitive forms of telescope had probably been in use earlier, in England and Italy, but with inferior optics. Whatever the answer, the telescope, especially in the hands of Galileo, ushered in a totally new dimension in astronomy.

Early telescopes had many optical defects, not least the fact that they showed coloured rings round every star and planet and were likely to show only a small central region in focus. To minimize these faults, astronomers constructed very long instruments, some over 96 ft (30 m) in length. Slung by block and tackle from a tall mast, they were most unwieldy. Much smaller telescopes could, however, be used satisfactorily with measuring instruments, to achieve a greater degree of precision.

It was the unwieldiness of the long telescopes that led Isaac Newton (1642-1727) to experiment with ways of overcoming optical defects. In the end he decided to gather light not by a lens at the front of the telescope but by a curved mirror at the rear, and such a reflecting tele-

scope could be quite short. In 1671, he built one which was only some 6 in (15 cm) long and almost 1 in (3.5 cm) in aperture, but which showed the moon clearly; another showed Jupiter '... as distinct and sharply defined as I have seen him in other Telescopes'.

Newton's reflecting telescope utilized a curved mirror to gather the light, and a small, flat mirror to catch this reflected light as it converged towards the eyepiece, which was placed at the side of the tube. This was considered an inconvenience by many astronomers and Newton's design was not used by many until the time of Herschel, then it became popular in the nineteenth century, at a time when astronomers demanded the most powerful telescopes so that they could probe ever deeper into space.

Newton's reflecting telescope was not the first. In 1616, Niccolo Zucchi, an Italian, had suggested using a curved mirror instead of a front lens but had found the result so poor in practice that he reverted to Galileo's lens design. Again, in 1636, Marin Marsenne in France proposed a different design and, although he never followed it through, it was later revived by a Monsieur Cassegrain almost 40 years later. Still another variation had been designed in 1663 by the Scots mathematician, James Gregory, but he was unable to construct an instrument, and professional instrument makers failed with a design that received severe criticism from Newton. In the 1740s, the design became popular but for no more than some 20 years.

The lens telescope or refractor had the promise of a new lease of life in 1729 when it was discovered, by Chester Moor Hall in England, that a front lens made of two components, each of a different type of glass and curved in a special way, could overcome the worst optical defects of the instruments. Much later, in the early nineteenth century in Germany, the optician, Joseph von Fraunhofer, constructed some beautiful examples of these new style refractors, one of which Bessel used in his measurements of the distance of the star 61 Cygni. Von Fraunhofer's success stimulated the construction of larger refractors culminating in two giant instruments in the United States: the 36 in (91 cm) aperture refractor at Lick Observatory in California in 1888, and the 40 in (1 m) at Yerkes Observatory near Chicago in 1895. These two American refractors not only represent a peak in optical workmanship but also a new phase in engineering. Whereas the new telescopes of Herschel and Rosse had to be moved by heaving on ropes and pulleys, the heavy engineering of the steam age could provide equatorial mounts of great sophistication that allowed astronomers to follow the curved paths of stars with just one movement of the telescope.

The large reflector had its advantages especially in measuring objects such as binary stars, but there was a limit to their size. The double-component front lens meant that four surfaces had to be precisely curved and polished, and the glass had to be thick if it was to retain its shape in all positions of the telescope, but this resulted in the glass itself absorbing significant amounts of light. Lastly, there was the problem of making large lenses free from bubbles and strains. Curved mirrors did not suffer from these limitations. Admittedly the mirrors used by Newton, Herschel and Rosse were not efficient light reflectors because they were made of a metal alloy; glass could not be used because there was no known way in which a reflecting surface could be laid on top of glass. (Glass mirrors with a reflecting surface behind the mirror were well known, but such mirrors were unsuited to telescopes because light passing twice through the glass of such mirrors distorted and gave ghost images.) The situation changed, however, and in 1856 the first silver-on-glass telescope mirrors were made, following a chemical method of depositing the silver invented in 1850 by a British manufacturer, and by the German chemist Justus von Liebig a few years later. This gave high efficiency — silver-on-glass mirrors can reflect about 90 percent of the light falling on them compared with only some 50 percent from a metal mirror.

With their increased efficiency coupled to the fact that very large mirrors could be constructed and mounted with mechanical competence, the large reflector began, in the twentieth century, to replace the refractor. This change was most marked in the United States, where the astronomer George Ellery Hale (1868-1938) had a flair for persuading rich businessmen to support astronomical research. For 30 years, from 1918 to 1948, his 100 in (2.5 m) reflector at Mount Wilson Observatory in California was the world's largest telescope, and it was this instrument that Hubble used in this fundamental research.

Large optical telescopes can only look at a small area of the sky at any one time, but with the invention of photography in 1826 and its first use in astronomy in 1840, a means of recording larger areas has evolved. The way to achieve this was devised in 1929 by Estonian optician Bernhard Schmidt, whose special design of reflector has been adopted since the end of the Second World War; it provides an area some 25 times greater than is possible with an ordinary telescope.

Photography itself has materially helped astronomy, not only because it allows greater

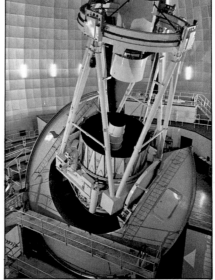
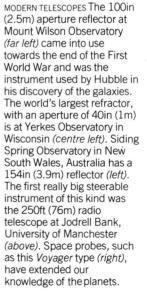

MODERN TELESCOPES The 100in (2.5m) aperture reflector at Mount Wilson Observatory *(far left)* came into use towards the end of the First World War and was the instrument used by Hubble in his discovery of the galaxies. The world's largest refractor, with an aperture of 40in (1m) is at Yerkes Observatory in Wisconsin *(centre left)*. Siding Spring Observatory in New South Wales, Australia has a 154in (3.9m) reflector *(left)*. The first really big steerable instrument of this kind was the 250ft (76m) radio telescope at Jodrell Bank, University of Manchester *(above)*. Space probes, such as this *Voyager* type *(right)*, have extended our knowledge of the planets.

accuracy in the determination of position — photographs may be measured under a microscope — but also because a photographic surface permits an image o be built up over a long period of time and thus objects that cannot be seen by the eye, even through the same telescope, are rendered visible. However, since the 1970s, developments in electronics have led to the design of light-sensitive devices that at present supplement photography; one day they may replace it. Some machines in Britain can today automatically measure photographs and even select for themselves items of a particular class for photographic examination.

The twentieth century has, perhaps, been most notable for the use of totally new ways of examining the universe. In 1931 Karl Jansky, an American radio engineer, first came across radio waves coming from space. In 1933 he confirmed his results but little notice was taken of them, except by Grote Reber, an amateur radio enthusiast, who built the first radio telescope in the form of a metal mirror, and obtained results which he published in 1940 and 1942. At the end of the Second World War, Reber's results were accepted by astronomers, partly because a little confirmation had been obtained in the United States and Britain during other wartime radio research. In the years that followed much progress was made, notably in Britain and Australia, both countries without large optical telescopes at the time. In Britain, research by Bernard Lovell at Jodrell Bank led to the solution of long-standing problems concerned with meteors, and in 1958 to the construction of the first large steerable dish-type radio telescope with a diameter of 250 ft (76 m) for studying specific sources. At Malvern, James Hey studied the sun at radio wavelengths and, in Sydney, Joseph Pawsey and colleagues did the same, as well as examining sources in the southern skies. Back at Cambridge University, Martin Ryle and colleagues charted the northern radio skies with astounding precision, which led to the discoveries of quasars and pulsars. In addition, following on work by the Dutch astronomer Henrik van de Hulst, all radio astronomy observatories studied emission from hydrogen gas in space that was too cool to glow and was detectable only by radio means. By the late 1950s, American astronomers were also taking part in this new and valuable research.

The extension of the spectrum into the invisible radio wavelengths ranges and the astounding and important discoveries arising from the use of radio telescopes has led to an appreciation of the importance of studying the universe in other 'invisible' wavelengths, especially those such as X-rays which never reach the earth's surface. This has now brought about the development of launching automatic telescopes and other equipment into space, with, once again, the most important consequences for our understanding of the universe.

Physics and Mathematics

The only way to ensure any precision in the description of the behaviour of the heavens, as the peoples of antiquity discovered, was to use mathematics. The motion and interaction of physical bodies in the world around us are also amenable to mathematical treatment, as are allied physical questions about the heat of bodies, the way they reflect or transmit light, become magnetized or conduct electricity. This ability to use mathematics to describe the physical world, and the development of special mathematical tools to make the descriptions more comprehensive, was the reason why physics took great strides forward during the 'scientific revolution' in the Europe of the sixteenth and seventeenth centuries. Progress without these powerful techniques, which included analysis and the testing of new ideas by experiment, is possible but slow, as evidenced by the pace of research in Ancient China and Greece.

In China during the fourth century BC, the Mohists — followers of the philosophy of Mo Ti — concerned themselves with measurement, with force and weight, and with pulleys and balances; they also developed ideas about what we now call 'the centre of gravity', about the strength of materials, hydrostatics, and especially light and the formation of images by mirrors. Their theories ranged over a wide area of physics. Unfortunately, their work was not continued and progress in these fields virtually ceased. However, the Chinese later made contributions to the study of sound and it may well be that the West first obtained a tempered musical scale from them.

In Ancient Greece, physics was periodically a subject of intense study. Sound interested Pythagoras and his followers from the late sixth century BC onwards. In the third century BC, that astonishing mathematician and physicist, Archimedes, did important work in pure mathematics and studied the principles of the lever and pulley blocks, while he also made considerable progress in hydrostatics. After the fall of Alexandria, however, most of Archimedes' work was lost and his mathematical approach forgotten. Instead, Aristotle's research, carried out in the fourth century BC, 100 years before Archimedes and contemporaneous with the Mohist work in China, is remembered. Aristotle's stature is in part due to the logical arguments he marshalled to support his physical views — his use of mathematics in this respect was not notable in any way — and in part because his ideas were consistent with his great conception of a synthesis within the universe, where all change occurred below the 'sphere of the moon'.

Aristotle's influence lasted well into the Renaissance, because it was his brilliant teaching that, in one form or another, survived the destruction of the Alexandrian library. His position was enhanced when the Western Church invested him with the mantle of scientific orthodoxy. His theories about the physics of motion acted as a stimulant to other ideas, not only on the question of motion but in allied fields such as the existence or non-existence of a vacuum.

With the onset of the new independence of thought that appeared in Europe during the sixteenth and seventeenth centuries, drawing on some novel ideas devised by Islamic scientists as well as Greek, other physical subjects began to attract attention. New and independent studies of how light behaves through a lens and in mirrors of various kinds — studies stimulated by the invention of the telescope — were made, and also about light's actual nature. These led to a determination of what constitutes colour. At the beginning of the nineteenth century, a novel theory of light had significant implications in other fields and was, in a sense, the start of that broadening of science whereby isolated subjects came to be understood as components of a great synthesis of the natural world.

The Greeks did not excel at the study of light; their mistaken belief that objects were seen

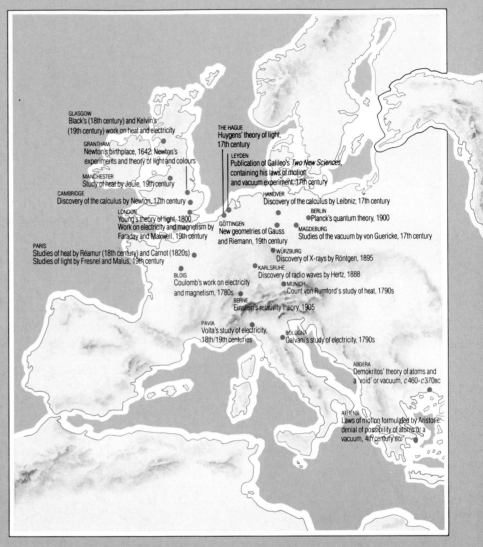

GLASGOW
Black's (18th century) and Kelvin's (19th century) work on heat and electricity

THE HAGUE
Huygens' theory of light, 17th century

GRANTHAM
Newton's birthplace, 1642; Newton's experiments and theory of light and colours

LEYDEN
Publication of Galileo's *Two New Sciences*, containing his laws of motion and vacuum experiment, 17th century

MANCHESTER
Study of heat by Joule, 19th century

CAMBRIDGE
Discovery of the calculus by Newton, 17th century

HANOVER
Discovery of the calculus by Leibniz, 17th century

LONDON
Young's theory of light, 1800
Work on electricity and magnetism by Faraday and Maxwell, 19th century

BERLIN
Planck's quantum theory, 1900

GÖTTINGEN
New geometries of Gauss and Riemann, 19th century

MAGDEBURG
Studies of the vacuum by von Guericke, 17th century

PARIS
Studies of heat by Réamur (18th century) and Carnot (1820s)
Studies of light by Fresnel and Malus, 19th century

WÜRZBURG
Discovery of X-rays by Röntgen, 1895

KARLSRUHE
Discovery of radio waves by Hertz, 1888

BLOIS
Coulomb's work on electricity and magnetism, 1780s

MUNICH
Count von Rumford's study of heat, 1790s

BERNE
Einstein's relativity theory, 1905

PAVIA
Volta's study of electricity, 18th/19th centuries

BOLOGNA
Galvani's study of electricity, 1790s

ABDERA
Demokritos' theory of atoms and a 'void' or vacuum, c 460–c 370 BC

ATHENS
Laws of motion formulated by Aristotle; denial of possibility of atoms or a vacuum, 4th century BC

DISCOVERIES AND CENTRES OF LEARNING Despite early studies in Greece and the more practical investigations by the Chinese in the fourth century BC, physical subjects such as light, heat and electricity became the focus for intense investigation only with the advent of the 'scientific revolution' in sixteenth- and seventeenth-century Europe. The development of geometry, algebra and calculus ran in parallel with advances in physics, and calculus, in particular, being devised to aid the analysis of certain problems. In the twentieth century, with the development of relativity and quantum theory, both physics and mathematics have emerged as powerful tools of abstract thought, challenging our concept of the physical world.

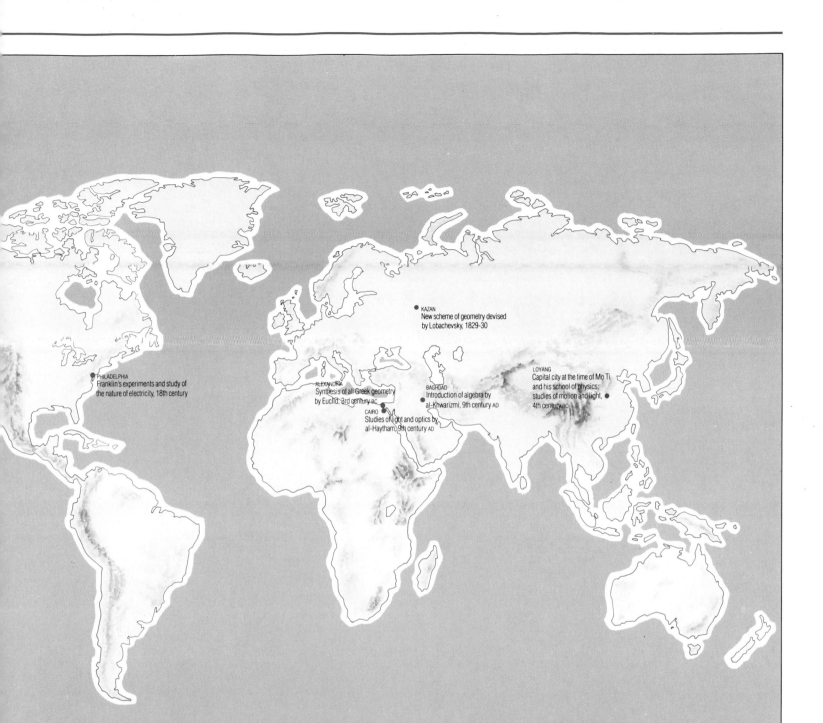

PHILADELPHIA
Franklin's experiments and study of
the nature of electricity, 18th century

KAZAN
New scheme of geometry devised
by Lobachevsky, 1829-30

ALEXANDRIA
Synthesis of all Greek geometry
by Euclid, 3rd century BC

CAIRO
Studies of light and optics by
al-Haytham, 9th century AD

BAGHDAD
Introduction of algebra by
al-Khwarizmi, 9th century AD

LOYANG
Capital city at the time of Mo Ti
and his school of physics;
studies of motion and light,
4th century BC

because of something emitted from the eye had an inhibiting effect on what later became obvious in the everyday world. Another physical study that seems to have failed to arouse curiosity was that of heat, and this subject only became analyzed scientifically from the late sixteenth century onwards. Again, this was to be incorporated into a broader scheme of physics during the nineteenth century. Similarly, it was only in the seventeenth century that a third aspect of what we now recognize as physics — the joint fields of electricity and magnetism — inspired enthusiastic exploration. The Greeks had recognized the existence of an electric charge — evident when amber is rubbed by another piece of amber (or any other insulating material) — but, again, had not pursued it. Despite later investigations into the subject, progress was slow until some astonishing research carried out in the nineteenth century. Interest in magnetism arose from investigations made in the first century AD in China; its connection with electricity was, however, a nineteenth-century development in the West.

Research was carried out into sound early in Ancient Greece and in China; vibrating strings, columns of air and surfaces were examined but the investigation was inspired by musical and aesthetic, rather than purely scientific, curiosity. The work began in Greece during the sixth century BC, with Pythagoras and his followers who recognized sound as a vibration but, after some Chinese studies, little was achieved until the recording of sound vibrations during the last years of the nineteenth century. After this, sound became a subject for the technologist rather than the pure scientist, while in architectural acoustics it developed into an applied art. Sound does not therefore feature in our description of purely scientific discoveries.

The development of mathematics ran alongside the study of the physical world and, from time to time, new mathematical techniques have been devised to accommodate and analyze particular problems. However, the development of mathematics soon led to abstract technicalities; it is only possible here, therefore, to sketch out general ideas.

Motion

The world around us is in a state of continuous motion. Trees and plants sway in the wind, rivers flow between their banks, fish swim, animals creep, slither or walk, birds fly and people can move or travel using many different modes of transport. Clouds scurry across the sky, while the sun, moon, planets and stars weave their regular paths. All this is part of everyday life and all easily taken for granted. When the earliest people used spears or shot arrows from a bow, the motion did not require analysis. Practice taught how to aim in order to hit the target and this was similarly true of the sling and, later, of the catapult; no one needed to study the trajectories of missiles in any detail. However, because motion was so ubiquitous, some intuitive ideas were bound to develop before long. Precisely what these were we cannot now be certain but they probably had little basis in science. Recent research in the United States has shown that some people still hold inherent beliefs about motion that are totally at variance with scientific laws.

The first coherent body of laws of motion were those drawn up by Aristotle (384-322 BC) in the fourth century BC. In keeping with his doctrine of the unchanging nature of the heavens — the heavens included everything beyond the innermost of all the celestial spheres, the sphere of the moon — Aristotle believed the motion of celestial bodies to be unique. Since he believed them to move in circles around the earth, he specified their nature as such that they moved in circles. They were, in short, governed by different laws from those governing bodies below the sphere of the moon. All objects had one thing in common, however: they were either in or seeking their natural place in the universe. The natural place for celestial bodies was one of the celestial spheres; the natural place for terrestrial bodies was the centre of the universe which, of course, was the centre of the earth in Aristotle's cosmos.

Material or 'earthly' bodies could perform three kinds of motion. The first of these was 'natural motion', the motion a body undertook when seeking its natural place. Since their natural place was at the centre of the earth, all falling bodies were in 'natural motion'. If a body were dropped, its natural motion took it towards the centre of the earth; it dropped vertically downwards. The speed at which a body fell depended on how 'ponderous' it was; heavier bodies falling faster than lighter ones because they had a greater urge towards their natural place.

The second kind of motion designated by Aristotle was 'forced motion'. This occurred when outside forces operated on a body, interfering with 'natural motion'. If an object was picked up from the floor, then its upward motion was a forced motion. An ox pulling a cart along the road was a forced motion; so was the motion imparted to an arrow when it was shot from a bow. Because such motion was not natural to a body, a force had to be applied constantly to cause movement in this way. For the cart to move, the ox had continually to pull it; stop the ox and the cart would stop, as was common knowledge. The speed at which a body travelled in forced motion depended on the amount of force used; again this seemed to be a self-evident fact of everyday experience.

The third kind of motion that Aristotle recognized was 'voluntary motion', that is, literally, motion imposed by will. It was a kind of motion possessed only by living creatures; by the ox which pulled the cart, by the person who picks up an object from the floor. Again, force had continually to be applied for this third class of motion to take place. The force was a result of the will to apply it and again the velocity of motion that resulted depended directly on the amount of force used.

Aristotle's analysis of motion was logical and seemed to explain experience. It also dovetailed perfectly into his explanation of the universe, its division into spheres and into four basic elements and a fifth essence. Indeed, it was so effective that it was accepted in the Islamic world and in the West, although questions began to be raised from the thirteenth century onwards.

The basic dissatisfaction that arose concerned Aristotle's explanation of the motion of an arrow. At the start of its forced motion from the bow, the arrow is driven forward by the bowstring, but what occurred after this? The answer was crucial and unsatisfactory. What Aristotle claimed, and his followers still proposed, was that as soon as the arrow left the bow, air would rush in to take up the space that the arrow had

PATHS OF A PROJECTILE The Aristotelian concept of the path of a projectile, illustrated in Satbech's *Problematum Astronomicorum* (1561) *(inset)* consisted of a series of straight separate motions as Aristotle did not believe that a body could undertake more than one motion at a time. In contrast, Descartes' idea, demonstrated by this illustration from his *Epistolae* (1668) *(right)*, was that a tennis ball falls to ground in a smooth parabola after being hit.

SPACECRAFT IN ORBIT *Skylab (above)* was launched into orbit in 1973, at a height of 270 miles (432km), ie just above the earth's atmosphere. The astronauts' primary mission was to study phenomena in space that are simply invisible to astronomers on earth; this is due to the protective atmosphere which only allows the detection of radiation of certain restricted wavelengths. The launch was timed to coincide with a period of quiet solar activity but as the solar 'wind' lessened, the atmosphere rose beneath the craft and the resulting drag gradually slowed it down. Only requiring relatively small amounts of fuel in orbit — enough to steer by — there was not enough to boost it into a higher orbit and in 1979 the craft had to be brought back to earth, earlier than intended. The *Apollo 9* command and service module *(left)*, which was in space for 10 days in March 1969, is shown here in orbit around the earth. The photograph was taken during the extensive 'extra vehicular activity' (EVA) that occurred during the voyage.

occupied, and this air would then act as a force to push the arrow along, causing the forced motion to continue. Once this force was spent, the arrow would seek its natural place and fall to the ground, unless, of course, it reached its target. However, the suggestion that the air pushed the arrow along seemed to contain an element of illogicality. Air, as both they and Aristotle knew, offered resistance to the movement of bodies — this was one of the reasons

Aristotle gave in his argument against the existence of a vacuum — so how could this resistive substance act as the driving force?

Many scholars gradually began to doubt Aristotle's explanation. One was Roger Bacon (c 1220-c 1291), whose ideas were influential in the thirteenth century although his research lay more in the field of optics. Those mainly concerned with discovering a viable alternative explanation were three men in the fourteenth century: Thomas Bradwardine, Jean Buridan and Nicole Oresme. Bradwardine made certain mathematical analyses of Aristotle's explanations and he was able to show that they did not stand up under all conditions. The Frenchman Jean Buridan, of the University of Paris, took the next step by using the concept of 'impetus', the idea that once a body is given a push, something inherent in the body itself was stimulated to keep the body moving. Buridan did not invent the concept — it had been used in the previous century by the Bavarian Albertus Magnus and had been discussed briefly in the sixth century — but was the first to suggest it could be a property of the moving body itself. The third important contributor to the discussion was Buridan's pupil, Nicole Oresme. He took 'impetus' to be not something inherent in a body but something impressed on it by a force and gradually used up as the body moved through a resisting 'medium' such as air or water. That was why an arrow, a stone from a catapult or even a cannonball would fall to the ground after a time.

This doctrine of impetus was an important step forward in understanding motion and, incidentally, was not confined to western Europe. In the tenth century AD, a view like Oresme's was proposed in India, although there was probably no intellectual contact between the two cultures and the Western concept appears to have been reached independently. Certainly, in the West, this was the natural, 'commonsense' view of many people. During the 1980s, research in the United States at Johns Hopkins University by Michael McCloskey and his colleagues, as well as research in Cambridge, Massachusetts and Pittsburgh, and also in Paris, has demonstrated that the idea of impetus is still widely held. What is more, they have shown that the path of a projectile is still not clearly understood by many people. Some still think, as did the eleventh-century Islamic physicist Ibn Sina, that a projectile such as a cannonball first travels in a straight line and then suddenly drops vertically downwards. Others follow fourteenth-century physicist Albert of Saxony (1316?-1390?), assuming that it first travels in a straight line then, as the impetus weakens and gravity takes over, there is a second stage in which the path curves before the body falls vertically to the ground. It has also been found that some people still believe bodies can travel naturally in curved paths, thinking that, for instance, when a body is whirled round

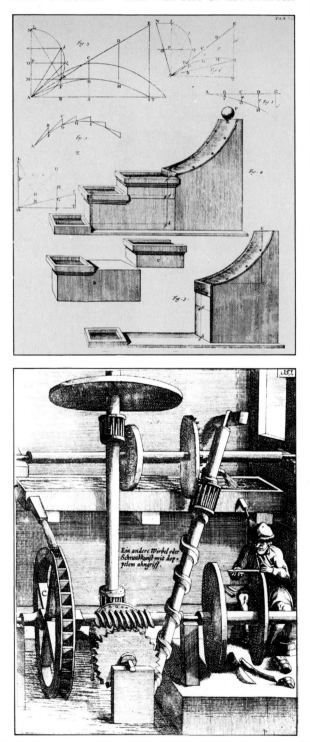

MOTION Perpetual motion in machines was a theoretical ideal that many scientists longed to achieve in the early seventeenth century. This illustration *(below)* from Böckler's *Theatrum Machinarum Novum* (1673) shows a water-wheel driving an Archimedean screw raising the water back to the reservoir. The system was designed to generate enough energy to keep the grindstones operating continuously in motion. Once Newton's laws of motion were developed and friction understood, it was realized that perpetual motion was not feasible in practice.
This drawing of a parabolic trajectory *(above)*, designed to investigate the motion of bodies, is taken from W.J. Gravesande's *Physices Elementa Mathematica* (1725). The ball would be rolled down the incline and its path traced on a board, so illustrating Newton's laws of motion as detailed in his *Principia*.

at the end of a string and then released, it will continue to move as if following a circular path.

These views are of great interest because they seem, to many people, to be a natural explanation of what they observe. Yet they differ markedly from the correct view of motion which was only discovered in the seventeenth century. The first steps in arriving at a totally new explanation came from Galileo (1564-1642), who was a staunch follower of Archimedes (287-212BC) and a stern critic of Aristotle. In a tract written in about 1590, Galileo rejected Aristotle's three classes of motion — natural, forced and willed — and also argued that all bodies took the same time to fall to the ground from a given point, irrespective of their weight. (Whether he did drop different weights from the Leaning Tower of Pisa in front of the whole university is now uncertain, although it seems likely he may have done the test with some colleagues.) Galileo also conducted experiments by rolling balls down sloping grooves in order to investigate motion and in his important book, *Discourses on Two New Sciences* (1638), he came close to what we now call 'Newton's first law of motion' and gave a correct description of the path of a projectile.

These ideas were followed up by René Descartes (1596-1650), who claimed that a body will continue its motion at a fixed velocity in the same direction indefinitely, unless it suffers a collision. This statement of what is now called 'the law of inertia' appeared in Descartes' *Principles of Philosophy* in 1644, and was read by Isaac Newton (1642-1727). But the great synthesis and complete alternative to Aristotle's theory of motion and the doctrine of impetus of the late medieval age, appeared in 1687 with the publication of Isaac Newton's *Principia (The Mathematical Principles of Natural Philosophy)*. Here he enunciated his now famous three laws of motion; first, that a body will continue in a state of rest or of uniform motion in a straight line unless acted upon by outside forces. Second, that the change in motion will be proportional to and in the direction of the outside force. Third, that to every action there is always opposed an equal reaction. In the remainder of the book he applied these laws with mathematical vigour, both to the motion of bodies on earth as well as to the motion of celestial bodies. This last was at variance with Galileo who, like those who still hold intuitive ideas of motion, believed bodies can move naturally in circles and thought this was the motion of all celestial bodies. Descartes had taken a different view because his ideas of motion applied to the whole universe he had fabricated in his *Principles*.

Newton's mathematical application of the new laws solved not only all problems of terrestrial motion but also those of celestial bodies. The basic problem of astronomy was solved because his laws led automatically to the elliptical orbits of the planets if one assumed a force

of a particular kind operating from the sun, a force that was also the same as that exerted by the earth on the moon. The power of his synthesis swept all before it and showed that intuitive ideas were incorrect and that the old physics of the Greeks and the medieval modifications were wrong. A body does not require a constant force to keep it moving.

Newton's laws, however, also showed the impossibility of a machine achieving perpetual motion — a myth that had seduced engineers for generations — and vindicated the mathematical approach to physical problems so strongly advocated by Galileo and Archimedes before him. Relativity, certainly, has modified the first law because one now has to define a state of rest with respect to a 'local frame of reference' — the earth, or the sun, for example — but the basic principles are not in doubt. It is no wonder that Newton's work is still looked on as of fundamental importance.

LEANING TOWER OF PISA Begun in 1174, the famous Leaning Tower itself illustrates the pull of gravity of a body — in this case a building without solid foundations. The tower started to lean during construction, so the top three storeys were added at a slight angle in an attempt at compensation. By the mid-twentieth century, the tower was 17ft (5m) out of perpendicular, and there were real fears that it would topple. Galileo, who was born in 1564 in Pisa, may have used the tower to illustrate, by dropping objects from the top, that all bodies fall at the same speed.

The Vacuum

In early times there seemed two possible ways to describe the universe: either it was full of matter, or it was composed of tiny particles or atoms with empty spaces in between them. Theories that there were atoms — particles which could not be further divided — partly developed in China and appeared in India and in Ancient Greece. In China, when the Mohists discussed the strength of materials and the way fibres break under strain, they referred to the substances concerned as if they were discontinuous, though they never quite reached an explanation in terms of atoms. Later, in the eleventh century AD, Indian thinkers began to develop an atomic theory, with each of the four elements — earth, air, fire and water — being conceived of as compilations of atoms of a particular kind, different arrangements of these atoms giving the various substances met with in everyday life. But the most highly developed atomic theory of early times arrived in Ancient Greece. Aristotle (384-322BC) severely attacked it and, in doing so, marshalled arguments against the existence of a possible emptiness or void; these were to exert a strong influence on Western science until the seventeeth century.

The Greek atomists and some other Greek philosophers had thought of a void or a vacuum as something 'bereft of body', but Aristotle argued that if such an empty space had three dimensions — length, breadth and depth — as he believed it must, it would be a body. Then, if a body was imagined to occupy this space, this would be equivalent to saying that it was possible to have two separate bodies in the same place. Again, Aristotle argued, to think of a three-dimensional empty space existing on its own was superfluous. What was the difference between thinking of a wooden cube and of its dimensions separately? If there was no difference, then it was possible to conceive of any number of coinciding cubical spaces.

Aristotle also thought of other arguments, based on his own ideas of the motion of bodies. He believed space to be continuous and every part of it equal to every other part. He argued that if space existed in its own right, there could be no natural motion in it: bodies would have no reason to seek a natural place if all places were the same. What is more, if motion did exist, then there was no reason for a body to stop; why should it stop at one point rather than another, since both points were the same? Aristotle also claimed that since such an empty space would offer no resistance, a body would move in all directions at once if it received a push. Furthermore, falling bodies would all drop at the same speed, whereas he believed they fell at speeds depending on their weight. Lastly, if a body moved in a void with no resistance, it would soon travel at an infinite speed due to the constant application of the moving force.

In the first half of the twelfth century, authors quote the now well-known phrase 'Nature abhors a vacuum', although its source is unknown. It may have arisen in discussions

MAGDEBURG HEMISPHERES The power of a vacuum is well illustrated by this picture from Otto von Guericke's *Experimenta Nova* (1672), which was published in Amsterdam. Two hollow copper hemispheres were joined to form a sphere of around 14in (36cm) in diameter and the air pumped out of it to create a vacuum — Guericke was the first man to devise a practical air pump. After the air had been evacuated from the sphere, the drawing shows how it would have taken more than the strength of two teams of horses pulling in opposite directions to break the suction and separate the hemispheres. This is due to the 'resistance of a vacuum'. Guericke is also credited with the invention of the first electric generator, in which the current was generated by the friction of a hand held against a rotating ball of sulphur.

about how or why it was possible to syphon liquid from a container. What we do know, however, is that 200 years later William of Ockham discussed a vacuum and wondered if it was a something or a nothing. At about the same time, Albert of Saxony (1316?-1390?) expressed the opinion that while one could discuss a vacuum, that did not necessarily mean it existed. This last view was important because the possible existence of a vacuum seemed to have religious implications: by the fourteenth century the idea that space extended outwards infinitely was being discussed. The orthodox belief was that such space would be filled by God, who was everywhere. The existence of emptiness or a vacuum was therefore a solemn matter.

In the sixteenth century, Galileo (1564-1642) developed new ideas of motion, rejecting Aristotle's teaching, and began to make way for the acceptance of a vacuum as a possibility on physical grounds. He argued against the old objections, including the notion that there would be infinite speed if a vacuum existed. But he did more than this. His break with Aristotle's physics led him to look anew at the concept of weight. He rejected the medieval view that bodies had an absolute heaviness and lightness; instead he used the idea of the relative density of bodies, what we might call their 'specific weight'. This was important because it meant that he treated all bodies alike. It became possible to discuss the behaviour of all bodies in the same way, whether they were in a vacuum or not. Indeed, he believed the existence of a vacuum had no influence on the way bodies would behave in it. Thus, he could discuss motion without being hindered by arguments about resistance, and concluded that all bodies would fall at equal speeds in a vacuum, irrespective of weight. This he expressed in no uncertain terms in his *Discourses on Two New Sciences*, where he also discussed 'the resistance of a vacuum'; he gives a diagram of a simple piece of equipment to demonstrate this. It consists of a plunger inserted as a tight fit into a cylinder, showing that a considerable effort is needed to pull it out.

Galileo's work had wide repercussions. His pupil Evangelista Torricelli experimented with columns of mercury in glass tubes sealed at one end, which led to the discovery of the vacuum at the sealed end and thus the barometer. Also, the international diplomat and sometime Mayor of Magdeburg, Otto von Guericke (1602-86), designed a pump to suck air out from containers and so create a vacuum without difficulty. He then carried out public demonstrations of the 'resistance of a vacuum'. Over the years von Guericke improved his air pumps and others also designed them, notably Christiaan Huygens (1629-95) in Holland and Robert Boyle (1627-91) and Robert Hooke (1635-1703) in England; they were not only used in physical experiments but also to investigate the biological process of respiration.

INVENTION AND USES OF THE VACUUM Galileo's first experiment to prove the existence of a vacuum involved pulling a wooden plug from the neck of a closed cylinder. This illustration *(below)*, from *Discorsi e Dimonstrazioni Matematiche, Intorno a Due Nuoue Scienze (Mathematical Discussions and Demonstrations about Two New Sciences)* (1638) describes a section through the cylinder (ABCD), and a section through the plug (EFGH) which is attached to a thick, hooked wire rod. Perhaps with the aid of weights, the plug was withdrawn against increasing resistance. No air could enter the closed cylinder, so a vacuum was created. Once the concept of a vacuum was understood, a variety of instruments was invented in the seventeenth century, including the barometer and the thermometer. This Florentine device *(left)* contained *acqua arzente*, or 'alcohol of wine' in a vacuum; the alcohol expanded and contracted according to the

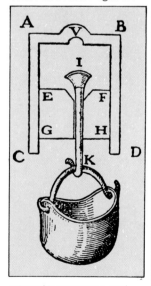

external temperature, and was measured against one of the 420 degree marks. Alcohol was used rather than water because it freezes at a lower temperature; water expands as it freezes and the thermometer would have needed to be very large to accommodate expansion during a frost.

Heat

Scientific studies of heat did not occur until the scientific revolution was under way. In ancient times, philosophers had distinguished between hot and cold, but no investigation into heat took place until the seventeenth century. Then, in keeping with the climate of the new scientific approach, attempts were made to measure heat. One of the pioneers in this was Galileo (1564-1642), although he was not alone; the Englishman Robert Fludd, the Dutch physicist Cornelius Drebbel and the Italian physician Santorio Santorio were all involved. One of them was probably the inventor of the first thermometer; Drebbel, we know, invented a thermostat to keep an oven at a constant temperature.

Certainly, people then began to experiment with devices to measure temperature. The members of the *Accademia del Cimento* (Academy of Experiments) in Florence, founded in 1657 and boasting two of Galileo's pupils among its membership, constructed thermometers using water, mercury or alcohol as fluids. They made other experiments besides those determining the degree of heat. They heated equal amounts of different liquids and found some more efficient than others at melting ice, and also investigated the way heat is conducted and retained in various bodies. In brief, they carried out much basic study, most of which was only followed up successfully later.

The first precise steps came in thermometry when the Danish astronomer Ole Roemer (1644-1710) realized that to be precise it was necessary to have two fixed points on a thermometer, a 'freezing point' and a 'boiling point'. Roemer himself devised a thermometer scale in 1708, using the melting point of snow and the boiling point of water, the same points to be used by the Swede, Anders Celsius (1701-44), some 50 years later. Roemer's thermometer contained alcohol as the expanding liquid and later he changed the zero to the point where a mixture of ice and ammonium chloride froze; this gave a lower freezing point. Roemer divided his scale into 60 degrees but it was soon replaced by a scale adapted from it by the Dutch physicist Daniel Fahrenheit (1686-1736). He seems to have mistaken or misunderstood Roemer's upper limit, thinking it was blood heat; this misunderstanding resulted in a measure of 212 degrees as the boiling point of water. By the mid-eighteenth century two other thermometric scales appeared: that of Celsius, which was altered by Linnaeus (1707-78), a Swedish biologist, to give 100 degrees as the boiling point of water (Celsius had made it 0 degrees), and a scale by the French physicist

INFRARED RADIATION These pictures, the first taken by normal light *(above)* and the second by infrared light *(right)* display how a hot iron gives off 'infrared' radiation. Also termed 'heat radiation' it is intensely radiated by all hot objects and is constantly used in the home for heating and cooking. It is also used in medicine to treat strained muscles and skin conditions.

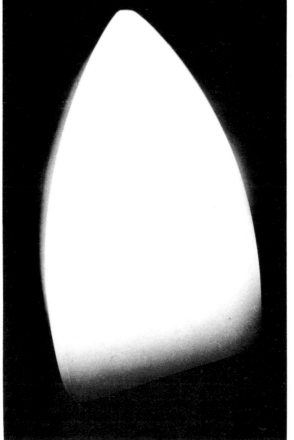

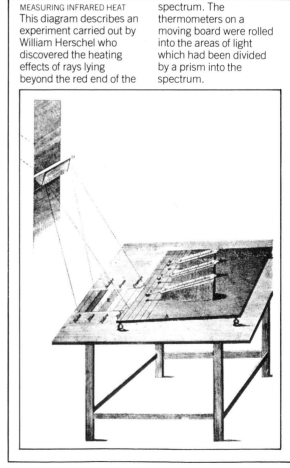

MEASURING INFRARED HEAT This diagram describes an experiment carried out by William Herschel who discovered the heating effects of rays lying beyond the red end of the spectrum. The thermometers on a moving board were rolled into the areas of light which had been divided by a prism into the spectrum.

René Réaumur which was based on the expansion of alcohol and contained 80, not 100, degrees between the freezing and boiling points of water.

The use of thermometers helped bring some precision into experiments in heat but the nature of heat itself remained a puzzle. During the seventeenth century, Robert Hooke (1635-1703) favoured the idea that heat was really some kind of vibration within a substance, while the astronomer Pierre Gassendi claimed that hot and cold were due to the presence of tiny separate particles, some hot, some cold or 'frigorific'. However, in the seventeenth century a different approach was made. Heat was thought of as an 'imponderable fluid', that is a fluid that could not be seen, weighed nor measured; this 'fluid' was called 'caloric' and was thought also to take part in chemical reactions.

While theories were being discussed, some sound practical experimental work was being conducted. The temperature of mixtures of hot and cold liquids was examined and it was discovered that bodies gave up heat to their surroundings. In the middle of the century, the work of the *Accademia del Cimento* (which had long ceased to exist — it was disbanded in 1667) was revived, but with a new precision, by the Scots physician, chemist and physicist Joseph Black (1728-99) at Glasgow and Edinburgh Universities. Black discovered that different bodies could possess different amounts of heat even though they were all at the same temperature, a view that opposed current thinking on the subject. However, his detailed research soon left no doubt, and his concept of 'specific heat' found a permanent place in physics. Again, Black also studied and measured the heat necessary to change a body from one state to another, such as ice to water or water to steam. This led him to the idea of 'latent heat', the heat required to cause such a transformation.

Black's work had important practical effects on the work of James Watt, who attended some of his lectures in Glasgow and who later invented the modern condensing steam engine. Black's work also had significant theoretical effects. The fluid theory received something of a setback in the 1790s when an American, Sir Benjamin Thompson, Count von Rumford, found that vast amounts of heat were generated when cannon were bored. He questioned where the heat could come from if it were a fluid and, therefore, favoured the vibration theory. In the nineteenth century, James Joule (1818-89) investigated the expansion and heating of gases and conducted a special paddle-wheel experiment which linked work done and the amount of heat generated.

Joule's important results were taken up by a Scotsman, William Thomson, later Lord Kelvin (1824-1907). Kelvin formulated mathematical laws to express Joule's results and to take into

BORING CANNON This picture from Vannoccio Biringuccio's *De la Pirotechnia* (1540) illustrates the machinery used in the early sixteenth century to bore cannon. While a two-man treadmill in the lefthand foreground turns the bore, the cannon is pulled slowly towards it. More than 200 years later, during a debate about the nature of heat, Sir Benjamin Thompson suggested that the heat generated by this boring method could not be an 'imponderable fluid'. He believed that heat is a vibration

account the fall in temperature in an engine which does work, a phenomenon which had been investigated in the 1820s by the French engineer Sadi Carnot. Kelvin faced difficulties, for he needed a new temperature scale in which work and heat generated are the same throughout the range.

It was at this stage, in 1850, that the Prussian Rudolph Clausius showed up flaws in Carnot's research, pointing out that 'caloric' could not be destroyed but was converted into mechanical energy. This led to the two famous laws of thermodynamics. The first one connected energy and work; the second stated that heat cannot pass from a colder body to a hotter one of its own accord — in other words, energy became increasingly unavailable for transformation (*trope* in Greek), often expressed as an increase of entropy.

Kelvin now had the link between the heat taken from a source and the heat absorbed to do work. Heat, clearly, was not a fluid but a form of energy, and his new scale of temperature — the 'absolute scale' that was very like the Centigrade (Celsius) scale — had its zero where no transfer of energy could take place, that is at −273.1 degrees C.

It also turned out that heat was not only a form of energy but also one that could be transmitted as radiation. As early as 1800, the astronomer William Herschel (1738-1822) had discovered heat rays existing below the red end of the spectrum, but this 'infrared' radiation was only to be explained later in a wider concept of energy that grew out of nineteenth-century studies of light and electricity.

Light

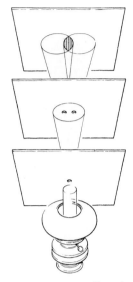

INTERFERENCE OF LIGHT Young's experiment *(above)* shows that when two beams of light from one source meet after travelling along close but different routes, the waves interfere. If coloured lights are combined, the eye sees new colours, while the result is white light where green, blue and red mix *(below)*. The colours in James Clerk Maxwell's photograph *(below right)* were created by combining three tinted lantern slides of a tartan ribbon. This was the first colour photograph.

Ideas about the nature of light and the parallel study of optics — the way light behaves when reflected and refracted as it passes through a transparent substance — go back to early antiquity. In the fourth century BC in China, the Mohists carried out research into the formation of shadows, the inverted picture obtained when light is passed through a tiny hole, and the effects of mirrors, both flat and concave. They also did some work on refraction, notably the apparent bending of a stick in a vessel partly filled with water. Their research seems to have been meticulous; unfortunately, it was taken no further at that time.

In Greece the subject was dominated and hampered by the teaching of Pythgoras (active *c* 530BC). He believed that objects were made visible when 'flux', emitted in a straight line by the eye, struck them. Not all philosophers accepted this; a few thought objects themselves gave off images. Euclid, who is known to have taught for some years at a school in Alexandria around 300BC, wrote 'theorems' on the behaviour of light at about the same time as the Mohists were at work in China, but what he is thought to have written about mirrors is lost. In the first century AD, Heron of Alexandria wrote on optics; Ptolemy, a century later, extended the subject of refraction to the apparent shifting of the images of stars at different heights above the horizon (due to the varying thickness of the air through which they are seen). This, however, is a difficult problem, solved only today by computers built into telescope controls; in Ptolemy's time there was no hope of a real solution. All that could be done was to put forward a theory, but this could not be verified.

Virtually no progress was made until the ninth century, when some remarkable work was carried out by the Islamic physicist Ibn al-Haytham, sometimes known in the West as Alhazen. He wrote a book on optics notable for its experimental and mathematical approach, in which he discussed not only the behaviour of 'rays of light' — a concept that he himself introduced — but pointed out that light bounces off a mirror and does not penetrate the polished surface at all. But al-Haytham did not confine himself to the behaviour of light rays. He discussed vision, rejecting the Greek explanation, but assumed, as the surgeon Galen had done seven centuries earlier, that sight begins at the lens in the eye, not as we now know at the retina at the back of the eye. Nevertheless, he did follow the optic nerve from the eye to the brain and, though his work had its faults, it was a notable step forward. Al-Haytham also tried to understand the nature of colours, which he believed to be different from light, coloured bodies radiating colour as well as light. As to light itself, he believed it to be something emitted in all directions from every luminous source and then emitted again from every body, be it a speck of dust or an illuminated object. In this he came very near to the theory of light to be proposed by the Dutchman Christiaan Huygens in the seventeenth century, the period when this and other subjects were tackled again in a scientific way.

Although theories of light were not developed after al-Haytham, some work was done in optics. In the thirteenth century, his results arrived in the West and were pursued by Robert Grosseteste (*c* 1168-1253) in Oxford

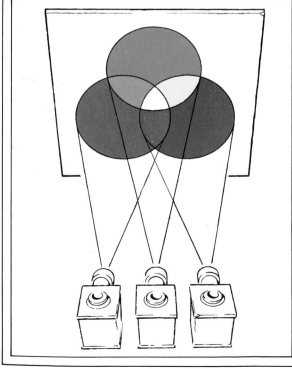

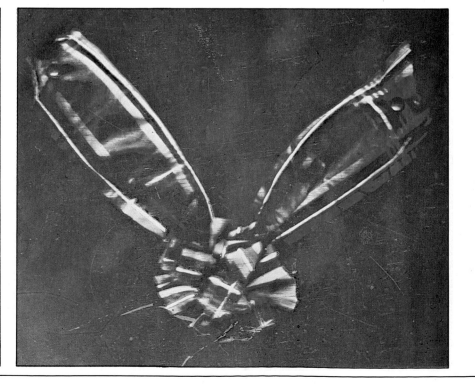

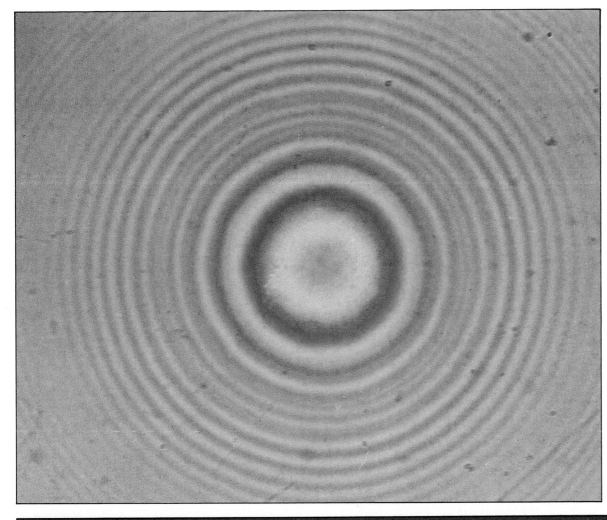

REFRACTION AND DIFFRACTION
Newton's investigation into light included an experiment in which he placed a slightly convex lens on a flat piece of glass. On observing it under white light *(left)* he found that at the point of contact nothing is reflected, but in rings around the centre different colours are visible. Newton attributed these rings to 'fits' of reflection and transmission. The theory held by Newton's followers that light consists of tiny particles or corpuscles was, however, countered by the phenomenon of diffraction *(below)*. Grimaldi first discovered and named diffraction, ie that a beam of light travelling through a fine slit will spread out on the other side; similarly, even using the finest light source, the edge of a shadow will never be absolutely sharp. Hooke observed the same phenomena and suggested that light was a kind of oscillation. It was only in the nineteenth century, however, after Young's interference experiment, that scientists began to understand how the wave theory more readily explains the behaviour of light than the corpuscular theory.

and by his pupil Roger Bacon (c 1220-c 1291). Both discussed the behaviour of rays of light, light reflected by mirrors and, a novel subject, light refracted by lenses, for simple lenses were beginning to appear as spectacles or eyeglasses before the century was out. Their work was pioneering in an experimental sense; in 1269 Roger Bacon described what sounds astonishingly like a simple telescope, although optically it would certainly have been far inferior to any of the numerous telescopes constructed in the seventeenth century.

Some investigation was made during the sixteenth century of the way lenses could correct defects of vision, but it was in the seventeenth that optics developed noticeably, with the use of the telescope and microscope (possibly invented at the time). This was also the period which was to see two notable theories of light, one by Christiaan Huygens (1629-95), the other by Isaac Newton (1642-1727). Huygens favoured a wave theory, conceiving light as a wave disturbance set going in every direction from an illuminated source. The waves were 'longitudinal' or pressure waves, moving through space by alternate compression and thinning out, each wave giving rise to secondary wavelets. It was a theory rather similar to, although more elaborate than, the one suggested by Ibn al-Haytham.

The waves in Huygens' theory travelled at a definite speed; he realized light did not travel instantaneously, even though its motion was very swift. Huygens based this opinion on the observations Ole Roemer (1644-1710) made of Jupiter's satellites. In 1675 Roemer had discovered that eclipses of the four bright moons by Jupiter's disc occurred late, when the planet was in the more far-off parts of its orbit, and realized that this was due to the extra distance light had to travel. With the timing methods then available and the distances of planets as determined in the seventeenth century, Roemer obtained a value for the speed of light of some 18,000 miles per second (190,000 km per second); although just over half the true value, it was nevertheless a great step forward because it showed light was something with a finite velocity, such as would be expected if it had a truly physical explanation.

Newton preferred to think of light consisting of tiny particles or 'corpuscles'. These particles seemed to explain reflection very well; to account for refraction when light passes from one substance or medium to another, Newton suggested the particles underwent 'fits' of easy reflection and easy refraction; some would be refracted, others reflected. Which action a particle would take depended on the way it was vibrating when it met the interface between the two substances. This allowed Newton to explain, for instance, why one could see one's reflection when looking into a window.

In addition to providing this alternative theory of light, Newton explained colours by saying that 'white light' or sunlight is composed of all colours. Experiment showed that when white light is passed through a glass prism, it is dispersed into separate colours — hence the formation of a spectrum. Newton's many experiments showed, first, that if the coloured spectrum was recombined using a second prism, white light again appeared. Secondly, he also demonstrated that if one colour of the spectrum was isolated and passed through a second prism, it could not be spread out into a further spectrum. Moreover, although in about 1621 Willebrod Snell had discovered the 'law of refraction' of a ray of light through any transparent substance, some 50 years later Newton was able to show that each colour was refracted by a slightly different amount. This last result led Newton to assert that no lens telescope could be built which would bring all colours to focus at the same point. Here he was mistaken because he assumed that each colour was always refracted in the same proportion, whatever the refracting substance might be; in fact, different substances — different kinds of glass, for instance — do disperse the colours to a slightly different degree, as the Englishman Chester Moor Hall was to discover in the early eighteenth century.

Newton and the astronomer Edmond Halley (1656-1742) criticized Huygen's wave theory, Newton questioning why, if light was a wave disturbance, it did not bend around objects in its path, just as ripples in water bend around a moored boat. In fact light does bend in this way, as the astronomer and physicist Francesco Grimaldi had proved by experiment; his results, published in 1665, showed that the edges of shadows are not sharp, but display fringes. However, Newton interpreted this 'diffraction' as evidence of refraction at the edge of an object where it meets a transparent medium (air, for instance). Moreover, Newton pointed out that Huygen's theory could not explain why a transparent substance like the mineral Iceland spar split a beam of light into two separate parts — but Newton himself never explained this phenomenon either. Newton published his theory and his experimental results in *Opticks* which appeared in 1705. By then his reputation was so great, due to his work on motion and gravitation, that his ideas on light became widely accepted and were not seriously challenged until new theories began to emerge at the beginning of the nineteenth century.

The challenge to Newton's theory that light is a stream of corpuscles was due mainly to Thomas Young (1773-1829), a physician who turned from medicine to pursue science more broadly. Young's theory of light arose out of his studies of the eye and of colour vision. By 1800 he voiced his criticisms of the corpuscular theory and suggested that Newton's idea of 'easy fits' of reflection and refraction, due to the way the corpuscles vibrated, came perilously close to a theory that light was indeed due to

INVERSE SQUARE LAW From any point in a flame, waves are emitted and further waves project from what may be called wavefronts. The intensity of radiation varies inversely with the square of the distance from the source.

vibrations. What Young therefore suggested was that space was not really empty but was filled with a 'luminiferous aether' — a perfectly transparent substance that could neither be weighed nor measured — in which light travelled as a pushing or compression type of wave. He incorporated Newton's idea of colours by supposing that each colour had its own particular wavelength. More importantly, he suggested that waves of light could interfere with one another, reinforcing each other when they were in step, but cancelling each other to give darkness if they were exactly out of step. He proved this point by a simple experiment which displayed bright and dark bands due to the interference of two light beams.

Young's theory still did not completely explain the effects of diffraction, or the discovery that the mineral Iceland spar could split light into two beams. Others took up the problem. In 1808 the astronomer and mathematician Pierre Laplace (1749-1827) found a way to explain the Iceland spar effect using the corpuscular theory but then, in the same year, the engineer Etienne Malus discovered that when light was reflected at certain angles from a polished surface, it was altered in some way and behaved just like one of the beams which emerged after the splitting of light in Iceland spar. Malus called this 'polarization', and found he could explain it using a corpuscular theory, but not Young's wave theory. It seemed that the new wave theory was doomed.

Within a few years the situation was radically altered by another French engineer, Augustin Fresnel (1788-1827). By a careful mathematical analysis of diffraction at the edges of objects and by equally careful experiments, he concluded light must be due to a succession of regular waves, and that these waves were not the longitudinal compression waves of Young or Huygens but transverse waves, similar to waves in the sea. One consequence of this view, which Fresnel proposed in 1819, was that the centre of the shadow cast by a small disc should show a tiny bright spot. Independent experiment confirmed this. The new theory was also able to explain polarization and the action of Iceland spar.

If the nineteenth century saw the overthrow of Newton's corpuscular ideas and the establishment of a new wave theory of light, a further change was to come in the twentieth century. In 1900 the German physicist Max Planck had suggested, for various reasons, that light and other radiation was not emitted continuously but in multiples of a basic unit of energy. His supposition was confirmed in 1905 by Albert Einstein (1879-1955) who studied the 'photoelectric' effect. This was a phenomenon where certain metals emitted electrified particles (electrons) when light fell on them. What puzzled physicists was that the energy of the emitted electrons did not depend upon the intensity of the light shining on the metal but on its

wavelength. Einstein showed that the wave theory of light could only explain this if it was coupled with Planck's idea that the light waves arrived in units of some basic energy. In other words, light seemed to be both a wave and a particle. Further studies in atomic physics were to extend this principle, now well established both in theory and by experiment.

EXPERIMENTUM CRUCIS Newton's own sketch of his 'crucial experiment' demonstrates that white light (sunlight), once split by a prism into its separate colours (seen on the screen behind), cannot be further split. Light passing through the screen and falling onto a second prism passes through as the same colour.

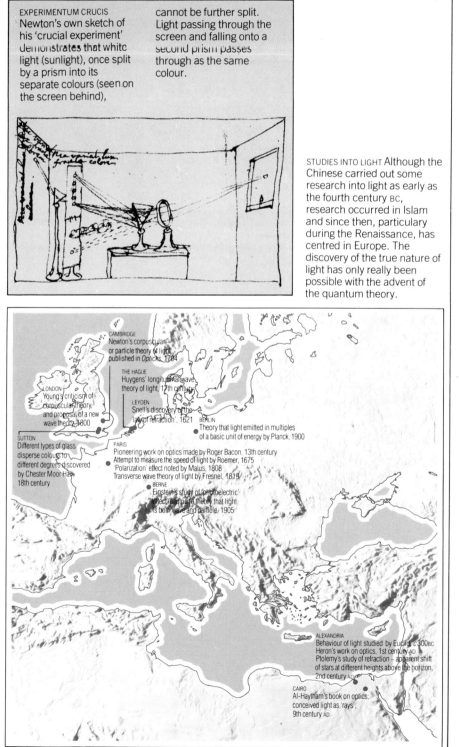

STUDIES INTO LIGHT Although the Chinese carried out some research into light as early as the fourth century BC, research occurred in Islam and since then, particulary during the Renaissance, has centred in Europe. The discovery of the true nature of light has only really been possible with the advent of the quantum theory.

CAMBRIDGE
Newton's corpuscular or particle theory of light published in *Optics*, 1704

THE HAGUE
Huygens' longitudinal wave theory of light, 17th century

LONDON
Young's criticism of corpuscular theory, and proposal of a new wave theory, 1800

LEYDEN
Snell's discovery of the law of refraction, 1621

BERLIN
Theory that light emitted in multiples of a basic unit of energy by Planck, 1900

SUTTON
Different types of glass disperse colours to different degrees discovered by Chester Moor Hall, 18th century

PARIS
Pioneering work on optics made by Roger Bacon, 13th century
Attempt to measure the speed of light by Roemer, 1675
'Polarization' effect noted by Malus, 1808
Transverse wave theory of light by Fresnel, 1819

BERNE
Einstein's study of 'photoelectric' effect leading to theory that light is both wave and particle, 1905

ALEXANDRIA
Behaviour of light studied by Euclid, c 300BC
Heron's work on optics, 1st century AD
Ptolemy's study of refraction - apparent shift of stars at different heights above the horizon, 2nd century AD

CAIRO
Al-Haytham's book on optics conceived light as 'rays', 9th century AD

Magnetism

Attraction, the basic property of magnetism, was noticed in very early times wherever lodestone was present, because lodestone (a naturally occurring form of iron oxide known as magnetite) attracts not only other pieces of lodestone but pieces of ordinary iron as well. This mysterious, almost magical, attractive power remained a curiosity, even though by the first century BC it was known that lodestone can attract over quite a distance, that it can hold pieces of iron in contact with it and that such pieces will retain the magnetic power themselves for some time. The earliest progress beyond this stage occurred, however, in China.

The study of magnetism in China is intimately linked with their discovery of the earth's magnetism. Between the second and third centuries AD, they found out that if a piece of iron is heated, then placed in the direction of the earth's magnetic field and quenched so that it cools quickly, it displays magnetic properties; weak properties it is true, but present all the same. They also found that while soft iron only retains its magnetism for a short time, steel remains magnetized for very much longer, a fact which led them to use steel needles in their magnetic compasses.

In the West, news of the magnetic compass did not arrive until the thirteenth century; a study of magnetism itself was far later. Galileo (1564-1642) had a magnet of lodestone and noticed its attraction was more powerful if its face and the face of the soft iron being attracted were polished. In 1643, Athanasius Kircher, the German, published *The Lodestone, or the Magnetic Art* which, besides describing magnetic toys and the magnetic compass, also contains his method of defining the strength of a magnet. The method entailed placing a magnet to weigh down a pan of scales and bringing a piece of iron into contact with it. The weight needed in the other pan to make a balance was his measure of the magnet's strength.

Descartes (1596-1650) also studied the subject and was the first to propose a scientific theory to account for the phenomenon. He conceived of some screw-like particles inside the vortexes with which he believed space was filled; they had left-handed or right-handed 'threads', depending from which pole of the vortex they came. In a planet, they entered through the north and south poles and screwed into holes or pores in its iron or lodestone interior, thus giving rise to the earth's magnetism. Lodestones offered least resistance to the circulation of these special particles by lining up their holes in the correct direction. Iron, he thought, also contained similar pores. It was an ingenious enough idea to account for all magnetic phenomena known at the time, 1644.

During the seventeenth century, no extensive attempts were made to follow up Kircher's determination of magnetic strength or any other magnetic qualities, although in the *Prin-*

cipia, Isaac Newton mentioned making some observations from which he deduced that magnetic force seemed to diminish with the cube of the distance (thus at twice the distance it would drop 2^3 or 8 times, at three times the distance 3^3 or 27 times, and so on). However, theories of magnetism were not entirely absent; Edmond Halley proposed an explanation based on 'effluvia' (a kind of aether) and in 1759 Franz Aepinus, a German physicist, proposed a one-fluid theory for both electricity and for magnetism, the fluids consisting of particles which repelled each other but attracted ordinary matter. A body became magnetized when the magnetic fluid accumulated at one end of it. But this theory met with difficulties when the repulsion of like magnetic poles was considered and a two-fluid theory, proposed by Anton Brugman, became more popular.

The two-fluid theory was the one accepted by the French physicist and military engineer Charles Coulomb (1736-1806), who investigated many mechanical forces such as cohesion, tension, flexure and torsion, as well as the efficiency and output of machines. Coulomb also carried out some notable work on electricity and magnetism, particularly his precise measurement of magnetic and electric forces. In his determination of magnetic force he used two independent methods. First, he suspended a magnetic needle and then beside it suspended a magnetized vertical steel wire some 25 in (60 cm) long in the same north/south line as the needle. One of the ends of the steel wire was level with the poles of the magnetic needle. The needle oscillated and Coulomb noted the oscillations, first in the earth's magnetic field alone and then with the steel wire held at different distances from it. By analyzing the

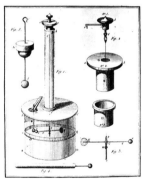

MODERN AND EARLY USES While carrying out an aeromagnetic survey in Thailand, the Thai Shell Exploration and Production Company used a DC-3 aircraft converted for survey work. The craft was fitted with a magnetometer clamped to the underside *(top)*; during the flight the instrument was lowered on a cable to reduce the influence of metal in the plane. The effect of this could be calculated partly because of Coulomb's work in the eighteenth century. He used a torsion balance *(above)* to measure the force between two electrostatic charges and concluded that the force is proportional to their magnitudes and inversely proportional to the square of their separation.

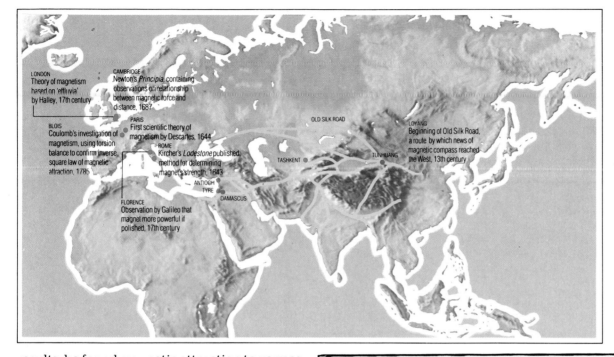

CAMBRIDGE
Newton's *Principia*, containing observations on relationship between magnetic force and distance, 1687

BLOIS
Coulomb's investigation of magnetism, using torsion balance to confirm inverse square law of magnetic attraction, 1785

PARIS
First scientific theory of magnetism by Descartes, 1644

ROME
Kircher's *Lodestone* published; method for determining magnet's strength, 1643

FLORENCE
Observation by Galileo that magnet more powerful if polished, 17th century

ANTIOCH
TYRE
DAMASCUS

OLD SILK ROAD

TASHKENT

TUNHUANG

LOYANG
Beginning of Old Silk Road, a route by which news of magnetic compass reached the West, 13th century

LODESTONE The Chinese art of geomancy often involved the use of a 'divining board'. This was constructed from two boards — one square to symbolize the earth *(below)* and one round for the heavens. The Plough was originally marked on this latter board, and its 'handle' was rotated around the apparent pivot point of the northern heavens. In about the second century AD, the Chinese replaced the upper board with a spoon made of lodestone. The shape of the bowl of the spoon allowed it to rotate, and the handle always pointed in one direction, south, which was later found to be in response to the earth's magnetic field. It was the earliest kind of basic compass. News of the compass only reached the West in about the thirteenth century, via Arabia, *(left)*.

results, he found magnetic attraction to vary as the inverse square of the distance. (At twice the distance, the force diminishes by 2^2 or one-quarter, at three times the distance, by 3^3 or one-ninth, and so on.) Coulomb confirmed these results using a torsion balance of his own design. This he built in two forms, one for measuring magnetic force, the other electric force; the magnetic balance was the simpler. Essentially it consisted of a vertical pillar, inside which ran a thin brass wire. At the bottom of the wire was suspended a bar magnet. A graduated dial at the top of the pillar allowed the suspended wire to be turned by a specific amount. Below the magnet was a second graduated circular scale. The strength of the earth's magnetic field was first determined by twisting the wire to turn the magnet through a given angle (measured on the larger scale), and then measuring the torsion needed to turn it through this angle; the torsion necessary depended on the strength of the field. The long steel magnet was then used at various positions and the torsion measured at each position. For electric measurements, the device was more elaborate and enclosed in a casing. Such a balance is extraordinarily sensitive; a force as small as one-fifty-millionth of a gram could be measured. The precision enabled Coulomb to confirm the inverse square law of magnetic attraction in 1785.

Coulomb's work in one sense completed measurements of magnetic force (but not of the earth's magnetism). But there was still the question of what caused magnetism and what really happened when a body became magnetized. No proper explanation was achieved until after magnetism and electricity were linked in the nineteenth century by Faraday and a full atomic theory appeared in the twentieth.

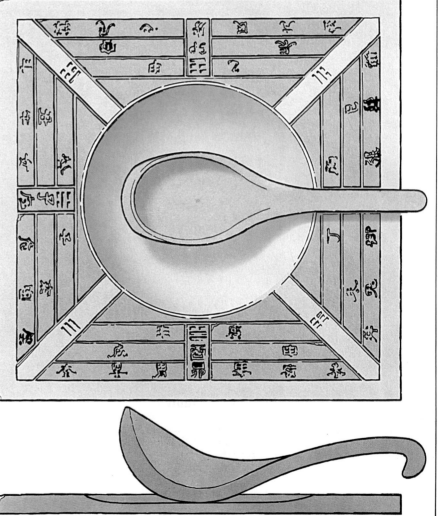

Electricity

The magnet is only one form of attraction between separate pieces of material; there is also electric attraction, where an insulating substance gathers small light non-metallic objects to it. The beautiful fossil resin amber was known widely in antiquity — it was found in China as well as in the West — and, when rubbed, its attractive power became obvious. The Greeks called the substance *elektron* but no further examination of such 'electric' properties was made. In fact, no research into this type of attraction was made until the seventeenth century, though William Gilbert mentioned it and concluded that the subject was too trivial for serious study! There the subject might have rested for a long time had it not been for Otto von Guericke (1602-86).

Von Guericke was intrigued by the problem of how celestial bodies affected one another; Kepler had suggested that there was some form of magnetic attraction and von Guericke decided to investigate this experimentally. Gilbert had used a spherical lump of lodestone to represent the earth in his investigation of terrestrial magnetism and the magnetic compass but von Guericke felt that he should use a sphere made of minerals, because he believed these were closer to the earth in composition. He therefore built a simple machine which consisted of a wooden base with two vertical arms, into which he could insert a sulphur sphere which was itself mounted on a iron rod. When von Guericke placed his hand on the sphere and then rotated it, the sphere became electrified

ELECTRIC PILES Volta's electric piles were the earliest kind of battery or cell, in which continuous rather than static electricity is generated. These piles consisted of damp wood or absorbent paper discs, separated alternately by copper and zinc discs. When metal plates were immersed into slightly acidified water, continuous electricity was also generated.

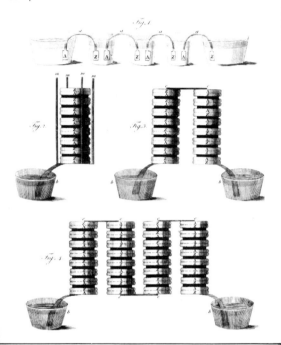

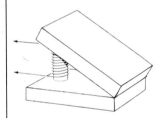

CONDUCTING ELECTRICITY Galvani, Professor of Anatomy at Bologna University, was in the process of studying muscle contraction, using electric shocks to cause frogs' legs to twitch *(right)*, when he made the interesting announcement in 1791 that electricity was present in every animal. Inspired by this discovery he found that even when the frogs' legs were touched with a knife blade held in the hand, while a Leyden jar was being discharged in the near proximity, contractions occurred. Galvani's view was, however, disputed by Volta who claimed that the frogs' legs only moved because of the contact of metal (the knife blade) with the moistness of legs and nerves.
Another method of generating electricity, first demonstrated by Faraday, is by using magnets. When the upper bar magnet is lowered to the position shown *(above)*, an electric current is induced in the coil of wire.

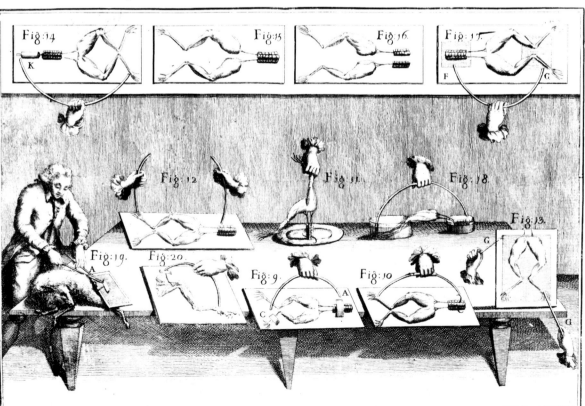

and attracted small pieces of paper, feathers and similar light objects, carrying them around on its rotating surface; 'just as the earth does', he remarked. When a finger was brought near the rotating globe, sparks were emitted and there was a luminous glow. Von Guericke also noticed that when a light body had been attracted to the sphere, it was later repelled and that two such bodies would still repel one another after they had left the sphere. In addition, he found that once a body had been affected or 'charged' by the sphere but had subsequently reached the ground, or been touched by a finger or even been brought near a flame, it could be attracted to the sphere again.

Von Guericke's electrical studies were particularly thorough. He discovered that the electrical charge would travel to the end of a linen thread and that bodies became electrified if merely brought close to the rubbed sphere; they did not have to touch it. Yet his experiments did not attract wide attention, possibly because his work on the vacuum was more dramatic.

The British scientist Robert Boyle (1627-91) read von Guericke's descriptions and repeated some of the experiments. This led him to speculate about the nature of electricity, which he did in typical seventeenth-century terms, speaking of electricity as an invisible emana-

tion of an 'effluvium' which was given out by an electrically charged body.

In the eighteenth century, further progress was made. During the 1720s Francis Hawksbee and Stephen Gray in London used a different type of electric — or more correctly 'electrostatic' — machine, having rotating discs of glass because these were more efficient. With this machine, they discovered that the electric charge could be transmitted long distance using threads of material such as silk, but that it leaked away if the material was unsuitable. Gray also extended von Guericke's results, showing that any charged body could electrify another, while in Paris Charles Dufay demonstrated that charged bodies either attracted or repelled one another; this led him to question whether, perhaps, there were two kinds of electric effluvia.

As electrostatic machines became still larger and still more effective at generating charges, more new discoveries were made. In Prussia, Ewald von Kleist (1715-59) found how to store an electric charge and add to it until it was powerful enough to ignite alcohol by its spark. His storage device was merely a small bottle coated with metal, but at Leyden in Holland, Pieter van Musschenbroek not only repeated the experiment but designed a more efficient storage device, a glass jar coated both inside

ELECTRIC POWER After the development of the dynamo — the electric generator — the transmission and distribution of electric power from a common power system to a number of different customers was an obvious step. In 1878, plans were proposed by Thomas Edison in the United States and St George Lane-Fox in England and the first successful electric distribution systems were constructed in 1882 in London and New York. However, the direct current was impossible to transmit over any great distance; effective distribution could not be achieved until the alternating current generator was developed in 1885 by George Westinghouse and William Stanley. In England, S.Z. de Ferranti was working on the problem and his first power station at Deptford (above) generated an alternating current that was carried to central London.

97

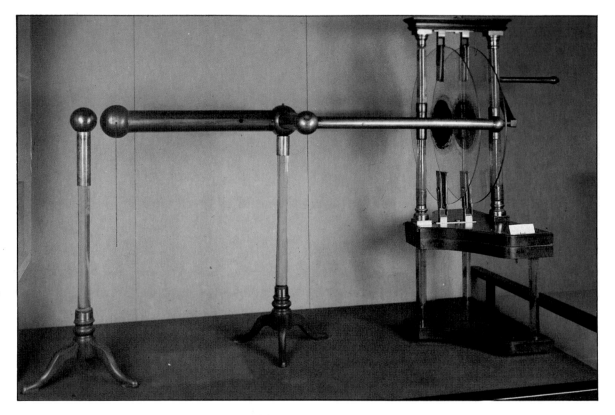

STATIC ELECTRICITY Von Guericke's simple electrostatic machine was made out of minerals, as he felt these would be close to the earth in composition. A sulphur sphere was therefore mounted on an iron rod. On rotation, the sphere became electrified and attracted small pieces of dust, hair, feather and paper, and carried them around on its surface. When von Guericke placed his finger near to the spinning globe, sparks were emitted. This machine from the eighteenth century is based on the same principle, but has a glass disc.

and out with metal. Known as the 'Leyden jar' it was, in fact, the first capacitor. Further studies showed that the spark it emitted increased, the thinner the glass walls of the jar. This last result could not be explained on the basis of Dufay's two-effluvia theory, although a modified form was devised to account for it.

The American, Benjamin Franklin (1706-90) conducted an ingenious experiment in which he connected a Leyden jar to a metal rod carried on a kite; he then flew the kite during a thunderstorm. From this he was able to demonstrate that lightning was nothing more than an electric discharge, as its spark-like shape had indicated. (The results of Franklin's experiment led directly to the development of lightning conductors to protect buildings.) Others, trying to increase the capacity of the Leyden jar, connected numbers of them together and obtained discharges that not only gave immense sparks, but were also strong enough to give a shock that would kill animals. Electrical discharges were also made through water; in London in 1747 a discharge was made by William Watson and others across the Thames, the discharge being sufficient to ignite 'spirits of wine' (ethanol — a product of the alchoholic fermentation of sugar). This activity was all part of the widespread interest taken in electrical discharges and electric shocks at the time. Electrical demonstrations, in fact, became a favourite entertainment for the rich, with the French Court of Louis XV being a notable centre for such novel kinds of displays.

During the eighteenth century, an aspect of static electricity that was increasingly pursued was the measurement of electric charges and the attempt to formulate some precise laws to describe their behaviour. There was even a theory that the 'electric effluvia' might cause an increase in weight and delicate weighings were carried out, notably by the French physicist, the Abbé Nollet, though no such increase was found. However, regarding the measurement of electrical charges and their action, success was achieved, mainly in England and France by Joseph Priestley (1733-1804), Henry Cavendish (1731-1810) and Charles Coulomb (1736-1806). In 1767, Priestley published the results of his attempts to try to prove experimentally that electrical attraction and repulsion vary with distance according to an inverse square law. Using a pair of very light balls made of pith and suspended on threads, and placing them in a tin container, he obtained a result which, he thought, pointed to the fact that 'the attraction of electricity is subject to the same laws as that of gravitation'. Priestley's attempts inspired Henry Cavendish to make a number of experiments; one of these enabled him to show that an inverse square law did indeed account for the facts. Unfortunately, Cavendish published very little and his important results remained unknown until 1879, by which time his work had been surpassed by others.

Charles Coulomb in Paris was not reticent about publishing his important electrical findings, which were made in 1784 with the aid of his torsion balance, a device already known to

L'ELECTRISÉE

33.

*Je le sçais, où se trouve mieux
Cette vertu presque magique,
Sçavamment nommée électrique;
Jeunes Beautés, c'est dans vos yeux.*

ELECTRICAL AMUSEMENTS
Experiments and demonstrations in static electricity became very popular at the court of Louis XV. Aristocratic games included the use of an electrostatic machine, as depicted on this playing card from c 1750. The romantic verse, however, implied that even the magical qualities of electricity could not eclipse the beauty of the young women at court.

be very sensitive when he was studying magnetism. Using it to measure the repulsion of electric charges, it proved to be delicate enough to show that the force between them did indeed vary as the inverse square of the distance, just as Priestley had suggested. Coulomb also investigated how electric charges are distributed over a surface, designing an experiment very similar to one carried out by Cavendish, although it is most unlikely he knew about Cavendish's work. Coulomb found that a charge was equally distributed over the surface of a conductor but, in the case of a hollow conductor, does not penetrate to the inside. To measure the quantity of an electric charge, Coulomb and others used devices — 'electrometers' — either based on Priestley's pith balls or utilizing two very thin strips of gold foil; in each case the separation of the balls, or of one ball from a charged body, or of the two gold strips, constituted a measure of the charge.

With Coulomb's work, the study of electricity reached the end of the first stage of its progress. The next was initiated, almost by chance, at Bologna University in Italy. Here Luigi Galvani (1737-98), the Professor of Anatomy, was studying contractions of muscles, using dismembered frogs' legs for his experiments. The use of electric shocks on animals had already

FRANKLIN'S KITE The American scientist-statesman Benjamin Franklin's interest in the nature of electricity led him to abandon his printing business in 1748 to devote himself to science. In 1752, he demonstrated the electrical nature of lightning by flying a kite in a thunderstorm. The kite was fitted with a metal rod, which was connected to a Leyden jar. When lightning struck the rod, sparks flew at the jar's connection, so demonstrating the electrical nature of the phenomenon.

made it evident that static electricity could cause muscle contractions and Galvani had an electrostatic machine in his laboratory. He was astounded to find that contractions could occur when the legs were touched with a knife blade held in the hand, provided the machine was emitting sparks or a Leyden jar was being discharged some distance away. Such contractions also occurred if the legs were hung outside on an iron fence or a brass hook. These and other experiments using two dissimilar metals to support otherwise insulated legs, led him to the view that electricity was present in every animal. The announcement in 1791 of his discovery of this 'animal' or 'Galvanic' electricity aroused immense interest.

Galvani's interpretation of his results was challenged by Alessandro Volta (1745-1827), Professor of Physics at Pavia University, who claimed that the evidence did not show that there was electricity present in animal bodies but that it was generated when two dissimilar metals are applied to a moist body. Volta proved his point by making some 'electric piles', which consisted of discs of moist material — wood, paper or porous tiles — separated by alternate discs of copper and zinc. When metal wires were connected to the ends of the pile, he found there was a flow of electricity. Volta continued this research by investigating which pairs of metals could be used satisfactorily to produce electricity; he noted that more electric stimulus could be obtained using a battery or series of piles or 'cells' (the name given to cups of liquid with metal 'electrodes' dipping into them). Volta's experiments were revolutionary; here, for the first time, was a continuous source of electrical energy.

The reason why piles and batteries produced electricity eluded Volta but others were only too ready to investigate the source of this 'voltaic' electricity, notably Humphry Davy (1778-1829), who later became president of the Royal Society in London. He discovered that no electricity was generated if the water in the batteries was pure, and only appeared when a substance was present which would cause the zinc electrode to be oxidized. In addition, Davy's assistant Michael Faraday (1791-1867) showed that the liquid between the electrodes decomposed with the generation of electricity and did so throughout the entire container, not just next to the metal plates, as some people believed. This work, carried out in 1833, when Dalton's new atomic theory had been accepted, led Faraday to suggest that the experiments showed how the atoms composing matter are probably associated with electricity. This association, he said, gives them their 'affinity' in chemical reactions. These very penetrating views were only expanded when the nature of atoms began to be understood.

Faraday next turned his attention to purely electrical experiments and made a number of notable advances. He showed that static and

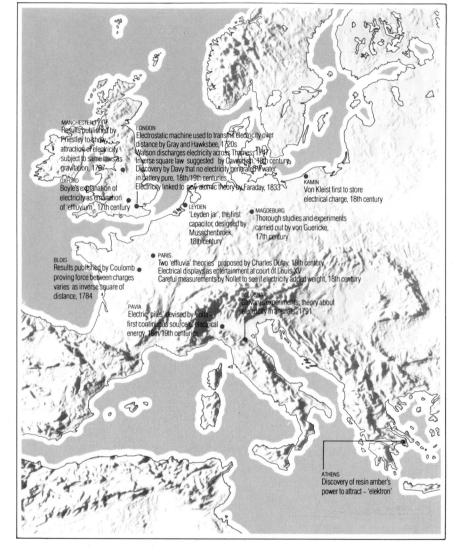

voltaic electricity were in no way different and then made further investigations on the results of the research by Hans Oersted and André Ampère. This led him to discover that an electric current from a battery flowing through a coil of wire could induce a current in a second coil. Faraday also showed how magnets alone could induce a current in a metal wire and that a flowing current always had an associated magnetic field.

The practical results of this research were immense, leading to the development of the electric motor, the dynamo or mechanical electric generator, to the transformer, and to the telegraph and the telephone. Faraday's work not only opened a new age in technology, it also ushered in a new understanding of matter. In describing the way magnetic and electric forces operate over empty space, Faraday conceived of the idea of magnetic and electric 'lines of force' stretching across space. Later research, aimed at elucidating this concept, extended our understanding of this revolutionary, but complex, theoretical concept still further.

RESEARCH INTO ELECTRICITY Since the attractive power of amber was first noted, electricity has been a fascinating source of inquiry. Its seemingly magical qualities of invisibility and unpredictability confused scientists until the eighteenth century, when simultaneous work was carried out all over Europe. Electricity is now a common source of power at work and in industry all over the world, and is used is many fields of research.

SCIENTIFIC FASHION Parisians have always been ready to adopt new and exciting fashions, not just in clothing but also in thought. They have been inspired by kings and queens, scientists and philosophers alike. The notion that it was necessary to attach a lightning conductor to one's hat when promenading appeared around 1778, when interest in electricity was widespread. Benjamin Franklin had shown, early in the eighteenth century, that lightning is an electric discharge; this led directly to the development of lightning conductors, and not just on rooftops!

Electromagnetic Radiation

After research by Michael Faraday (1791-1867) on electricity and magnetism in the 1830s, it became increasingly evident that some fundamental theoretical study was needed to try to bind together in a coherent scheme all the diverse facts about the subject. At the beginning of the nineteenth century, Hans Oersted and André Ampère had discovered and investigated a link between voltaic electricity and magnetism; in the 1820s, Georg Ohm (1787-1854) had discovered and measured the resistance of metal wires to the flow of this electricity. Now, with Faraday's establishment of further links between magnetism and electricity, the need for a comprehensive analysis of the phenomena had become urgent.

Such an analysis required not only a comprehensive theory but a deep mathematical analysis if it were to be acceptable. Faraday, largely self-taught, had never had the benefit of a university training and could not tackle this; the immense progress he had been able to make in research was astounding in any case. His concept of lines of electrical and magnetic force was brilliant; it fitted the results he had obtained but needed a mathematical foundation.

A Scots physicist, James Clerk Maxwell (1831-79) became interested in the problem; a Cambridge graduate in mathematics, he was ideally suited to meet the challenge. Maxwell's interest in the subject arose both from correspondence he had with Faraday and from some work which Lord Kelvin had carried out in 1842 while a student at Cambridge. Kelvin, who was interested in the study of heat, had compared the way an electrostatic charge of electricity spread over a body with the way heat spreads over a very large body, large enough for its edges to be ignored when dealing with this particular, more local problem. (Only in this way could Kelvin simplify the problem sufficiently to come to grips with it). Two things interested Maxwell: the first was that the mathematical solutions of the two cases — the spread of heat and the spread of an electric charge — were very similar, and the second was the fact that in obtaining his results, Kelvin had made use of the idea that the electrical effects spread out over a continuous 'medium'. They were of interest because they fitted in with the lines of force and electric and magnetic 'fields'.

Kelvin looked again at electricity a quarter of a century later. This was at a time when the wave theory of light had become accepted and the belief in an 'aether' to carry the waves had become commonplace. In this second piece of electrical research, he compared electrical effects in such an aether with the strains that would be imposed in a solid body, suggesting how these effects might possibly be transmitted across space or, rather, through an aether.

The stage was now set for a complete synthesis of electricity and magnetism. In 1855, Maxwell attempted to find mathematical expressions to describe precisely what happened when a magnet influenced the area around it. This attempt to deal with a magnetic field and its lines of force was successful, yet it was only a beginning. Five years' more work was required before Maxwell at last obtained complete mathematical solutions. In 1864 he published his results, which tied magnetic and electric fields into one all-embracing scheme, using an 'aether' as the transmitting medium.

RADIANT ENERGY This term describes electromagnetic radiation, ie the form in which energy travels through space. Known to be a wave motion, this type of energy can be subdivided into various categories, of which gamma rays, X-rays, ultraviolet radiation, visible light, infrared radiation and radio waves are all part. These are listed in order of increasing wavelength as may be seen in the diagram (right). The atmosphere acts as a screen against very short waves, from gamma rays to some ultraviolet radiation. Also water vapour in the air blocks out much of the infrared; mainly only optical waves and some radio waves can penetrate to the ground. This X-ray radiograph of some mummified bones (below) shows how the rays penetrate through the tissues but are absorbed by the bones themselves. For this reason, X-rays are used extensively in medicine and also in engineering to show up structural faults.

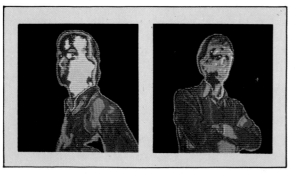

ELECTRONIC PORTRAITURE The two portraits (left) were constructed on an electronic system that first scanned the subjects, measuring the intensity of the light radiation being given off. The scans of different light frequencies were then superimposed. Different types of radiation have varying wavelengths (below), which can all be registered on a computerized display for further study.

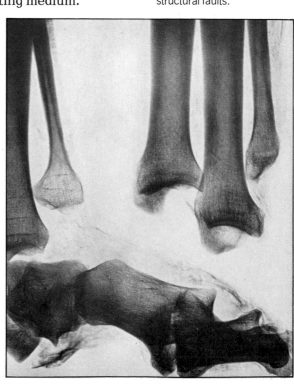

| gamma rays | X-rays | ultraviolet | infrared | radio waves |

1/10 million mm | 1/100,000 mm | 1/10,000 mm | 1/1,000 mm | 1/100 mm | 1/10 mm | 1 mm | 1 cm | 10 cm | 1 m

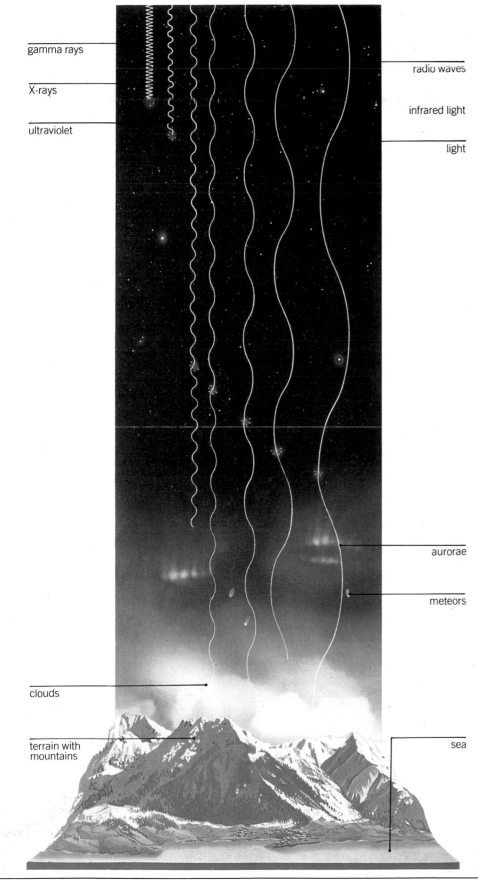

gamma rays

X-rays

ultraviolet

radio waves

infrared light

light

aurorae

meteors

clouds

terrain with
mountains

sea

The importance of Maxwell's results was due to the fact that the mathematical equations he had derived from electrical and mathematical experimental results were similar in every way to those equations which had already been derived to express the behaviour of light; it seemed undeniable that light was only one aspect of electromagnetic phenomena. Once this astounding conclusion was accepted, it then seemed evident that electromagnetic radiation should extend to both longer and shorter wavelengths than those of light itself, and also be subject to reflection and refraction.

Some waves of this kind had already been discovered. In 1800, the astronomer William Herschel (1738-1822) had discovered rays coming from the sun that were below the red end of the spectrum; they had a longer wavelength than light. Although invisible to the eye, the rays clearly carried heat — they cause the mercury in a thermometer to rise. Dispersed by a prism, they could, Herschel thought, also display other optical effects. Placing a lens in front of a fire, he found that these infrared rays could indeed be refracted. At the time of his discovery, the result was little more than a curiosity but now, in the light of Maxwell's work, it assumed more significance. What was true of Herschel's discovery was true of another: the discovery of ultraviolet radiation by Johann Ritter a year later in Vienna. This radiation, he found, lay beyond the violet, as its name implied; although invisible, it blackened light-sensitive material, like silver chloride, and could be reflected and refracted.

With all scientific theories, it is their power to foresee other results previously unknown that establishes their validity, and discovery of radiation at other invisible wavelengths was now required to firmly establish Maxwell's results. The first breakthrough came in 1888, although Maxwell was by then dead. At Karlsruhe in Germany, the physicist Heinrich Hertz discovered radio waves; these were far longer in wavelength than Herschel's infrared waves and so supported Maxwell's result that waves were to be expected extending far beyond the visible range. The second independent confirmation came 7 years later, in 1895, when at Würtzburg, also in Germany, Wilhelm Röntgen discovered the existence of what he called 'X-rays'; they proved to have a very short wavelength indeed. In 1900, the French physicist Paul Villard detected gamma rays, which were even more penetrating and still shorter in wavelength.

These confirmations of Maxwell's most important theory have had their own implications. X-rays and gamma rays have been used in medicine for diagnosis and treatment, while it is now realized how important such invisible radiation is in the study of the universe. Spacecraft are now launched to observe those wavelengths which can never reach earth-based observatories.

The Art of Geometry

The meaning of the word 'geometry', literally 'the measure of the earth', gives a clue about its origin. Geometry was first used to apportion land, to enclose areas that were to be cultivated, or to measure stone or wood for building. To begin with, it was no more than a collection of methods, diverse and separate, by which various tasks could be performed. The prime example is the '3-4-5' rule, the rule that describes how to space out knots, say, along a cord so that when the cord is stretched around two stakes in the ground, a third stake can be placed so that the three form a right-angled triangle. In this way the corners of a square or rectangular field may be laid out. The 3-4-5 rule is not geometry; it is an age-old practical rule of procedure, yet it formed the basis of the mathematical discipline of geometry.

For such a mathematical discipline to develop, it was necessary to first extract and organize the general ideas that lay behind the practical procedures. For instance, not only is the triangle whose sides measure 3, 4 and 5 one which contains a right-angle; so too are those whose sides are multiples of these numbers — triangles with sides of 6, 8 and 10, or 9, 12 and 15, and so on. Even this does not exhaust the possibilities. If a triangle can be defined by a figure on a flat surface bounded by three straight lines, and a right-angle by using two intersecting straight lines, it is then possible to draw other right-angled triangles. It is also possible to extract a general rule about triangles of this kind: that the sides are all related by the squares of the numbers representing their sides. Thus, in the 3, 4, 5 triangles 3^2 plus 4^2 is equal to 5^2; in other words $3^2 + 4^2 = 5^2$ or $9^2 + 12^2 = 15^2$ or $81 + 144 = 225$.

This can be generalized by saying that the

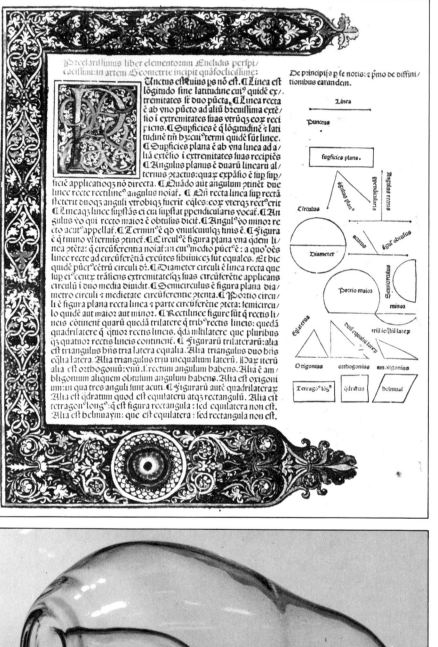

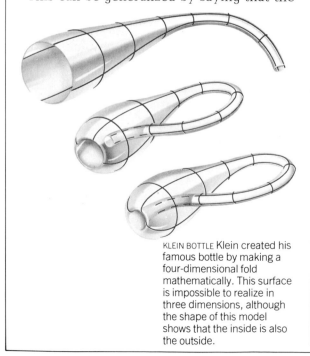

KLEIN BOTTLE Klein created his famous bottle by making a four-dimensional fold mathematically. This surface is impossible to realize in three dimensions, although the shape of this model shows that the inside is also the outside.

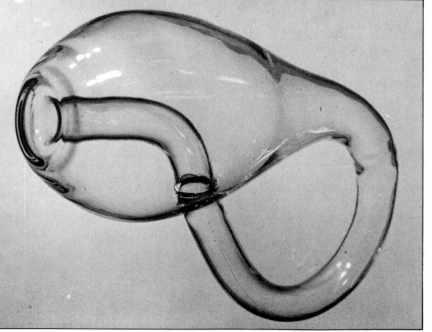

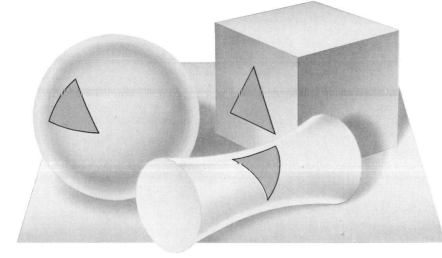

which have equal sides and equal angles between them. But progress in geometry did not rest there. During the third century BC Apollonios wrote on the curves obtained by taking slices through an upright cone. These curves are the circle — the most beautiful of all plane figures according to the Pythagoreans — the ellipse and the open curves (those which do not return on themselves), the parabola and hyperbola. These were to have great importance later, the ellipse in explaining planetary motions, the parabola for some cometary paths and the hyperbola in geometry itself.

Research in geometry was carried out by most Greek mathematicians, who concerned themselves with difficult problems such as finding the areas of plane figures, particularly the circle, and the areas of solid figures such as the sphere. However, the most famous name in Greek geometry is probably that of Euclid, who worked in Alexandria during the third century BC. He synthesized and organized all Greek geometry up to this time, laying down a logical system of definitions, axioms and proofs; these held throughout the Western world for more than 2,000 years.

Despite his genius, Euclid was unable to formulate a logical proof for two of his theorems, one connected with parallel lines and the other with segments of a straight line. Formal proofs continued to evade every other geometer after Euclid's time. While trying to prove the theorems, Giorolamo Saccheri came close to developing a new 'non-Euclidean' geometry in the eighteenth century, but most mathematicians were convinced of the truth of Euclid's geometry.

The great nineteenth-century physicist and mathematician Carl Friedrich Gauss (1777-1855) tried replacing Euclid's two theorems with a simpler one and came to the same result, but did not publish his findings. Only in the 1830s did two mathematicians go through the whole process of developing a new geometry. One was the Hungarian Janos Bolyai, who, because Gauss had already achieved such a geometry, only published his work as an appendix to a mathematical book by his father. It was not generally known until the late 1860s. However, Nikolai Lobachevsky, in Russia, also achieved a similar feat. His geometry was published between 1829 and 1830. It is not a geometry of ordinary space, although it has all the Euclidean elements except the two unprovable theorems; it is the geometry of hyperbolic space. An alternative geometry, again using the same Euclidean material, was invented by the German, Georg Riemann (1826-66) and published posthumously in 1867; this gives a spherical space. Thought at the time to be the products of the imagination and to have nothing of the real world in them, these non-Euclidean geometries are now seen to provide a truer picture of the universe and to represent an important development in mathematics.

GEOMETRIC FIGURES Some of the subject matter in Euclid's famous work, the *Elements*, was drawn from other geometricians, but Euclid himself arranged the information logically and developed many of the ideas, adding theorems and explanations. A page from the Latin translation *(left)* — *Opus Elementorum* — shows clear illustrations. The triangles on the sphere and the hyperbola *(above)* require a different geometry from that of Euclid, however. In the first, the angles of the triangle add up to more than, and in the second less than 180° This is the sum of the angles on the cube.

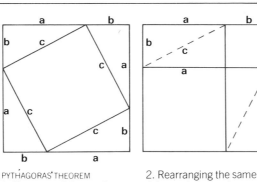

PYTHAGORAS' THEOREM
1. The area of the smaller square (c^2) + the area of the four right-angled triangles = the area of the larger square.

2. Rearranging the same right-angled triangles within the large square gives: $a^2 + b^2$ + the area of the larger square. Therefore, $a^2 + b^2 = c^2$.

square of the hypotenuse is equal to the squares of the other two sides added together, and this rule brings us to a strange fact. It was first noted by Pythagoras in the fifth century BC and worried him considerably. In a right-angled triangle, where the two short sides are at right-angles to one another, each only one unit long, the length of the hypotenuse is the square root of the other two sides added together: the square root of 2 (because $1^2 + 1^2 = 1 + 1 = 2$). The puzzle began here for Pythagoras, because the square root of 2 (ie the number which multiplied by itself equals 2) is not a whole number but a fraction. It is 1.14213...; the Pythagoreans called it an 'irrational' number, meaning that it could not be expressed as the ratio of two whole numbers. Their concern was that they believed whole numbers and rational numbers (such as $1/2$, $3/2$, $2/3$, etc) had an important mystical significance in the universe. However, whether they are irrational or not, the relationship between the sides of a right-angled triangle can be proved by geometric argument.

It was the Pythagoreans who discovered the 'five regular solids', those geometrical figures

Algebra

Counting is the basis of arithmetic and of all mathematics; it enters into geometry — the laws of right-angled triangles show that — and into many practical fields of endeavour. Counting schemes were invented by all early civilizations. The counting system we now use is based on 10; we count from one to 10 and then change the position of our number symbol and start again. But the decimal system is not the only system. Some races count in 12s — a duodecimal system — while the peoples of Mesopotamia had a number count of 60 — the sexagesimal system. Astonishingly enough, this counting system is still with us some 4,000 years later; we continue to use it for the degrees of a circle and for fractions of those degrees, as well as for our subdivisions of time into minutes and seconds.

To develop mathematics it is not only important to be able to count but also to write down the results of counting; if we are to add, subtract, multiply or divide numbers — whether decimal, duodecimal or sexagesimal — then it is essential that we can write down our results in a clear fashion. The Mesopotamians used wedge-shaped or cuneiform strokes; one stroke for one, two for two and so on, changing the stroke from vertical to horizontal at 10,600 or other combinations of 10 x 60. The Chinese also used horizontal and vertical lines, singly or together; they had single vertical strokes from one to five, then again from six to nine but joined at the top by a horizontal line; 10s were horizontal lines, and so on. The Chinese system seems to have been derived from the use of counting rods of bamboo placed in appropriate positions on a counting-board, these positions showing whether a number was among the digits, 10s, 100s, 1,000s or whatever. This, of course, is what we do today; thus 1 is one, 10 is one shift to the left; 100 a second shift further to the left and so on. The Mesopotamians also used a positional system with their cuneiform number strokes but the Egyptians and the Romans did not, except that IX was nine (X minus I) and XI was 11 (X plus I).

How important positional arrangements of simply written numbers can be becomes evident in the light of further developments. The Egyptians and Romans had many different signs for numbers but paid little attention to position, whereas the Mesopotamians and Chinese had simple number writing and were more concerned with position. The result was that in Mesopotamia and Ancient China relationships between the numbers were used in arithmetical operations and in due course both cultures were able to express more complicated relationships, to draw up what we would call equations. Such equations, expressions of relationships in the natural world, are the essence of algebra.

The word 'algebra' is derived from Arabic, for it was in Islam that algebra was really developed. One factor that aided this development was the adoption of an ingenious system

of writing numbers devised by Hindu mathematicians, who as early as the sixth century AD had a sign for zero, as did the Chinese — the invention of the zero sign is still a matter of some debate. Since the West inherited this number system from the Arabs rather than directly from the Hindus, it is still often called the system of 'Arabic numerals'. With the Hindu numbers, which were adopted in Islam in the ninth century, the mathematician Abu Jafar al-Khwarizmi was able to explain how the equations relating to problems could be reduced to six simple forms using two standard procedures. One was to transfer terms from one

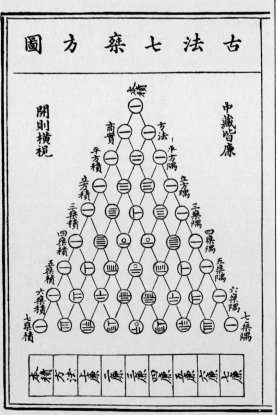

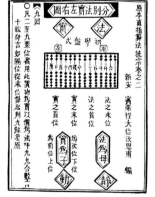

EASTERN ACHIEVEMENTS The Chinese were able to calculate quickly with the abacus *(above)*. The diagram shows their version of what we know as the 'Pascal Triangle' entitled 'The Old Method Chart of the Seven Multiplying Squares', tabulating the binomial coefficients up to the eighth power *(left)*. The open-air observatory at Jaipur in India has giant instruments based on Muslim designs for accurate observing *(top)*.

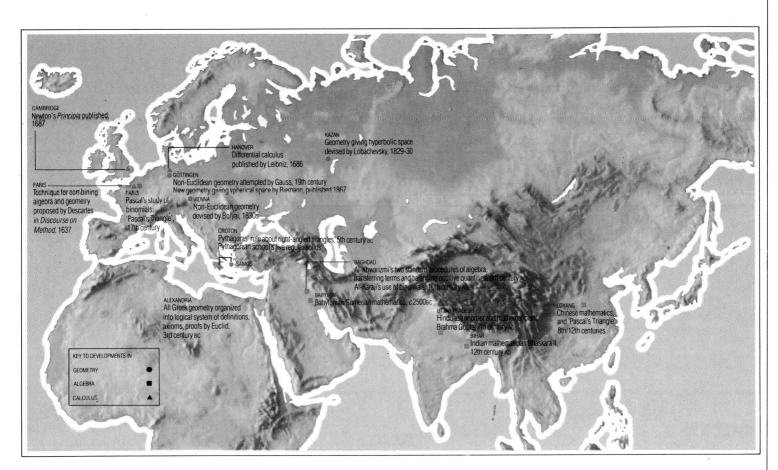

CAMBRIDGE
Newton's *Principia* published;
1687

KAZAN
Geometry giving hyperbolic space
devised by Lobachevsky, 1829-30

HANOVER
Differential calculus
published by Leibniz, 1686

GÖTTINGEN
Non-Euclidean geometry attempted by Gauss, 19th century
New geometry giving spherical space by Riemann, published 1867

PARIS
Technique for combining
algebra and geometry
proposed by Descartes
in *Discourse on
Method*, 1637

PARIS
Pascal's study of
binomials;
'Pascal's Triangle',
17th century

VIENNA
Non-Euclidean geometry
devised by Bolyai, 1830s

CROTON
Pythagoras' rule about right-angled triangles, 5th century BC
Pythagorean school's five regular solids

SAMOS

BAGHDAD
Al-Khwarizmi's two standard procedures of algebra,
transferring terms and balancing positive quantities, 9th century AD
Al-Karaji's use of binomials, 10th century AD

BABYLON
Babylonian/Sumerian mathematics, c 2500 BC

ALEXANDRIA
All Greek geometry organized
into logical system of definitions,
axioms, proofs by Euclid,
3rd century BC

UTTAR PRADESH
Hindu astronomer and mathematician
Brahma Gupta, 7th century AD

BIHAR
Indian mathematician Bhaskara II,
12th century AD

LOYANG
Chinese mathematics
and 'Pascal's Triangle'
8th/12th centuries

KEY TO DEVELOPMENTS IN

GEOMETRY ●

ALGEBRA ■

CALCULUS ▲

side of an equation to the other in order to eliminate the negative quantities (thus $2x = 100 - 3x$ becomes $5x = 100$); the other to 'balance' the positive quantities which compose the equation (thus $x^2 + 100 = 8x + 93$ would become $x^2 + 7 = 8x$). The Arabic for this transferring of terms was *al-jabr* and it is from this word that 'algebra' is derived.

Much progress followed al-Khwarizmi's work; 150 years later, Abu Bakr al-Karaji expressed the essence of algebra when he explained it as 'the determination of unknowns' from known facts. Algebra has proved to be a powerful mathematical technique which has been developed to astonishing lengths ever since and is of immense importance in helping to pursue modern science.

Al-Karaji is also remembered today for his use of binomials, that is of 'two number' expressions. These are important in applying mathematics to the real world but they can be tedious to work out. There is, however, a 'shorthand' way of dealing with them devised by Chinese mathematicians in the twelfth century. This is known in the West as 'Pascal's Triangle' after Blaise Pascal (1623-62) who studied binomials in his work on calculating the probabilities of events. To explain the Triangle is simple enough. In the binomial expression $(x + 1)$, the (unwritten) number 'coefficient' is front of x is 1; if the expression is squared we obtain $(x + 1) \times (x + 1) = x^2 + 2x + 1$ and the coeffi-

cients are 1, 2, 1. Cubing the expression gives us $(x + 1) \times (x + 1) \times (x + 1) = (x^3 + 3x^2 + 3x + 1)$, where the coefficients are 1, 3, 3, 1; this continues when we go to higher powers. In fact we need not bother to do the multiplication at all, we can get the results merely by writing down all the coefficients for power 1 — that is for $(x + 1)$ — for power 2 — that is for $(x + 1) \times (x + 1)$ — and so on. This gives:

power 1	$1 + 1$
power 2	$1 + 2 + 1$
power 3	$1 + 3 + 3 + 1$
power 4	$1 + 4 + 6 + 4 + 1$
power 5	$1 + 5 + 10 + 10 + 5 + 1$

The rest can be worked out by a triangle with numbers derived by adding up those in the previous line.

Methods like this would not be possible without the use of a simple way of delineating numbers, as possessed in China, Islam and the West, nor without the use of unknowns (such as x) which need the technique of algebra. Algebra and its later developments enabled scientists of the seventeenth century onwards, and particularly those concerned with the physical sciences, to tackle a vast number of complicated problems with an efficiency and precision that would be quite impossible without such techniques and mathematical short cuts available at their command.

DEVELOPMENTS IN NUMERIC SYMBOLISM Simple arithmetic and geometry have been vital methods of calculation since the earliest times. The Greek civilization, however, was the first to use a logical, complete system of geometry. As science developed, calculations were needed and algebra was invented and adopted in the Islamic world while, during the Renaissance in Europe, Newton and Leibniz put forward the invaluable method of the calculus.

The Calculus

When the *Principia* by Isaac Newton (1642-1727) appeared in 1687, readers who could understand it discovered that its mathematical text was geometrical. The paths of planets and projectiles, the motion of bodies through resisting media, were all described in geometrical terms. Yet Newton had not worked out his original ideas using geometry; he had used the new techniques of algebra and his own mathematical invention, the calculus or, as he termed it, the method of 'fluxions'. The reason he gave for writing the text in geometrical terms was clear enough: if he had presented the results in a totally unfamiliar form of mathematics the book would not have been read at all.

Geometry as a way of mathematical reasoning had ruled Western mathematics for so long that, although algebra and algebraic techniques were being developed, it seemed the natural form in which to tackle problems such as planetary motion in an ellipse — which, after all, was a geometrical curve. Yet as early as 1637, in an appendix to his *Discourse on Method*, René Descartes (1596-1650) had proposed a technique for marrying geometry and algebra, a method that has since become known as 'analytical geometry' because it uses methods of algebraic analysis to study geometrical figures.

The method may sound esoteric and complex but most people are familiar with its basis if they know how to read a map grid reference. To specify the position of a place on a map grid one uses two sets of numbers, one set to specify the east or west position of the place with respect to some given point or 'origin', the other to specify its position north or south of this origin. Descartes adopted a similar method, although instead of using numbers, the 'east-west' direction is given in x units, the north-south direction in y units. A simple example will

show how this works. Suppose we wish to measure the length of a line between two points A and B, we can now do this algebraically. If we draw a right-angled triangle having AB as its longest side, then its other two sides can readily be made to lie in the x and y directions. Then, using Pythagoras' right-angled triangle theorem, and fixing the origin of measurement at one end of the line · — at A, say — the result is $AC^2 + CB^2 + AB^2$ or, putting it in algebraic terms, $x^2 + y^2 + AB^2$. By taking the square root of AB^2 we find AB.

The analytical geometry of Descartes can deal with much more complex geometrical figures than straight lines and triangles. It can, for instance, formulate an equation to represent all the points on the circumference of a circle, or all the points around the edge of an ellipse. By means of this technique, Newton could express the behaviour of a point moving around an ellipse; in other words, he could transform his problem into one expressible in analytical, that is algebraic, terms.

However, in trying to deal with motion in an ellipse under the force of gravitation operating from the sun, Newton faced a very difficult problem. The distance from the sun of a body orbiting in an ellipse is constantly changing; it is only a certain value at any particular instant. In this case, what the mathematician has to do is to deal with a quantity in his equations that is in a continual state of flux. The answer to this defeated other mathematicians of the time; they knew of no technique for dealing with such a varying quantity; Newton's triumph was that he invented one.

Some idea of Newton's technique can be gained by looking at the line AB again. Moving along the x direction from A to C, for each step — for each very tiny increase in x — the value of y changes too. How large this increase is depends on the slope of AB; the steeper the

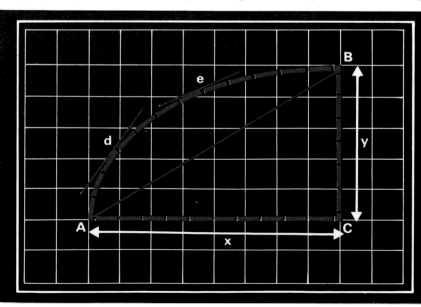

THE CALCULUS As the diagram shows, calculus, a powerful technique combining algebra and geometry, makes it possible to calculate constantly changing qualities *(left)*. Thanks to the calculus and gravitation theory, the prediction of the behaviour of rockets and other spacecraft is relatively straightforward. *Columbia (right)* was first launched from Cape Canaveral in Florida in April 1981; since then it has been launched on four other occasions. These successive launchings prove the precision with which scientists can programme and monitor the Shuttle with the aim of protecting and maintaining it in re-usable condition.

slope, the larger the increase of y for every step along x. In the *dotted* curve which connects A to B, the increase in y varies for equal steps along x; to begin with it is large, later on it is much less. We can measure this change of increase by drawing straight lines which just touch the curve at various points. Let us take two points, *d* and *e*. The point *d* is at a place of large change of y and the steep slope of the dotted line through *d* illustrates this. On the other hand, if we go along the curve to *e* and draw a line through there, we can see that the slope is very much lower, indicating that the rate of change of y for equal steps along x is much less. Newton's achievement was that he invented a method for calculating this change continually around an ellipse, and any other curve for that matter, without having to stop each point and without having to draw slopes on the curve. His method was purely algebraic.

The problem that Newton solved faced many mathematicians. Gottfried Leibniz (1646-1716), in Germany, invented a similar technique, publishing his 'differential calculus' in 1686. Encouraged by others, Newton accused Leibniz of stealing his ideas: there was a bitter dispute. Despite this, research has shown that Leibniz came to his methods independently.

The calculus was certainly a powerful technique, developed and applied in following years to a vast number of scientific and engineering problems. Initially, most progress took place in France and Germany. Much of this was because the mathematical notation that Leibniz used in his calculus was far more explicit than the notation adopted by Newton; this made Leibniz' calculus somewhat easier to use and certainly easier to develop. Because of the old controversy, British mathematicians refused to forsake Newton's notation; only after the 1820s was the Leibniz method adopted and then developments also occurred in Britain.

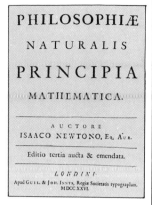

PHILOSOPHIÆ
NATURALIS
PRINCIPIA
MATHEMATICA.

AUCTORE
ISAACO NEWTONO, Eq. Aur.

Editio tertia aucta & emendata.

LONDINI.
Apud Guil. & Joh. Innys, Regiæ Societatis typographos.
MDCCXXVI.

MOTION IN AN ELLIPSE
Principia (above) first published in 1687, explains the whole question of planetary motion by a single mathematical law — gravity. The sun's gravity has the effect of making an orbiting planet move at its fastest at the perihelion, which is its nearest point to the sun — between A and B on this diagram *(below)*. When the planet travels away, the sun's influence lessens and the planet's motion slows down. The aphelion is its furthest point from the sun, and the point where it moves at its slowest speed — between C and D. Kepler's second law stated that the radius vector — the line from the sun to a planet — sweeps out equal areas in equal times. Thus the area SAB is equal to the area SCD. Hence the planet moves the greater distance AB in the same time as it takes to go from C to D.

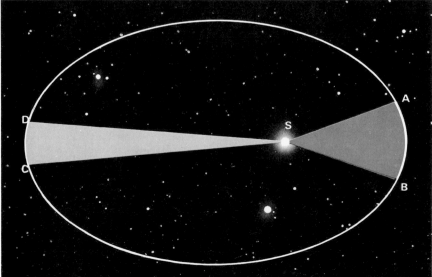

Chemistry

The science of chemistry did not arrive until after the scientific revolution and then only rather slowly and laboriously. But chemical knowledge is as old as history, being almost entirely concerned with the practical arts of living. Cooking is essentially a chemical process; so is the smelting of metals and the administration of drugs and potions. This basic chemical knowledge, which was applied in most cases as a rule-of-thumb, was nevertheless dependent on previous experiment. It also served to stimulate a fundamental curiosity about the processes themselves. New information was always being gained as craftsmen and artisans improved techniques to gain better results.

The development of a scientific approach to chemistry was, however, hampered by three factors. The most serious problem was the vast range of material available and the consequent difficulty of organizing it into some system. Secondly, there were social and intellectual difficulties. Chemistry is nothing if not practical; those who practise it must use their hands, they must have a certain practical flair. Yet in Ancient Greece, and in other civilizations as well, where practical tasks were primarily the province of a slave population, the thinker or philosopher stood above and apart from this mundane world. The practical arts were beneath his dignity and thus his interest; they appeared to lack any intellectual content. The Chinese have a delightful story to illustrate this; it concerns a philosopher who was having a house built. The builder did not want to use new unseasoned wood, but the philosopher insisted, arguing that as wood hardens with age and lime softens with the passage of time, all should be well. The builder could not counter this argument so he used new wood, and in due course the house fell down. This tale was often told by the Taoists who did not accept this attitude of superiority to manual ability and who, indeed, practised chemical research.

The third problem for early chemical science was the element of secrecy. On the one hand, craftsmen who were experts in specific trades using their own techniques, guarded their knowledge to prevent others from stealing their livelihood. In the West, the medieval guilds were just such an example of organizations jealous of their specialized trade secrets. The other motive for secrecy was the esoteric and often magical knowledge of those alchemists who were pursuing the chimera of being able to transmute base metals into gold, or were concerned with the hunt for the elixir which would bestow the blessing of eternal life. In one sense, the second was the more serious because the records of the chemical processes which the alchemists uncovered were, in the West at least, written down in symbolic language intelligible to very few, or in symbols that were purposely obscure.

During the Renaissance, attitudes began to alter gradually; with the advent of paper and printing, which came from China by way of Islam in the fifteenth century, the publication of technical books began and chemical techniques were made known to a wider audience. Although the cult of esoteric alchemy continued, it slowly began to become less secretive; by the time the scientific revolution was underway, serious attempts were being made to put chemistry onto a more truly scientific footing. Research began into processes hitherto unexplained and little examined; combustion was just such a subject, the study of which was to have immense repercussions. New concepts were needed; a new look was taken at what is meant by an 'element' and the novel idea of a 'gas' began to be used.

By the eighteenth century, the new scientific approach was starting to bear fruit. Chemists introduced a vital degree of precision in their work, weighing and measuring the results of experiments meticulously. There was a move to

MANCHESTER
Priestley's work on the chemistry of gases, 18th century
Dalton's atomic theory, 1802

STOCKHOLM
Chemical nomenclature devised by Berzelius, 19th century

GLASGOW
Promotion of atomic theory by Black, 18th century

CAMBRIDGE
J. J. Thomson and Rutherford's work on the nature of the atom, 19th century
Gowland Hopkins' work in biochemistry, 19th/20th centuries
Sanger's work on construction of protein molecules, 1940s
Dirac's work on quantum theory, 20th century

COPENHAGEN
Neils Bohr's model of the atom, 1912

VILVORDE
Study of gases by van Helmont, 16th/17th centuries

BERLIN
Stahl's phlogiston theory, 1697

LONDON
Boyle's definition of elements, 17th century
Mayow's experiments with burning objects in containers, 17th century
Cavendish and Hooke's work on the chemistry of gases, 18th century
Invention of aniline dyes by Perkin, 19th century
Hofmann's work on organic chemistry, 19th century

NEUILLY-SUR-SEINE
De Broglie's work on quantum theory, 19th/20th centuries

LEIPZIG
Heisenberg's work on indeterminancy and quantum theory, 1927

PASADENA
Work on chemical molecules by

PARIS
Establishment of scientific chemistry by Lavoisier, 1789
Discovery of radioactivity by the Curies, 1900

HEIDELBERG
The benzene ring discovered by Stradonitz von Kekulé, 1857

BASEL
New chemical principles devised by Paracelsus, 16th century

TURIN
Avogadro's hypothesis of combination of atoms, 18th/19th centuries

MADRID
Proust's discovery of the law of combining proportions, 18th century

ATHENS
Aristotle's Lyceum, 4th century BC

ACRAGAS
Birthplace of Empedokles, 5th century BC

DISCOVERIES AND CENTRES OF LEARNING The beginnings of chemistry are rooted in the ancient and practical arts of cooking, smelting metals and administering drugs. The science of chemistry, as we know it today, did not begin to emerge until the time of the scientific revolution in Europe; before this period, the pursuit of chemical knowledge was almost entirely the province of either craftsmen or alchemists, both groups intent on preserving a high degree of secrecy about their work. After research in the seventeenth century, a new look was taken at the subject; precision, clear notation and new terminology laid the basis of the science.

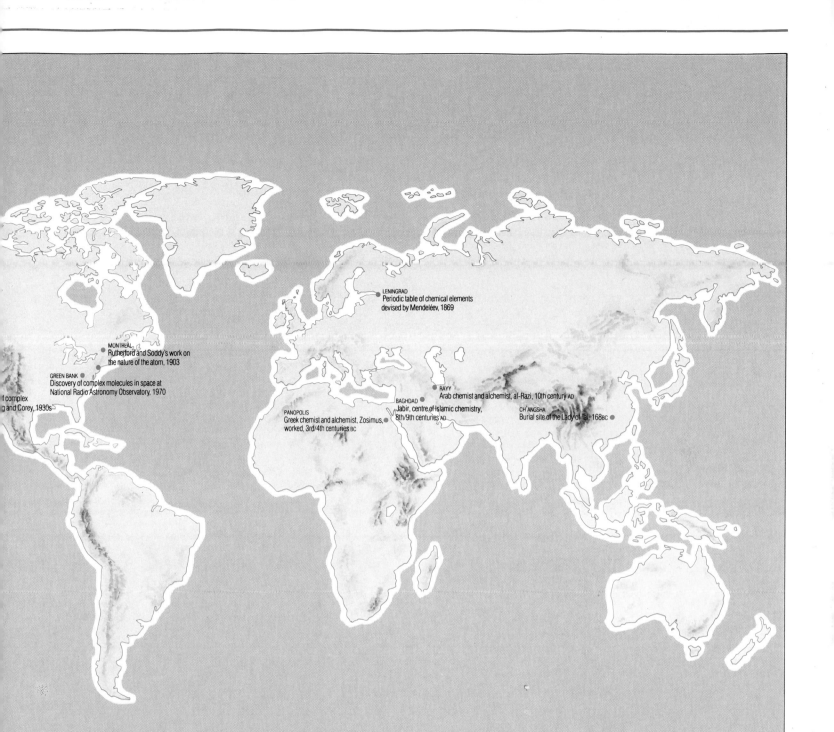

LENINGRAD
Periodic table of chemical elements
devised by Mendeléev, 1869

MONTREAL
Rutherford and Soddy's work on
the nature of the atom, 1903

GREEN BANK
Discovery of complex molecules in space at
National Radio Astronomy Observatory, 1970

complex
g and Corey, 1930s

RAYY
Arab chemist and alchemist, al-Razi, 10th century AD

BAGHDAD
Jabir, centre of Islamic chemistry,
8th/9th centuries AD

PANOPOLIS
Greek chemist and alchemist, Zosimus,
worked, 3rd/4th centuries BC

CH'ANGSHA
Burial site of the Lady of Tai, 168BC

use new names for chemical substances that describe the elements present: 'vitriol' became 'sulphuric acid' and 'aqua fortis' was more descriptively named 'nitric acid'. Just as in mathematics, where clear notation made progress possible, the new descriptive terminology in chemistry had the same effect.

Scientific chemistry was almost immediately given a new impetus by John Dalton's atomic theory, produced in the first decade of the nineteenth century. Not only was this a marked improvement on any previous atomic theory but its application soon showed a way to gain still greater precision and, very significantly, led to an understanding of what was happening during chemical reactions. It also became possible to see a complex series of relationships between all the different chemical substances found in nature. Another nineteenth-century development was the discovery that the laws and techniques of chemistry, so far confined to in-

animate material, could in fact be applied to substances present in living things. The scope of chemistry was broadened immensely and its applications widened to cover almost all the branches of natural science.

By the twentieth century, chemistry was not only treated as a science in its own right, but was also beginning to be related to other scientific disciplines. The understanding of the internal construction of chemical substances has led to the development of ways of synthesizing complex materials; this has had purely utilitarian results in the production of plastics and man-made fibres, but its applications in the formulation of new drugs has not only helped medical treatment but also brought about a deeper understanding of the chemistry of living creatures. The growth of the new discipline of biochemistry has been a notable development in this century, leading to the discovery of the chemical basis of heredity.

Early Chemical Arts

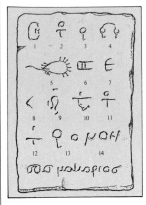

TRANSMUTATION For centuries, the idea of transmutation of base metals into gold dominated the thoughts of the first chemists. The Formula of the Crab *(above)*, given in the writings of Zosimos of Panopolis, a Greek philosopher of the third and fourth centuries BC, was thought by many to embody this secret.

The very earliest chemistry was concerned with the needs of the community: smelting metals, cooking, dyeing clothes, preparing cosmetics and providing materials for the artist. All demanded specialist techniques and involved some basic chemical knowledge.

The smelting of metals was important and widespread; indeed, early ages are known by the descriptions 'bronze' and 'iron'. In civilized times gold may have been the first metal to attract attention; it is malleable as well as beautiful and so ideally suited to making ornaments. Certainly available in Egypt, there is also evidence that its use goes back at least to Neolithic (Stone Age) times. Silver was another ornamental metal that was used early on, although copper may have antedated both gold and silver. Copper, often in combination with tin and zinc to give the alloy bronze, has a long history; tin bronze has been found at Ur in Mesopotamia in remains dating from 3500BC. Some iron, alloyed with nickel and possibly obtained by digging up meteorites, seems to have been known quite early, but the Iron Age did not arrive in the West until about 1300BC. Iron came into use so much later because of the much higher temperature needed to melt it compared with the temperatures required for copper, silver, tin and zinc.

In China the Iron Age was some seven centuries later, but progress was quicker and cast-iron was being produced in the fourth century BC, 17 centuries before the West. This use of true liquid iron was due partly to a naturally occurring iron which was rich in phosphorous — or had phosphorous added — and so melted at a lower temperature. It was also partly the result of the presence of good clays for making small but adequate furnaces and the invention of efficient bellows. The Chinese developed steel-making before the West, appreciating the need to remove carbon from molten iron in order to obtain this valuable metal.

In the Middle East glazes were used on pottery and glass was manufactured — not clear glass but coloured glass used for decoration and for making vases and jugs. Dyes were also known, especially the blue indigo dye obtained from the indigo plant and the expensive and exclusive Phoenician Tyrian purple', obtained from tiny marine molluscs. But more significant than the availability of dyes was the use of mordants — metallic compounds which fixed the dye in the fabric. This showed a somewhat sophisticated degree of chemical knowledge.

These practical chemical arts were developed over long periods of time. There was some concept of pure substances and of compounds, although no chemical elements as we understand them were known. Yet, the idea of a basic substance or a series of basic substances was not far away. As early as the sixth century BC, the Greek philosopher Thales suggested that water was the basic element. Thales had visited Egypt and doubtless seen the way previously parched and barren land became full of plant life after inundation by the waters of the Nile. However, others had different views; Anaximenes thought air the prime element and Herakleitos, fire. A step forward came in the fifth century BC when Empedokles introduced the idea of four basic 'roots' — earth, air, fire and water — and two fundamental forces — attraction and repulsion. This was a worthy attempt to systematize the materials of which the world is made.

Aristotle (384-322BC) took matters a stage further, suggesting a basic substance, *hylee*, to which different forms can be given. Such forms were the 'elements', earth, air, fire and water — not elements in the modern chemical sense, but rather 'elementary properties'. With them went four qualities: coldness, dryness, heat and moistness.

The fourth section of Aristotle's book *Meteorologica* goes beyond a mere introduction of these terms. (It is now thought that Aristotle may not have written this section himself and that the text is a later addition, made in the third century BC by Straton, a pupil of Aristotle's Lyceum, although probably there only after Aristotle had retired.) In any event,

DISTILLATION As man developed his desire to understand the mechanics of what we today call chemistry grew. The beginnings of the science were intensely practical; these Chinese cooking pots could be converted into basic stills, the distilled vapours collecting in the upper vessel.

the fourth section comprises a discussion on what types of materials bodies contain, the decay of these substances, their solidification and melting and, especially, the question of whether when various substances are brought together they just form mixtures or combine into something essentially new. Is it possible that new forms are actually created?

The chemical discussion in the Aristotle's *Meteorologica* is very impressive but it is theoretical. Many scholars believe that the real beginnings of chemistry in the West took place in Alexandria. Here the industrial arts of Ancient Egypt — metallurgy, dyeing and glass-making — were allied to some theoretical speculation and not a little mysticism. Many of those practising chemistry seem to have been Gnostics. Gnostics, both inside and outside Christianity, believed in a divine source of knowledge available to those initiated into its mysteries. Those investigating some of the technological achievements in chemistry, and especially those concerned with making imitation precious metals and artificial gems, thought they began to see the presence of new forms and totally new substances. Chemistry

soon became looked upon as a 'divine' art, which could lead to the making of real gold and silver by the mysterious process of transmutation of lesser metals.

Treatises on this divine art were certainly in existence in Alexandria by the first century AD. They were sometimes falsely ascribed to famous authors of the past, and often contained many mystical references, but they also discussed chemical technology and described many factual experiments and tests. The most significant work was probably that written by the Gnostic Zosimus of Panoplis. He wrote what was in essence an encyclopedia of chemical knowledge, describing and illustrating chemical apparatus and the uses to which it was put. He distinguished between 'bodies' — usually metals — and 'invisible spirits' — probably vapours of substances such as sulphur, arsenic and mercury, which can have a powerful action on metals. These 'spirits' may be bound to 'bodies' and then freed again by suitable processes. His language is often mystical and sometimes obscure, a characteristic that was to colour the literature of the developing subject of alchemy for centuries.

BASIC CHEMICAL ARTS A knowledge of basic chemistry is a hallmark of many civilizations, both past and present and consciously and unconsciously applied. These women in Nigeria are painting patterns on cloth with starch, before dyeing it with indigo in a starch reverse process.

The Growth of Alchemy

ALCHEMY The immediate precursor of the science of modern chemistry was alchemy, in which many of the principles that later formed the basis for proper scientific investigation were established, even if not fully understood. Renaissance alchemists were as obsessed with mysticism and astrology as they were with chemistry, as this elaborate seventeenth-century frontispiece shows.

STILLS AND FURNACES These were vital items of equipment for any striving alchemist (above). Distillation (top) played a key part in early chemical industry as well as in the quest for the mysterious elixir of life; while furnaces were also used industrially and to help in transmutation.

The derivation of the word 'alchemy' throws an interesting light on the history of chemistry. *Al* means 'the' in Arabic, but *chemi* is not originally an Arabic word and its source is more difficult to determine. It seems first to have been used by Zosimus or an earlier author of Alexandrian chemical texts and to have been a tribute to Egyptian knowledge, for *Chemia* was the Egyptian name for the country — it meant 'black' and referred to the extreme darkness of the soil. However, more recent research has suggested that *Chemia* was the personal name of an alchemist. A more likely explanation is that the word is derived from a Chinese word pronounced *kêm* and referring to 'gold'. At the time of Zosimus this term could have been transmitted to the West along the Old Silk Road, a trade route that ran from Loyang in northeast China across Turkestan to Alexandria itself. It might even be that the personal name referred to in the Alexandrian writings was itself derived from the Chinese *kêm*, one meaning of which was to transmute base metals into gold.

Whatever the derivation of 'chemy', it is now clear that much Chinese alchemical work was being done in the third century BC, possibly even in the latter part of the fourth, in the hope of making gold and silver out of baser metals.

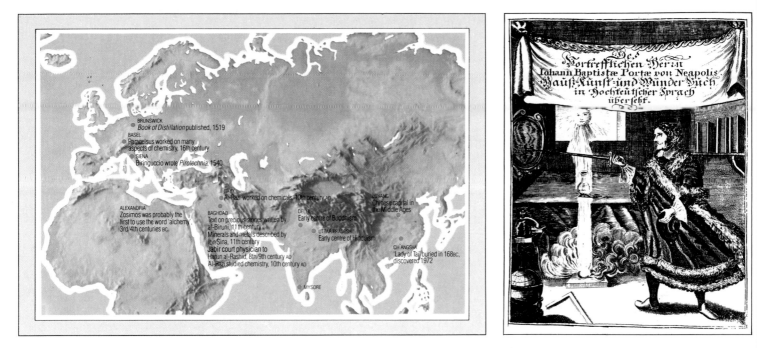

This was not specifically due to a desire to become rich, though financial reward was certainly a motive for the practitioners of alchemy who, at this time, were hermits of the Taoist religion living in poverty in mountain retreats. In fact, both in China and the West, the transmutation of base metals into valuable ones was sometimes carried out with the altruistic aim of relieving poverty in a wider sense. Another reason for these endeavours was the belief that the spiritual and physical disciplines necessary to make such transformations would create a better product as well as help the alchemist to attain eternal life.

As time passed the desire for bodily immortality and the belief in its possible attainment became firmer. The connection of this quest with 'aurification' or transmutation into gold came about because gold was not only beautiful in itself, it also seemed imperishable because it never tarnished and did not appear to age. In practice, this connection led to the use of gold and other metallic substances in the potions or 'elixirs' — the word is probably derived from the Chinese — some of which were dangerous concoctions. Yet if this hunt for physical immortality, the desire to preserve the body in as youthful a state as possible, seems an illusion now, it is sobering to realize how far the Taoists progressed, in one sense at least. In 1972 a tomb was unearthed in Honan Province, China and the body of the 'Lady of Tai' found in a sealed coffin. Although buried in 168BC, more than 2,000 years ago, the body was in a perfect state of preservation and the flesh, when pressed, returned to normal, just as it does in a living body, but does not on a corpse more than a couple of weeks old. Yet the body had not been embalmed, nor undergone mummification or tanning, but was buried in a sealed coffin under what

today we should call anaerobic conditions (free from oxygen).

As with so much early endeavour, in this case magic and science were working together; this was a characteristic combination of all alchemy, where incantations and rituals were as much a part of the many processes as the actual chemical reactions. On the scientific side, the Chinese were aided by their concept of five elements — earth, water, wood, metal and fire — and their belief in links between these and mineral substances. In addition, they were assisted by their belief in the universe as an interdependent organism in which the two forces 'yin' (passive femaleness) and 'yang' (active maleness) played their part. The perpetual waxing and waning of these forces led to an appreciation of cyclic change.

The alchemy and early chemistry practised by the Chinese called for the development of special equipment, as it did elsewhere. Some of the Chinese apparatus is particularly important because it seems to have found its way west, probably along the Old Silk Road or by sea through Arab trading with the south Chinese ports. Among these items were special ovens, stoves and small furnaces. Although the Chinese never developed thermometers, they seem to have been well aware of the importance of temperature in chemical reactions, for they built efficient water-baths and temperature stabilizing devices. It is also of interest to see that they used bamboo piping to connect one piece of chemical apparatus to another, similar to the modern use of glass tubing. Chemical processes were often carefully timed, using sundials and especially water-clocks which the Chinese developed so successfully, and careful weighing was also practised. In these ways the Chinese clearly showed a scientific attitude.

THE SPREAD OF ALCHEMY Both the equipment and the methods of early Chinese alchemists seem to have spread westwards along trading routes, such as the Old Silk Road (above). In this way, their alchemy probably reached India and Arabia. From the latter source, during the twelfth century, the West finally also gained alchemical knowledge, some aspects of which proved important when chemistry began to be developed as a true science.
ALCHEMIST'S TOOLS An alchemist is seen surrounded by the tools of his trade in this illustration from Magica Naturalis, (above) published in Nuremberg in 1715. These include the philosopher's egg, to which the alchemist is pointing, and the hermetic vase on the work bench. The sun represents gold.

ALCHEMICAL SYMBOLISM The drawings here all have alchemical significance. The sun and moon *(top)* symbolize gold and silver respectively, the dragon linking the two standing for mercury and volatility. In the second illustration, the fish represent the soul and spirit of metals, while the third shows symbolically the process of transmutation. After killing his father, the king (gold), mercury is shut in the tomb (vessel) to be transmuted into gold. The final illustration is of the tree of universal matter. As well as the sun and moon, Mars (iron), Venus (copper), Mercury (quicksilver), Saturn (lead) and Jupiter (tin) are shown.

Perhaps their most significant development in the field of chemical apparatus was what has come to be known as the 'East Asian' type of still. This is very different in design from the distilling equipment devised in Alexandria. It was derived from a Chinese Neolithic cooking vessel built in two parts, the lower with three hollow legs that stood in the fire and an upper that stood on this, a grating supporting it. The alchemists or 'proto-chemists' placed a container with cold water on the top of the upper vessel, which served to cool the lid, condensing the vapours there; these then dripped into a cup placed on the grid. Developed in China in the seventh century AD, this still is more self-contained than the Alexandrian type in which the distilled condensed liquid passes through an external arm to a collecting vessel. The design of the modern molecular still is very similar to the East Asian still, a device which enabled the Chinese to prepare strong concentrations of alcohol some four or five centuries earlier than was possible in the West.

On the practical side, Chinese alchemists studied minerals for medicinal use, devised advanced techniques for extracting copper and gained considerable knowledge about certain elements, notably potassium and sulphur. Experiments with these two substances, one in the form of saltpetre (potassium nitrate), in combination with charcoal, formed a material which they found to be highly explosive. Known later as 'gunpowder', it was first used in China for military purposes as early as the tenth century AD, though it took until the thirteenth century to reach Islam and another 100 years to arrive in the West. As far as theory is concerned, in an attempt to understand more clearly what went on in chemical reactions, the Chinese tabulated their chemical substances and the reactions between them, coming close to the tables of chemical affinities devised in the chemistry of modern times.

Alchemy was practised in the Indian subcontinent, although not until the seventh century and almost certainly due to outside influences. These may well have come from China; there had been cultural contact between the two countries ever since Buddhism had spread to India in the first century AD. Some aspects of alchemy would have been of interest to Tantric Buddhists, whose mystical ideas were first in evidence during the sixth century. It was also the East Asian not the Alexandrian type of still that the Indians adopted. Yet, whatever the original source, Hindus as well as Buddhists showed interest in alchemy, which became strongly associated with a male-female principle. Much attention was paid to the chemistry of mercury.

In Islam, alchemy assumed many of the characteristics it was later to display when it reached the West in the twelfth century. There was much symbolism. There were connections with the sun, moon and planets — the moon was linked with silver, Venus with copper, the sun with gold, and so on — but this was not new; the connections had been present in Alexandrian and Persian alchemy, from which sources Islam had inherited many of its alchemical ideas. What the influx of this knowledge did in Islam was to channel interest mainly towards metals and minerals. In the eleventh century both Abu al-Biruni and Ibn Sina were producing encyclopedic texts, al-Biruni on precious stones and Ibn Sina on minerals and metals. The greatest of all the Islamic alchemists, however, was Jabir Ibn Hayyan who laid the foundations of the subject during the late eighth and early ninth centuries. Usually known simply as Jabir, he was court physician to the famous caliph Harun al-Rashid, who was immortalized in the *Arabian Nights* and who, incidentally, had close diplomatic contacts with China.

Jabir adopted a philosophical outlook which embraced the whole of nature. He staunchly believed in the interaction of cosmic forces with terrestrial phenomena and advocated the microcosm-macrocosm concept, an idea that sees man and his soul as a microcosmic counterpart of the universe at large and of its soul or guiding influence. This is a view of considerable antiquity, dating back at least to Greece in the fifth century BC. Jabir also accepted Aristotle's four elements and four qualities, obtaining from them two active principles which he called 'mercury' and 'sulphur'; these were not the metals themselves, but principles of action and reaction, similar in a way to the yin and yang of the Chinese, or the male-female principle of the Indian alchemists. By marrying these two principles together in various proportions under the correct celestial influences at the right time, Jabir was able to account for all the metals found in nature. Jabir's alchemy also contained some number mysticism, as well as this astrological aspect.

Not all Islam accepted alchemy. The theologians did not welcome it — they had no liking for mysterious occult qualities — but most medical and scientific men accepted the idea of transmutation if not the rest of the teaching. The rationalist physician Abu al-Razi totally rejected the mystical side but was, rightly, interested in the actual chemistry involved.

When the West began to receive Greek teaching from Islam in the twelfth century, however, the whole corpus of Islamic alchemical mysticism accompanied it. This was heightened in the fifteenth century by the discovery of what were supposed to be the teachings of the Ancient Egyptian Hermes Trismegistus, Hermes the 'Thrice-great'. These texts, which seemed to have received the blessing of some Church fathers and so to be of unassailable authority, contained much Alexandrian alchemy; following their publication there was a vast upsurge in alchemical work, people applying themselves avidly to the 'divine Hermetic art'. Transmutations were

UNIVERSAL KNOWLEDGE
Alchemists saw their science as fitting into an elaborate system governing man's relationship with nature and the heavens, shown in the two illustrations *(left)*. Astrology and magic were two important influences in the nature of their work.

TENDING THE FURNACE An alchemist seen at work in his laboratory. Though many alchemists worked in secret, guarding their formulae and experimental notes by writing them in symbolic language and sometimes even in cipher, their search for the secret of transmutation was not through greed. They believed that gold was the purest of metals.

pursued and sometimes successes claimed — in retrospect these appeared to have been no more than successes in obtaining a surface colouration. The hunt was also on for the elixir of eternal youth and books on alchemical technique were published that were usually so obscure in language and symbolism that they could be read, if at all, only by the adept. Some of the experiments described were of great duration, taking weeks or even longer, for there was a strong belief that minerals and metals gestated over long periods in the womb of the

earth and that the alchemist needed to copy this procedure.

Out of all this mysticism and magic, some useful chemical results did emerge, while there was also a move to make known the practical chemical techniques used in everyday technical processes. Two notable examples were the *Book of Distillation* (1519) published in Brunswick, Germany, and the *Pirotechnia* (1540) by the Italian metallurgist, Vannoccio Biringuccio. which contained a wealth of useful material from metallurgy to gunpowder manufacture. Written in clear, simple language, they were soon followed by others.

This marriage between the practical and esoteric is epitomized in the work of Paracelsus (c 1490-1541), a man known universally by this nickname, although his real name — Theophrastus Philippus Aureolus Bombastus von Hohenheim — is as romantic as any in the history of science. He studied general science, metallurgy, the occult arts, alchemy and medicine and, even though he was both a braggart and a Hermetist, he made considerable advances in medical treatment and medical theory. In chemistry Paracelsus carried out processes of drug-making that were of use to later generations of medical chemists, found how to prepare concentrated alchohol and discovered a new way of making nitric acid. He even tried to formulate a new system of chemistry using three 'principles' — salt, mercury and sulphur — and while this was only an extention of Islamic alchemy, his scheme did focus attention to some aspects of chemistry that were to prove important as the age of scientific chemistry dawned in the following century.

The Discovery of Gases

The practical treatises which dealt so openly with chemical processes and made no reference to mysticism were studied closely by the new men of the scientific revolution, who examined not only the *Book of Distillation* and the *Pirotechnia* but also other books on mining and metallurgy, notably Lazarus Ercker's *Description of Leading, Ore Processing and Mining Methods* (1574) and Georg Bauer's *Metallurgy* (1555). But there was also a growing interest in wider aspects of scientific chemistry, and this was catered for in 1597 with a book called *Alchymia*, written by the physician Andreas Libavius. In spite of its title, this was really an up-to-date textbook on the chemistry of its time.

New research was carried out, most importantly by the Belgian Jan van Helmont (1577-1644) who, admittedly, accepted the three principles of Paracelsus, but stressed the immense significance of careful measurement and, equally noteworthy, carried out some experiments on what he called 'gases'. An example of his care in measurement was his experiment to try to determine what basic elements actually exist in nature. He took a tree weighing some 5lb (2.25kg) in a 200lb (100kg) pot of earth, which had previously been carefully dried in an oven. The tree was regularly watered over the next five years, after which everything was again measured. The earth had lost some 2.5oz (60g) but the tree had gained more than 160lb (70kg) and van Helmont logically concluded that the excess had come from the water added.

It seemed, then, that water was indeed the main basic substance.

As far as gases were concerned — van Helmont coined the term either from the Greek *chaos*, meaning 'empty space' or the Dutch *gasen* 'to ferment' — these were smokes and vapours either produced after combustion or fermentation or to be found in grottoes and caves. He noticed a vapour he called 'wood gas' (our carbon dioxide), as well as other gases, but he was hampered by their being no known technique for collecting them for further examination. Van Helmont's work was studied in particular by Robert Boyle (1627-91), his assistant Robert Hooke (1635-1703) and by Isaac Newton (1642-1727) but, as van Helmont's description of the gases was not always clear, some 5lb (2.25kg) in a 200lb (100kg) pot of earth, what later were called 'airs'.

Van Helmont's research stimulated an interest in two new areas — respiration and combustion — and experiments were undertaken using, among other equipment, the recently developed vacuum pump. The problem that faced experimenters was that air was not then known to be composed of various chemical substances and it was to be some time before methods of analysis began to make this clear. However, Boyle's own experiments on combustion followed directly on from van Helmont's work and were nothing if not ingenious. Using an efficient air pump devised by Hooke, he put such things as heated charcoal and burning

EARLY EQUIPMENT This illustration of a sixteenth-century assay laboratory shows some of the various pieces of laboratory equipment then in common use. They include various types of furnace, such as an athanor, a self-stoking furnace used for cementation and a barrel-shaped one, being used to test copper. In this, the draught is supplied by the steam rising from the boiling water being heated by the hot charcoal. A crucible can also be seen being heated by a ring of burning coals; to increase the heat, the coals are raked into a smaller circle.

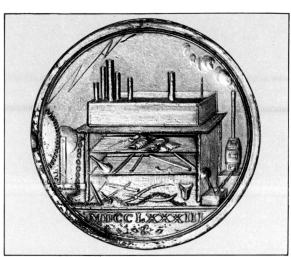

PRIESTLEY'S APPARATUS The English chemist Joseph Priestley carried out extensive research into the nature of gases, devising an efficient method of collecting them over liquid *(left)*. More of his apparatus is shown *(above)*. Priestley's greatest scientific discovery was oxygen, but, as a champion of the idea that a tangible fire element — phlogiston — existed, he failed to recognize its importance.

coals into it and observed what happened when the air was exhausted around them. He then repeated his experiments, this time without removing any air at all. He found, naturally, that if substances were burned in a confined space, such as the glass bowl of his pump, combustion ceased after a time. This was a well-known fact, but what was not well known and came to be realized only after Boyle's experiments with the vacuum pump, was that combustion also ceased immediately the air was removed. This observation enabled Boyle to demolish the generally accepted idea at the time that the fumes generated during burning caused the process to stop. Air, Boyle showed, was vital if combustion was to occur. It was necessary, too, for respiration, since not only did animals die if left too long in the glass container of the air pump but did so as soon as there was no air to breathe.

Robert Hooke, who left Boyle's employ in 1662 to become 'curator of experiments' to the newly formed Royal Society in London, conducted a host of experiments on air and published more than 200 'queries' on the subject in his *Micrographia* (1665), his marvellous book on the microscope and microscopic objects. Although there were many things yet to be discovered — the large number of his 'queries' shows that — Hooke was not averse to formulating some tentative theoretical ideas of his own. Indeed, he went so far as to produce a complete theory of combustion and respiration, which was nothing if not novel.

He considered that when a body burned one should think of it as dissolving under certain specific conditions, an unusual, albeit reasonable, view considering that part of the original material does disappear. However, since com-

bustion can only happen when air is present, Hooke very sensibly concluded that air must contain something that acted as a solvent. This was in many ways a very penetrating idea, for we now know that it is oxygen in the air reacting with the burning substance that gives a by-product of combustion; although we do not see combustion as bodies dissolving, the concept is very much the same. Hooke knew nothing of oxygen — its discovery lay in the future — but he did refer to a 'sulphurous' part of the air which, he suggested, was what dissolved the sulphurous parts of the bodies being burned. (Like his contemporaries he was still influenced by the Paracelsian principles of sulphur, salt and mercury.) He also suggested that the dissolving action generated heat and that this heat is 'that which we call Fire'. He even went on to make the bold hypothesis that the sulphurous part of air might perhaps be 'like, if not the very same' as that which is to be found in saltpetre, since saltpetre (potassium nitrate) is a very strong oxidizing agent he was very near the mark.

As to respiration, Hooke actually suggested that there must be some other component of the air which, as he put it, supplies whatever it is that is necessary for the 'fire of life'. But Boyle did not agree, either with Hooke's view of respiration or that of combustion, preferring to believe that the whole of the air was involved in both processes, and that as far as saltpetre was concerned, it contained tiny pores which were full of air. His experiments showed no loss of pressure when substances were burned in a container yet, if Hooke were correct, then there should be, Boyle argued, because some of the air would have been used up.

Boyle and Hooke were not alone in this field

of study. John Mayow, a medical man, also experimented with burning objects in closed containers and devised an important technique of collecting gases. He allowed them to collect in a glass container, open at the bottom but partly immersed in water, which acted as a seal. The gases could be drawn off using a U-shaped glass tube, one end of which protruded into the container above water level, the other end going out of the water outside the container. He discovered that Boyle was wrong; there was a change in the weight of air after combustion and during respiration, and he suggested that air contained 'nitro-aerial' particles.

Boyle's views prevailed, however. In 1661 he published his book *The Sceptical Chemist* which contained some very important ideas. Boyle pointed out that fire did not break up substances into their basic 'elements', as was then generally believed, and went on to emphasize that no one had really defined what they meant by a chemical element. As a supporter of an atomic theory rather along the lines of that held by the Ancient Greeks, Boyle claimed that to investigate the nature of chemical elements and prepare a proper definition should be the first task facing scientific chemistry.

Burning and the process of 'calcination' — when a metallic substance is reduced to a powdery residue (a 'calyx') on heating — were still great puzzles. In 1673 Boyle suggested that some 'effluvium' surrounding fire combined with a metal to cause this result, the effluvium being able even to penetrate through glass (for calcination was observed also to occur in a closed container). This view was taken up by others, and led to the concept of 'phlogiston' (from the Greek, meaning 'burnt'). The theory was first put forward by Johann Becher, a follower of Paracelsus, who separated minerals and metals into three new 'elements' — a transparent glassy element, an element that could vaporize readily and a third one that was oily and fatty. Substances containing this last element burned readily and it was the presence of the element in minerals and metals that made calcination possible. The next step in developing this theory was carried out by Becher's compatriot Georg Stahl, who published his ideas in 1697. What Stahl suggested was that there was one basic element, present not only in metals and minerals but also in all other combustible material; this was the fire element phlogiston. This was a direct extension of Becher's concept and meant that metals and everything that would burn must be compounds of the metal (or whatever the substance was) and phlogiston.

The phlogiston theory caught on because it seemed to explain all kinds of experimental results; for instance, paper, wood and charcoal changed on burning because they lost phlogiston, combustion stopped when things were burned in a closed container because the air became saturated with phlogiston and, so far as respiration was concerned, exhaled air became so full of phlogiston that it gradually became unfit to breathe. However, there was one experimental result that raised great difficulties. This was that some metals, such as lead, gain weight on calcination. According to the theory, they should lose weight if phlogiston were given off, and the only conclusion seemed to be that phlogiston must cause substances to be lighter than they would ordinarily be, in other words that phlogiston had negative weight!

In due course, the phlogiston theory was rejected but only after a new series of careful and penetrating experiments. A set of measures of the weight of materials and the 'air' they gave off on burning made by Stephen Hales led him to suggest that air particles were contained within all solids and were released on heating. He published his results and his views in 1727 and they met with general acceptance. Next, some decades later, Joseph Black (1728-99), known for his study of heat, discovered that while lime-water (calcium carbonate) kept in a stoppered bottle remained unchanged, if left open to the air, it formed a crust on its surface. More study convinced Black that air was a compound, one component of which became fixed in lime-water to give a crust; he called this 'fixed air'.

Henry Cavendish (1731-1810) also became intrigued with the problem and found that when an acid reacted on a metal, 'air' was released. This air burned readily; was it phlogiston? Theory said it could be but Cavendish preferred to call it 'inflammable air'. He also passed electric sparks through a variety of liquids and discovered the fact, astounding at the time, that water was not a basic substance but a compound, made of inflammable air and some other air. In 1784, he described his results as research on 'factitious (artificial) airs'.

At the same time as Cavendish was experimenting in 'airs', Joseph Priestley (1733-1804) was also at work on the subject using his new, efficient invention, the 'pneumatic trough'. Gases were collected first over water and then over mercury which, he found, reacted with fewer of the gaseous products. Priestley isolated a number of gases and found that plants could restore the air breathed by a mouse or altered by a candle burning in a restricted space. His greatest discovery was this air, which supported both respiration and combustion, just those things which phlogiston would not do. He called it 'dephlogisticated' air.

A new situation had now arisen. Various experimental results had shown that there were different types of 'air' released during chemical reactions, and that each of these had specific properties. In particular, it had been discovered that there was a gas necessary for breathing and combustion, and another that was itself inflammable. In addition, it had been found that neither 'air' itself nor water were single substances; they were compounds. The phlogiston theory could not explain these results; a fresh approach was really required.

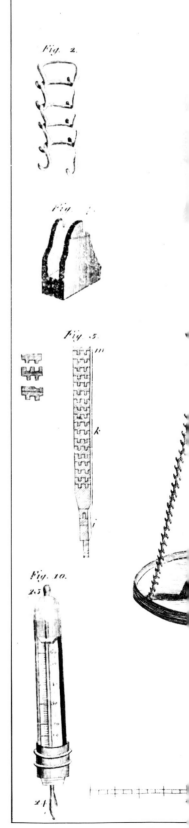

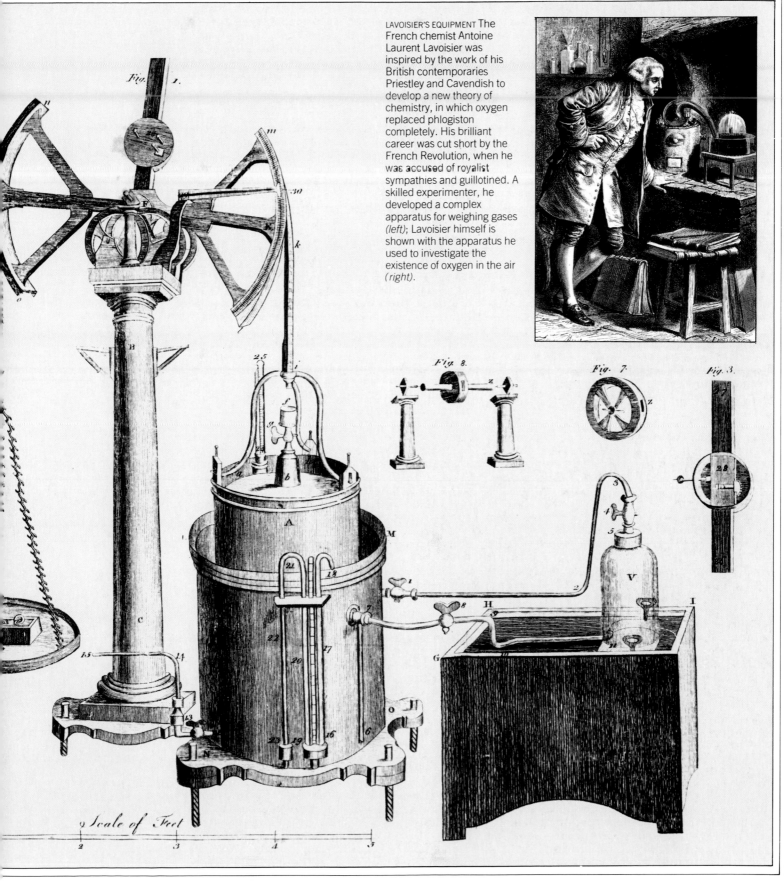

LAVOISIER'S EQUIPMENT The French chemist Antoine Laurent Lavoisier was inspired by the work of his British contemporaries Priestley and Cavendish to develop a new theory of chemistry, in which oxygen replaced phlogiston completely. His brilliant career was cut short by the French Revolution, when he was accused of royalist sympathies and guillotined. A skilled experimenter, he developed a complex apparatus for weighing gases (left); Lavoisier himself is shown with the apparatus he used to investigate the existence of oxygen in the air (right).

The Growth of Chemical Science

Looking back, it is evident that the progress of chemistry depended on a new insight into the subject but this was not at all easy. In spite of its shortcomings, the phlogiston theory had become the basic theory of chemistry, and to discard it and find some new unifying principle required a great intellectual effort. The man who achieved this was Antoine Lavoisier (1743-94), a French scientist and administrator imbued with the new freedom of outlook that was part of the Enlightenment — a period in seventeenth- and eighteenth-century European thought which extolled reason as the guiding principle in human affairs. A man who set great store by meticulous measurement, Lavoisier's main chemical research started in the late 1760s when he was commissioned by the city authorities to examine the purity of the Parisian water supply.

To begin his analysis, Lavoisier heated a sample of water in a closed container, weighing the sample carefully both before and after heating; he found no change. He also noticed that sometimes the water he heated left an earthy residue and sometimes it did not. Both results led him to reject the current idea that water turned into earth when heated for long enough. He next turned his attention to combustion and 'airs'. He carefully repeated Joseph Black's experiments and found that when a metal was heated in a closed container until it was a crumbly mass — a calyx — it did become heavier because it absorbed some air, but he was puzzled by what kind of air this could be. Further experiments made it clear to him that it did not absorb an effluvium as Boyle had suggested, nor 'fire particles', nor was the absorbed air Black's 'fixed air'.

It was at this juncture that Lavoisier was visited by Priestley, who explained how in experiments on combustion and respiration he had discovered 'dephlogisticated air'. With this result in mind, Lavoisier himself conducted his own experiments on respiration and became convinced that the phlogiston theory was no longer viable. He therefore set about formulating a totally new theory of chemistry in which phlogiston recieved no mention whatsoever. By 1779 Lavoisier was ready to claim that air was composed of two components — an 'eminently combustible' part and an unbreathable part. He also suggested that Black's 'fixed air' contained charcoal in some way. As charcoal is a form of carbon and Black's 'fixed air' was what we would call 'carbon dioxide', Lavoisier was very near to what we now know to be the case.

Still more experimentation led Lavoisier to connect the 'eminently combustible' or 'inflammable' air with acids and he finally concluded that it was indeed an integral part of every acid. He therefore named it *principe oxygine* or 'oxygen principle', deriving the word oxygen from the Greek word, *oxus*, meaning 'acid'.

Lavoisier's view, his invention of the oxygen principle, did not convince all chemists. Some, such as the very able German chemist, Carl Scheele, who like Priestley had come across oxygen, still preferred to retain the phlogiston theory and think of dephlogisticated air. More research was required before the old views could really be overthrown.

The results that were finally to persuade other chemists were experiments into the nature of water. Lavoisier's interest in the subject was aroused by a visit to Paris in 1783 of Charles Blagden, Secretary of the Royal Society in London, which was about to publish Cavendish's discovery that water was a compound. Blagden explained to Lavoisier that when 'inflammable air' was burned in a closed container, dew formed, and that Cavendish had proved that the dew was water. This was of great interest, not only on account of its chemical significance but also because inflammable air was being used to fill some of the balloons flown by aeronauts at that time. Blagden, Lavoisier and the mathematician Pierre Laplace began investigating the matter further.

They placed inflammable air and ordinary air together into a closed container; when combustion occurred, they found that water was indeed produced. When Cavendish's results were published, he tied them into the phlogiston theory and assumed the water came from the condensed air. But Lavoisier was able to do better — he linked up this experiment with the evidence he had already gathered about how an acid acts on a metal to produce inflammable ('eminently combustible') air. His inspiration was that he saw how everything could now fit together provided one assumed that every acid contained water (H_2O), because then, when an acid reacted with a metal, the water could be imagined to break up, giving its oxygen to the 'salt' which was formed and releasing the inflammable air. Since the inflammable air came from water, Lavoisier named it the *principe hydrogene* (from the Greek word *hudor*, meaning 'water').

The whole process of combustion as well as other chemical reactions could now be explained using Lavoisier's two 'principles' which turned out to be the gases oxygen and hydrogen, substances that could be weighed and measured. This explanation was now seen to be superior to anything before it and, even though some traditionalists clung to the old beliefs, as early as 1784 Black was teaching the new theory in Edinburgh.

These new ideas were energetically followed up by a trio of French chemists, Claude Berthollet, Guyton de Morveau and Antoine Fourcroy. They decided that terms such as 'oxygen' and 'hydrogen' were far preferable to the old descriptions of 'airs' and that chemical names should refer to the qualities of the chemicals themselves. 'Oil of vitriol' gave way to 'sulphuric acid', 'aqua fortis' became 'nitric

FOUNDING FATHER Robert Boyle was one of the leading lights of the scientific revolution of the seventeenth century. In his laboratory *(right)*, he developed his law on the pressure and volume of gases and laid many of the foundations of modern chemistry, including establishing precise definitions of the nature of the chemical element, a reaction and chemical analysis. The laboratory *(below)* belonged to Ambrose Godfrey Hanckwitz (1660-1741), who was Boyle's assistant for a period. Hanckwitz went on to produce and investigate the properties of drugs.

PLATE XXXIX.

acid', 'Scheele's green' became a copper hydrogen arsenite. To extend this further meant finding out which elements made up various substances. They first decided that an element was defined as a substance that could not be further decomposed; then they drew up a list of 55 such substances which included oxygen, hydrogen and carbon. This also included 'light' and 'heat' or *calorique* (from the Latin word meaning 'heat'); since light was then thought to be composed of corpuscles and heat was considered to be a fluid, clearly these could be decomposed no further and were therefore elements.

Lavoisier wrote a book about this new nomenclature; it appeared in France in 1789, and a year later in Britain, under the title *Elements of Chemistry*. Written with masterly clarity, this book accomplished just what Jabir and Boyle had advocated long before. It gave a clear definition of an element.

The Atom

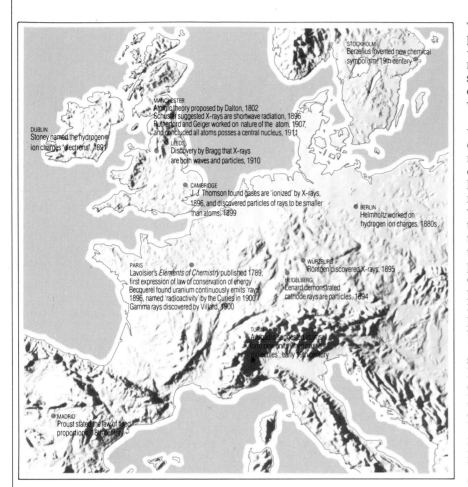

On the map (reading by city):

STOCKHOLM
Berzelius invented new chemical symbolism, 19th century

MANCHESTER
Atomic theory proposed by Dalton, 1802
Schuster suggested X-rays are shortwave radiation, 1896
Rutherford and Geiger worked on nature of the atom, 1907, and concluded all atoms posses a central nucleus, 1911

DUBLIN
Stoney named the hydrogen ion charges 'electrons', 1891

LEEDS
Discovery by Bragg that X-rays are both waves and particles, 1910

CAMBRIDGE
J. J. Thomson found gases are 'ionized' by X-rays, 1896, and discovered particles of rays to be smaller than atoms, 1899

BERLIN
Helmholtz worked on hydrogen ion charges, 1880s

PARIS
Lavoisier's *Elements of Chemistry* published 1789; first expression of law of conservation of energy
Becquerel found uranium continuously emits 'rays', 1896, named 'radioactivity' by the Curies in 1900
Gamma rays discovered by Villard, 1900

WÜRZBURG
Röntgen discovered X-rays, 1895

HEIDELBERG
Lenard demonstrated cathode rays are particles, 1894

TURIN
Avogadro suggested atoms form new units when mixed 'molecules', early 19th century

MADRID
Proust stated the law of fixed proportions, 18th century

THE ATOMIC AGE Dalton's atomic theory and subsequent work in the nineteenth and early twentieth century on the nature of the atom brought about a radical change both in our concept of matter and in our capacity to change the world. Aside from Rutherford and Soddy's discovery in Montreal in 1903 that it is possible to change the elemental structure of a material, the important early discoveries and research were carried out in Europe.

Lavoisier's *Elements of Chemistry* (1789) both laid down the foundations for a new chemistry in which elements were unambiguously defined and also expressed his belief that 'nothing is created in the operations of art and nature'; in other words, the total quantity of matter never changes during an experiment. This important 'law of the conservation of matter', as we now call it, was also held by both Cavendish and Black, though Lavoisier was the first to express it so clearly. The result of the enunciation of this law was to make all chemists even more careful to obtain measurements of as high a precision as possible in every experimental result they obtained. For Louis Proust (1754-1826), it led to the 'law of constant proportions'.

A compatriot of Lavoisier, Proust carried out most of his work in Spain, where he had been commissioned to examine the country's mineral wealth. This led him to make many chemical tests, in all of which he noticed that materials always combine in the same proportions. Proust's law of fixed proportions was important, particularly once a new atomic theory had been proposed. To begin with, however, it met with some scepticism. The famous French chemist Claude Berthollet, who exerted a wide influence among his contemporaries, especially in France, strongly disagreed with Proust. Berthollet believed that the proportions in which substances combined depended upon the physical conditions at the time of combination — on the heat or the pressure, for example — rather than on something inherent in the substances themselves. In support of his views, he cited some experiments, the results of which were, however, mistaken. Proust won his case.

This whole issue of combining proportions was given new significance by research carried out by John Dalton (1766-1844), a schoolmaster from the north of England, around the close of the eighteenth century. Paradoxically enough, Dalton's primary interest was meteorology and Lavoisier's discovery that air was composed of at least two gases had intrigued him. If one gas was really heavier than the other, Dalton argued, surely gravity ought to make them separate out — the earth's atmosphere should consist of two layers, the upper one of the lighter gas. He knew that the atmosphere does not behave like this — it is an even mixture — and he set about trying to find an explanation. Dalton began by considering particles or 'atoms' of the two gases surrounded by 'caloric' which, he thought, might prevent them settling down into separate groups. Gradually, he extended the atomic idea, assumed that every gas has its own kind of atoms and that the heavier the gas, the heavier its atoms. Such atoms, he suggested, attracted one another but, in the atmosphere at least, they were surrounded by 'caloric' which kept them apart; the result was that the gases acted like vapours. What, in fact, Dalton had formulated was a concept which would explain the state of matter as well as why one substance differed from another in weight and chemical behaviour.

Dalton now extended this notion to every substance in all its various physical conditions — gaseous, liquid or solid — and went on to claim that 'no new creation or destruction of matter is within reach of any chemical agency' — a more specific form of Lavoisier's statement on conservation. The theory became public knowledge in 1802 and was seen to explain the reason behind Proust's law of combining proportions. In one sense, Dalton had only revived atomic theory of the Greeks and of Boyle, but he had given it a new precision; by weighing the products of every chemical reaction the relative weights of the atoms involved could be determined.

Dalton's theory did not suit every chemist but it gained support over the years as new evidence was brought forward in support of it. Two chemists who laboured to do so were Joseph Gay-Lussac (1778-1850) and Amedeo Avogadro (1776-1856). Gay-Lussac, with the assistance of the Prussian naturalist and explorer Alexander von Humboldt, analyzed water by passing an electric current through it and found that, whenever this was done, twice the volume of hydrogen was released compared with the volume of oxygen. Extending this work, in 1811 Gay-Lussac was able to state that gases always combine in volumes that are in a simple relation to one another, just what should happen if Dalton's atomic theory were correct. Avogadro followed up this discovery and overcame an apparent difficulty — the fact that when gases combine they occupy less space. This type of result appeared to go against the atomic theory but Avogadro overcame the problem by suggesting that atoms combined together into new units when gases were mixed. Avogadro did not use the word 'atom' but the term 'molecule' from the Latin *mole*, meaning 'mass', a name that was to be used for groups of atoms by all later scientists.

After this reasearch, much work on determining atomic weights was carried out, especially by the Italian Stanislas Cannizaro and the Swedish chemist Jöns Berzelius (1779-1848), who also invented a new symbolism in chemistry, and one superior to Dalton's own. Berzelius' system was simplicity itself; he used the capital letter (or the first two letters) of each element as its symbol. It immediately became accepted because it showed clearly the nature of a substance — H_2O indicates at once that a water molecule has two hydrogen atoms and one of oxygen — and could describe precisely what occurred in a chemical reaction. As Berzelius was not only a good research chemist but also a brilliant teacher, his work and Cannizaro's led to virtually universal acceptance of an atomic theory by the mid-nineteenth century.

John Dalton's atomic theory was a way of explaining chemical reactions, but what of the atoms themselves? They had been defined as the smallest units which could take part in a chemical change but they could not be observed directly; their existence could only be inferred. However, it soon became evident that their reality was being confirmed at every turn. There was, however, a dilemma; by definition the nature of atoms could not be discovered from chemical experiments and evidence had to be sought elsewhere. In the event, it came from a new and unexpected quarter.

In the 1850s there was great interest in investigations of the way electricity could be made to pass through gases. It had been realized for some time that gases could conduct electricity; Faraday had made some studies on the subject, while those who had begun to use the spectroscope to analyze the light given from chemicals when heated had found it very useful to place a thin trace of an unknown gas in an evacuated glass tube and set it glowing by an electric discharge. The technique became so important that in 1855 the German physicist Heinrich Geissler (1815-79) developed a special method of sealing metal electrodes (which carried the electricity) into the glass of which the tubes were made. Geissler also devised a much improved vacuum pump for exhausting air out of the tubes before gas was allowed to enter. In 1856 Hermann Sprengel designed an even bet-

ter version. Because the Sprengel pump and Geissler's efficient sealing allowed very high pressure vacuums to be obtained, the scene was set for some momentous discoveries.

Physicists became intrigued after it was discovered that glowing discharges occurred when electricity was fed to an exhausted tube and they noticed that the discharges altered, the higher the vacuum. In particular, they were puzzled by a glow that appeared on one end wall of a tube; this appeared to be caused by rays of some kind emanating from the electrically negative metal electrode or 'cathode' at the other end. In 1879 an attempt to explain this was made by the British physicist William Crookes, who conducted many experiments with tubes of this kind. He suggested that the rays were caused by the few remaining molecules of gas still left in the tube even after exhaustion. Such particles would, he thought, become electrically charged and then by repelled by the cathode.

Crookes' explanation seemed satisfactory for almost 20 years. However, in 1895, Wilhelm Röntgen discovered X-rays. Using what had become known as a 'Crookes tube', he found invisible rays being emitted and it did not seem that odd electrified gas molecules were the answer. The very next year, Arthur Schuster (1851-1934) at Manchester University decided to investigate these rays further and, remembering Maxwell's ideas about electromagnetic radiation, he came to the conclusion that they were a very short-wave radiation. He arrived at this view because the 'rays' could not be deflected by magnets or by electric fields, as would have happened if they had been particles or molecules with an electric charge on them. On the other hand, they could not be reflected by mirrors or refracted by a lens, although Schuster conjectured that might happen if these were waves of extremely short length.

While Schuster was at work in Manchester, other research of a similar kind was being carried out at the Cavendish Laboratory at Cambridge University under J.J. Thomson (1856-1940), the Professor of Physics. (Joseph John Thomson, always known as 'J.J.', was no relation to William Thomson, Lord Kelvin.) Working with J.J. was a brilliant student, the New Zealander Ernest Rutherford (1871-1937). To begin their research they examined very carefully the effect of the new X-rays on gases and in 1896 found, to their surprise, that they caused a gas to conduct electricity even when it would not ordinarily do so. To explain this J.J. took an analogy of a liquid conducting electricity; Faraday had suggested there were 'ions' or electrified molecules of the liquid that allowed this conduction, so J.J. suggested that the gas was being 'ionized', or turned into 'ions'. Since Crookes tubes not only produced X-rays but also cathode rays, J.J. next turned his attention to these cathode rays in an attempt to try to discover what they really were. He left Ernest Rutherford to look further into X-rays.

THE ATOM REBORN John Dalton made a major contribution to the advance of science with his new atomic theory, which he put forward in his *New System of Chemical Philosophy*. However, his use of symbols *(above)* to indicate the various individual elements was soon discarded as cumbersome. The numbers in the table indicate the atomic weights Dalton assigned to each element.

One of the reasons why J.J. wanted to turn his attention to cathode rays was that in 1894 the German physicist Philipp Lenard had demonstrated that they could pass right through a thin sheet of metal foil. No gas molecules could do this and so, once again, it seemed Crookes' explanation was incorrrect. What is more, Lenard was able to demonstrate that the rays could be deflected by magnets placed outside the glass tube, showing that they were not rays of electromagnetic radiation, they were particles. But what kind of particles could they be if they could pass through metal foil? This was the question J.J. tackled. He immediately discovered that the particles could be deflected not only by magnets but also by an electric field; this enabled him to measure an important ratio involving the electric charge on the particles and their mass, although he could not determine these quantities separately. He also measured their velocity, which he found to be far less than that of light and so confirmed, once again, that cathode rays were indeed particles, not a form of electromagnetic radiation.

The measurement of this ratio (the electric charge divided by the mass) turned out to be more than 1,000 times greater than the same ratio for electrified atoms ('ions') of hydrogen. As the electric charges were similar, it was evident that the cathode ray particles were very much less massive than hydrogen ions. In 1899 J.J. studied other particles, particularly those released from metals by the action of ultraviolet light and from the carbon filaments in electric lamps, then a recent invention. In each case his value for the ratio was almost identical to that for the cathode ray particles. From all these measurements and experimental results, he concluded not only that the particles must be small compared with ordinary atoms or molecules, but also that 'the so-called (chemical) elements are compounds of some primordial element'. Meanwhile, earlier in the 1880s, work had been carried out independently by Hermann von Helmholtz and by George Stoney on the electric charges associated with hydrogen ions, and it seemed there was a basic charge associated with them. In 1891 Stoney had named this unit the 'electron'; this became the term used for J.J.'s cathode ray particles.

In addition to the work just described, a different kind of investigation was underway in France but one that turned out to have an important bearing on the electron and its nature. In 1896 the physicist Henri Becquerel (1852-1908) discovered that the very heavy chemical element uranium continuously emitted 'rays' which, like X-rays, enabled a gas to conduct electri'ity even under ordinarily nonconducting conditions. The question then arose whether there were other elements besides uranium that behaved in a similar way; in 1898 the physicist Pierre Curie (1859-1906) and his Polish-born wife Marie (1867-1934), who was a chemist, decided to look into the problem. The research was difficult and slow and they had to work under poor laboratory conditions, but in 1898 they discovered that thorium acted in this way, as a German chemist, Gerhard Schmidt, also found working independently.

The Curies and their research student Gustave Bémont also discovered that the uranium compound, pitchblende, appeared to contain very active ray-emitting components,

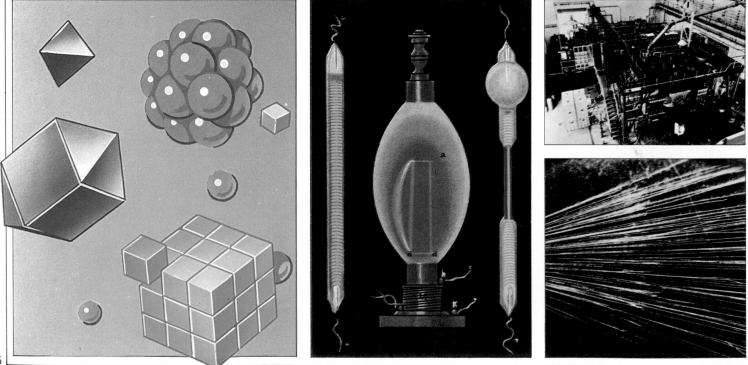

ACCELERATING THE ATOM An atomic accelerator in operation. The device is designed to make atoms move at extremely high speeds so that, when they strike other atoms, detailed studies can be made of the reactions involved and the nuclear particles produced.

ATOMIC PATTERN This diffraction pattern was created by passing atomic particles through a tiny hole in a gold sheet. The pattern demonstrates that the particles behave like waves and have a wave structure.

They were, in fact, ionized helium atoms. However, the beta ray particles were much lighter in weight and investigation showed that they had the same mass and the same (negative) electric charge as electrons, so they must be electrons.

As radioactive elements disintegrated they did more than emit ionized helium atoms and electrons, however; they also emitted a very penetrating radiation, discovered in 1900 by the French physicist Paul Villard, who named them 'gamma' rays. But since the alpha and beta emanations were particles, not rays, doubt was expressed about Villard's conclusions, and the question was not fully answered until 1910 when William Bragg (1862-1947) at Leeds University discovered precisely how X-rays and gamma rays ionize a gas.

Bragg's work was complex and important. He discovered that X-rays do not ionize a gas directly but cause its atoms to emit electrons at a high speed — to emit beta rays, in fact — and that it was these emitted electrons that hit neighbouring gas atoms, knocking off electrons which moved more slowly and so left ionized gas atoms scattered throughout the gas itself. It was a two-stage progress. This may not sound very remarkable but the energies involved certainly were, because Bragg found that there was no energy lost at the X-ray stage. The high-velocity cathode ray electrons generated X-rays which, in their turn, caused beta ray electrons, but these had an energy equal to the original cathode ray electrons. The only way of explaining this was to consider the X-rays as particles not waves, yet Bragg had also shown that the shorter the wavelength of the X-rays the higher the velocity of the beta ray electrons. In the end Bragg had to conclude that X-rays are both waves and particles at the same time. Later research was to show how to account for this apparent dual personality of X-rays and, as it turned out, for all electromagnetic radiation.

All the evidence — J.J.'s work on the electron, Rutherford's research on radioactivity, the results on the ionization of gases by Bragg — now seemed to point in one direction. J.J. and Rutherford were correct; the atom might be the smallest unit to take part in a chemical change, but it was not the ultimate unit of matter. Beta rays and cathode rays demonstrated the existence of negatively charged particles (electrons) and alpha rays, which turned out to be positively charged helium ions and, therefore, positively charged particles as well. Various ideas were suggested to account for this but, in 1911, Rutherford solved all difficulties by suggesting that all atoms possess a central nucleus which is positively charged and contains most of the atom's mass, and that outside this nucleus are electrons, sufficient in number to balance the positive electric charge of the nucleus by their own negative charges. The nuclear theory of the atom had arrived.

and in the same year isolated what turned out to be the two active elements, polonium (named in honour of Marie Curie's homeland) and radium. Radium proved to be the more active of the two. However, it was not until 1902 that a little (0.02oz/0.5g) pure radium chloride had been extracted from several tonnes of pitchblende. The Curies did more than isolate these elements; they also discovered that the power to emit rays was unaffected by all the chemical processes involved in isolating them and, as radium was the most powerful emitter, in 1900 they gave the name 'radioactivity' to the emission process.

From 1897 onwards Rutherford, first at Cambridge and then at McGill University in Canada, began to study the radioactive emissions of which two kinds were then recognized and which, 'for simplicity', he named 'alpha' and 'beta'. With the help of the chemist Frederick Soddy (1877-1956), he confirmed that radioactivity was indeed a property of radium, thorium and uranium and that both the alpha and beta 'rays' were particles. In 1903 Rutherford and Soddy published a revolutionary idea: the theory that the emission of the particles meant that the atoms of these elements were breaking up and turning into different basic elements in doing so. Here was the alchemists' dream come true but in a rather more prosaic way than they had ever imagined, for the transformation turned the substances into the base metal lead, not into gold!

The next step was to discover what kind of particles the alpha and beta rays were. Rutherford continued to work at this question when he moved back to England to Manchester University in 1907. Here, with a young German colleague Hans Geiger (1882-1945), who is famous now for the invention of the 'geiger counter', Rutherford discovered that the alpha particles always gave the spectrum of helium, whether they came from radium, thorium or uranium.

Quantum Theory

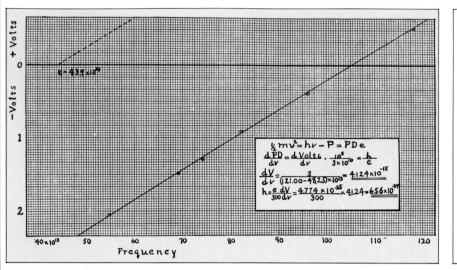

$$\tfrac{1}{2}mv^2 = h\nu - P = PDe$$
$$\frac{dPD}{d\nu} = \frac{d\,Volts}{d\nu} \cdot \frac{10^8}{3\times10^{10}} = \frac{h}{e}$$
$$\frac{dV}{d\nu} = \frac{3}{(121.00-48.25)\times10^{13}} = 4.124\times10^{-15}$$
$$h = \frac{e}{300}\frac{dV}{d\nu} = \frac{4.774\times10^{-35}}{300}\times4.124 = \underline{656\times10^{-27}}$$

ATOMIC MODEL The Danish physicist Niels Bohr devised this model of the atom while working with Rutherford in England in 1913. It shows the specific pattern in which electrons move around the nucleus; it demonstrates that they are arranged in shell-like layers.

THE PHOTOELECTRIC EFFECT The American physicist Robert Millikan's work on the photoelectric effect, the emmission of electrons from a surface that is being struck by electromagnetic radiation, such as light, won him a Nobel Prize. His experiments, shown in the diagram (above), demonstrated that it was the wavelength, or frequency, of the radiation, not its intensity, that determined the voltage produced. Millikan's findings confirmed Einstein's photoelectric law, which is one of the foundations of quantum theory.

In 1900 the German physicist Max Planck (1885-1947), who had been studying phenomena connected with radiant heat (infrared radiation) had come to the conclusion that radiation is not emitted continuously but that it arrives in discrete units or 'quanta'. Five years later, Albert Einstein (1879-1955) investigated what happened when short wavelength (ultraviolet) radiation falls on a metal surface, causing electrons to be emitted. He found surprisingly that the energy of the electrons in this 'photoelectric' process did not depend on the intensity of the ultraviolet light but on its wavelength, being greater the shorter the wavelength. Inexplicable on any wave theory of light, it could readily be accounted for if the ultraviolet arrived as if it were particles. This all fitted in precisely with the experimental results Bragg was to obtain five years later, by which time it seemed that Planck's concept of particles or quanta, together with the proviso that when examined they displayed the attributes of waves, might well be correct.

The consequences of such a view had now to be worked out in detail and a number of mathematical physicists investigated the subject, notably Louis de Broglie (1875-1960), Erwin Schrodinger (1887-1961), Paul Dirac (b 1902) and Werner Heisenberg (b 1901). The theory that was developed was essentially mathematical, expressing the behaviour of particles and the emission and absorption of energy in quanta, but remembering that each quantum behaves as if it were a packet of waves. The 'wave mechanics' that developed had many important consequences, not least the prediction of the existence of other atomic particles, besides the electron and a simple positively charged nucleus, particles which physicists have since observed. The wave-like properties of quanta and of particles mean that, as Heisenberg pointed out in 1927, there is an essential 'indeterminacy' in the sub-atomic world. It is impossible to specify precisely where an electron, say, will be at a precise moment; it is only possible to specify a volume of space for any particular instant, or a number of possible instants, if the position is precisely defined. This is not because of inadequacies in our ability to measure with sufficient exactitude but because of the nature of the physical world.

Meanwhile, in 1912, the Danish physicist Niels Bohr (1885-1962), the mentor of Heisenberg and a pupil of Rutherford, began to develop Rutherford's nuclear theory of the atom in order to account for the way an atom absorbs and emits radiation. Essentially, the theory supposed that electrons orbit the nucleus and that when an atom absorbs energy from radiation, this energy is distributed among one or more electrons, causing them to take up orbits further out from the nucleus. After a minute fraction of a second, the electrons fall back to their original orbits, emitting energy in the form of electromagnetic radiation. The wavelength of the radiation absorbed or emitted depends upon the distance over which the orbits change.

Bohr's hypothesis fitted in well with quantum theory, provided the electrons are restricted to moving only in specified orbits and not in any orbits in between. The specified orbits depend on the nature of the atomic nucleus and are different for each element, since each element has its own specific nucleus. Such a theory accounted well for all kinds of observed facts. For instance, it explained the strange results obtained in 1885 by the Swiss physicist Johann Balmer, who had found out that the wavelengths of the hydrogen lines in the spectrum were such that they formed a mathematical series of numbers. This could now be seen to be due to the specific jumps of electrons from one quantum orbit to another.

The Bohr theory, and Rutherford's for that matter, had made the number of electrons dependent upon the charge on the nucleus, which was larger the more massive the atom. This too made sense out of the 'periodic table' of the elements, drawn up in 1869 by the Russian chemist Dmitri Mendeléev (1834-1907). This was a table in which the chemical elements were arranged in order of increasing atomic weight (in increasing mass of the atomic nucleus), and also laid out in such a way that those of similar chemical properties were spaced at regular recurrent intervals along the scale of atomic weights (hence the name 'periodic'). It was now seen that the different weights and properties were a consequence of the different number of electrons. Its understanding paved the way for a deeper appreciation of chemical reactions and of nuclear physics.

Rutherford continued experimenting at Manchester, now using the new Bohr theory. In 1918 he had bombarded nitrogen atoms with alpha particles (helium nuclei) and found that the nitrogen emitted heavy positively charged atomic particles. These he was to call 'protons'. In 1919 he moved to Cambridge to take over from J.J. and was able to extend this work. With the help of James Chadwick (b 1891), he bombarded other atoms in similar fashion and the same year was able to publish his astounding results, showing that the nuclei of atoms could be broken down. His work was taken further at Cambridge in 1932 by both John Cockroft (1897-1967) and Ernest Walton (b 1903), using a very high voltage (710,000 volts) to accelerate

alpha particles to extremely high velocities to break up lithium, a comparatively lightweight atom. Not only did they break lithium atoms but found these to be transmuted into helium with the release of energy. This was a true nuclear transformation by artificial means. In the same year Chadwick discovered the neutron, a heavy particle that had no electric charge but was a component of the nucleus of many atoms.

The techniques of Rutherford, Cockroft and Walton have been extended and atom smashers working at thousands of millions of volts are now in regular use to break down nuclear particles so that their constituents can be observed. Modern atomic and nuclear theory is almost embarrassed by the large number of nuclear particles discovered. This led to the belief that scientific research has not yet discerned the most fundamental building bricks of matter. The existence of more basic particles called 'quarks' is being pursued most energetically in many locations.

Techniques of breaking up not only light but also heavy atomic nuclei were devised in the 1930s. According to relativity theory the energy released would be immense — it could be calculated from the famous equation $E = mc^2$ — and so it proved to be. In practice, this has led to nuclear weapons and also to the generation of nuclear energy for peacetime purposes.

THE PROBABILITY FACTOR
Influenced by the seventeenth-century vogue for games of chance (below), the French mathematician Blaise Pascal devised his law of probability. This established that there is a statistical relationship between the number of particular results and the number of possible results in a given set of circumstances. Probability theory plays an important part in atomic physics.

Chemistry of Complex Substances

The development of scientific chemistry in the eighteenth and early nineteenth centuries was concerned primarily with metals and acids and with such everyday materials as sulphur, phosphorus and nitrogen. There was no detailed attempt to deal with the chemistry of living substances, which, it was realized, were probably very complex. Certainly, chemists spoke of 'animal chemistry' and also 'vegetable chemistry'; the first comprised substances such as gelatin, blood, saliva, urine — which, when described at all, were discussed from a purely medical point of view. As for vegetable chemistry, various substances such as gums, sugars, indigo, the 'bitter principle' and the 'extractive principle' were described, but that is as far as it went; again, there was no sound analysis. Few substances could be turned into crystals for examination, and neither chemical theory nor chemical practice had developed sufficiently for any real attack on the problem of what came to be called 'organic chemistry', to distinguish it from the 'inorganic chemistry' of non-living things.

A few organic substances, especially those containing carbon (well known from charred wood) were recognized in the West from medieval times onwards, but it was not until Antoine Lavoisier's time that a more purely scientific chemical approach was taken. It then became evident that organic substances contained carbon, hydrogen and nitrogen united with oxygen. Indeed, by the end of the eighteenth century and the early decades of the nineteenth, some analysis of organic acids was carried out in France, and then by Berzelius in Sweden, who wanted to ensure that the usual laws of chemical combination still applied to organic materials.

In 1828 Wohler discovered that urea, which is present in the urine of animals, birds and some reptiles, as well as in milk and blood, had the same chemical composition as ammonium cyanate $(H_2N.CO.NH_2)$, a well-known inorganic substance. However, although the chemicals were the same, the chemical reactions of ammonium cyanate were simpler and different from its organic counterparts. This proved to be only one example of such a difference between organic and inorganic substances — Berzelius named it 'isomerism' or 'sharing equal parts', a term still in use today. Berzelius also tried, unsuccessfully, to account for it by claiming it was due to electric charges on chemical atoms but, though his theory was wrong, the importance of his study was the fact that he drew attention to the problem.

The other possible explanation of isomerism was that, in substances displaying it, it was a result of the way the atoms were arranged within the molecule, those in the inorganic form having a different pattern from those in the organic. This discovery required still further analysis and developments in the techniques used. It was Justus von Liebig (1803-73) to whom many new methods were due. Liebig carried out some research with Wohler and took a great interest in agricultural chemistry but, above all, he was a magnificent teacher who inspired a whole generation of research chemists with an all-consuming interest in organic chemistry. It was due to one of these pupils, August von Hofmann (1818-92), that some vital organic research was stimulated.

In 1845 Hofmann moved to London to take charge of the Royal College of Chemistry, founded by some other pupils of Liebigs, later to be absorbed into the Imperial College of Science and Technology. Hofmann's own interest lay primarily in organic chemistry; with his pupils he initiated an active research programme into coal-tar, a range of products derived from distilling coal and very rich in hydrogen and carbon. Such 'hydrocarbons' form an important class of organic compounds.

Of all Hofmann's pupils who took part in this work, two became so enthusiastic that they established their own laboratories at home. One of them, William Perkin (1838-1907) followed what was to turn out to be a very promising new development. Perkin investigated the relationship between quinine — derived from the bark of the cinchona tree and then familiar as a medicine — and a coal-tar derivative known as quinoline. In 1856, during this research, Perkin came quite by chance on a by-product which was a beautiful purple colour. This turned out to be a very effective dye and, being a man of great practical sense, he realized the commercial aspects of his discovery. A purple dye was at that time a rarity; prepared since Roman times from vast numbers of small sea-snails, it had been a dye only for the very rich. Now Perkin could manufacture it from comparatively inexpensive materials and give it a permanence the natural product never possessed. He set up an appropriate plant and shortly was producing a whole range of synthetic dyes — the 'aniline' dyes — which had a coal-tar basis,

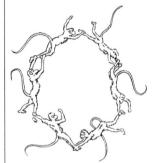

SIX WISE MONKEYS A cartoonist's drawing of the structure of benzene *(above)*, established by the German scientist Kekulé von Stradowitz, the father of modern organic chemistry. Kekulé's experiments showed that benzene's six carbon atoms were arranged in a ring.
MAN-MADE FIBRE Rayon was the first artificial fibre to be manufactured *(below)*. It was a product of the work or organic chemists, using cellulose as the basic material from which they derived the fibre.

thus initiating a great industry.

Perkin's dyes not only had commercial value; there was also a scientific aspect to the research that had led to their discovery. This aspect concerned the way the atoms of the substances are arranged within the complex molecule; the chemical components were known, as were some of the reactions into which the substances readily entered, but their arrangement was still a mystery. Various chemists tackled the problem, but the man who solved it was August Kekulé von Stradonitz (1829-96) of Heidelberg University. In 1857 Kekulé began to study in detail the replacement of hydrogen in organic materials by other chemical elements and this led him to appreciate that, while chemists had been placing different substances into groups according to their chemical behaviour, a more satisfactory way would be to classify them according to the way atoms or groups of atoms were replaced when chemical reactions occurred. In other words, he was interested in the way atoms combined and broke away — the combining power or 'valency' (from the Latin word *valens*, meaning 'strength') of chemical elements.

Such a concept of combining power must, Kekulé realized, be an indication of the way the atoms were arranged, for those at the outside or at the ends of a molecule would be available for combination or replacement. He followed up this idea with a detailed study of carbon compounds, for these seemed to have a great importance in organic chemistry and lay, for instance, at the basis of all coal-tar products, synthetic or otherwise. In particular, he was

THE OIL INDUSTRY The cracking tower of this modern oil refinery complex dominates the photograph *(below)*. Organic chemistry plays a vital role in the reduction of crude oil to its various component parts, or 'fractions'. Products range from petroleum spirit to the raw petrochemicals used in the manufacture of plastics and other complex substances.

interested in the four-fold power of carbon to combine with other elements — its 'tetravalency' (from the Greek *tetra*, meaning 'four'). One of the carbon-based substances he experimented with was benzene, which he knew contained six carbon atoms, but he was puzzled because it did not combine with other substances as if it were a chain of six tetravalent atoms. He turned the matter over in his mind until, suddenly, the answer came to him: the six carbon atoms were arranged in a ring.

The 'benzene ring', as it has come to be called, lies at the basis of a vast range of organic chemicals. Solving the benzene puzzle opened up a whole new range of possibilities. When chemists learned, especially after the middle of the twentieth century, to handle and even reorganize such structures (ie long molecules with chains of ring structures attached to one another) as well as the long 'straight' chain molecules of carbon atoms (butane, ethane,

methane and so on) it became possible to synthesize new materials. The best-known examples of these are the man-made fibres and the huge range of plastics and detergents.

It may seem strange that it is possible to determine the layout of atoms within a molecule, even though it is not possible to see individual atoms using a microscope. One technique — that used by Kekulé — has already been indicated; a study of valency and chemical behaviour, knowledge of molecular and atomic weights, provides a basis for some careful analysis that can lead to a picture of the situation. Another method, devised in 1912, was due to William Bragg (1862-1947) and his son Lawrence (1890-1971): this is the technique of X-ray crystallography. The Braggs showed that when a beam of X-rays is passed through the crystals of a substance, a photograph can be taken of the pattern in which the atoms are arranged. This happens because, first of all, the

PROTEIN MODEL This complex model shows the three-dimensional nature and the size of a single molecule of myoglobin, an animal protein which is found in the muscles. Closely related to haemoglobin, it works in the same way, combining with oxygen to assist in its transfer to the muscles from the blood.

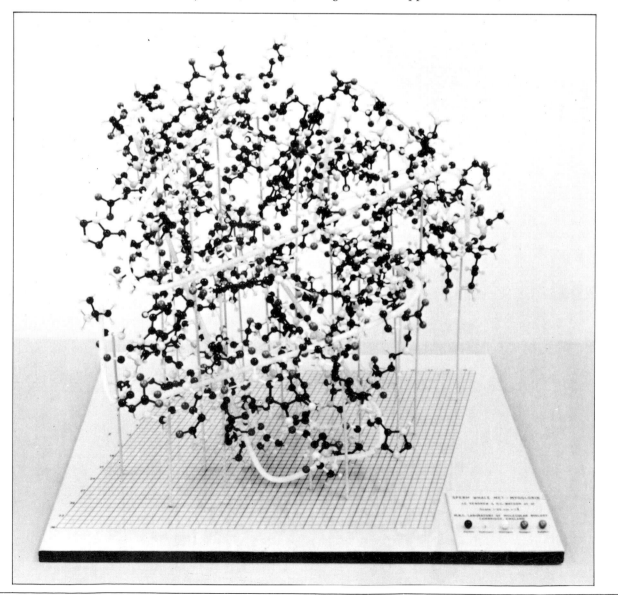

atoms in any crystal are arranged in the form of a lattice — a regular geometrical pattern — in three dimensions (since a crystal is a solid not a flat body). The second reason is that whereas ordinary light will readily pass through a crystal, X-rays are of such a short wavelength that the atoms forming the crystal lattice scatter them. The image so obtained displays the three-dimensional atomic arrangement.

The whole subject of the chemistry of living material has developed remarkably during the twentieth century as biologists and chemists found common ground in trying to solve problems such as respiration and metabolism (the way the body handles and makes use of its chemical intake). Progress along these lines began before 1900, by which time there was already enough specialization for the word 'biochemistry' to be coined. One early leader in this new subject was Gowland Hopkins (1861-1947) at Cambridge University, who not only discovered many of the substances used in metabolism but also studied 'proteins'. Proteins were so-named by Berzelius because he recognized them as basic or 'primitive' organic substances (from the Greek *proteios*, meaning 'primitive') — and found that some of their essential components, known as amino-acids, could not be built up in the body. They had to be taken in from outside and were called 'vitamins' because they were vital for life.

Two other aspects of biochemistry were the study of the way living cells break down molecules of fatty substances and carbohydrates to produce energy for the body, and detailed analysis of proteins leading to the discovery of 'enzymes' (from the Greek *zymosis*, meaning 'leaven', because they were originally known as 'ferments'). By the beginning of the twentieth century two ideas about proteins had emerged; that they were large collections of small groups of molecules of other substances or that they were giant molecules in their own right. One of the supporters of the giant molecule view was Emil Fischer (1852-1919), a pupil of Kekulé, who by 1907 was able to synthesize a molecule composed of 18 amino-acids. It became clear that proteins were indeed large molecules; using the new technique devised by Fischer, others discovered just how big they were. For instance, in 1917 the Danish chemist Soren Sorensen (1868-1939) obtained a molecular weight of 35,000 for egg-white (hydrogen has a weight of 1.008 on the same scale).

Further progress in this analysis was helped by the development of two new techniques. In Sweden in 1925 Theodor Svedberg (1884-1971) invented the ultra-centrifuge which spun chemical solutions at very high speeds. The denser the molecule the quicker it separates at a given speed of rotation. This was of vital importance in determining molecular weights and Svedberg was able to show that proteins such as haemoglobin (found in the red blood cells of vertebrates) have weights of some 65,000. The other was based on the invention by the Russian chemist Mikhail Tswett (1872-1919) who, in 1907, had separated components of organic dyes by letting them move up a strip of absorbent paper or a column of absorbent grains; the distance the components moved depended on the mass of the molecules involved. In the 1940s this technique of 'chromatography' began to be used in protein analysis.

Progress continued. In the mid-1930s the Americans Linus Pauling and Robert Corey at the California Institute of Technology discovered that long protein molecules seemed to be coiled on themselves in the shape of a helix; a decade later Frederick Sanger and colleagues at Cambridge University were able to show conclusively that all proteins are long-chain molecules of amino-acids, linked together by special chemical bonds. This result was of immense importance in biology.

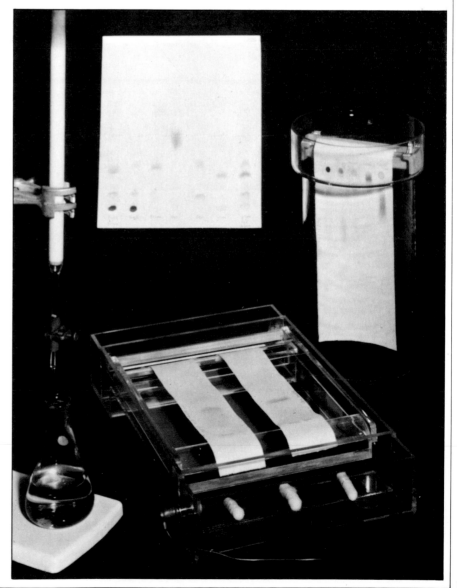

CHROMATOGRAPHY These items of equipment are all used in chromatography, a technique used in chemical and protein analysis. In the column, the component materials are absorbed by a very fine powder at various specific heights, depending on their molecular weights. This principle applies to all the other methods shown here, as in the case of the special absorbent paper.

Organic Chemicals in Space

JOURNEY INTO SPACE This view of the Horsehead nebula in the constellation of Orion, some 1,100 light-years away, was photographed through the Anglo-Australian wide-angle telescope at Siding Spring Observatory. The obscuring clouds of dark matter contain vast numbers of complex organic molecules.

The idea that organic substances or indeed life exist far out in space is in one sense not new; mankind has speculated about the subject from early times. In the first century AD, the Greek writer Plutarch thought the moon was like the earth and conjectured that it was inhabited; within 50 years the Greek satirist Lucian of Samosata wrote a story about visiting the moon. The subject received more serious consideration from time to time, though mainly on the question of the possible existence of other inhabited worlds like the earth. This speculation could only be based at best on such understanding as there was of the way stars and planets were formed, a subject on which there are still, however, some differences of opinion. Yet the idea of life elsewhere in the universe has always held some attraction, so much so, in fact, that when reports appeared in 1835 in the New York *Sun* newspaper reporting observations by William Herschel's son John (1791-1871) of a lunar civilization, the hoax was widely believed for a time.

The subject, not of life on the moon but of the possible existence of advanced civilizations elsewhere in space, has now become a serious scientific possibility. Radio telescopes have been used from time to time to try to detect messages from space. Spacecraft making close approaches to the outer planets of the solar system, in paths that will eventually take them out into deeper space, have been equipped with messages and artefacts characteristic of our own civilization. But the prerequisite for any civilization elsewhere in space is the existence of complex molecules under stable conditions. With developments in chemistry and nuclear physics it has become clear that there are no more than 92 naturally occurring elements; it is evident that organic materials must be composed of these. Further modern research has shown that all long complex molecules, which are necessary to make living material, are based on carbon as the linking element.

For organic and complex molecules to exist in space, conditions must not be too extreme as far as temperature is concerned; in addition, they have to be protected from intense short-wave radiation, especially from X-rays and gamma rays. Bombardment by nuclear particles such as those from cosmic rays — first discovered during balloon flights made in 1911 and 1912 — must also be avoided. Exposure to these particles and protracted exposure to very short-wave radiation will break up most organic substances. These requirements also introduce another complicating factor; the organic molecules being sought must not be heated sufficiently to radiate light, otherwise they will break up and be consumed. This means that we cannot expect any direct radiation to be received, although it does not rule out cool organic molecules being visible when lit by more distant starlight. Some very simple carbon-hydrogen compounds such as cyanogen (CN_2) and the carbon-hydrogen compound CH, both discovered in 1937 in interstellar clouds of gas by Walter Adams (1876-1956) and Theodore Dunham Jr. at the Mount Wilson Observatory in California, are a case in point.

During the years following the Second World War, studies of comets, particularly by Fred Whipple in the United States, resulted in the discovery of some more organic molecules, and led Whipple in 1950 to propose his cometary 'model' containing frozen water, ammonia, methane, carbon dioxide and carbon monoxide. Then, in 1967, carbon monoxide was detected in interstellar nebulae in Orion and associated with the formation of stars by Eric Becklin and Gerry Neugebauer at Mount Wilson Observatory. However, optical observations are limited in what they can detect; for more complex organic molecules much lower wavelengths must be used, and it was not until after the development of radio astronomy in the 1950s and 1960s that the search could be made. This is because radio telescopes can detect the radiation emitted by cool gas, by organic and complex molecules that produce no visible radiation at all. The power of radio techniques was demonstrated both at the appearance of comet Kohoutek in December 1973, for radio astronomers detected hydrogen cyanide (HCN) and the more complex molecule methyl cyanide (CH_3CN), and also in investigation into the cool gas clouds in interstellar space. Indeed, methyl cyanide had first been detected in 1971 by a radio telescope of the National Radio Astronomy Observatory (NRAO) of the United States, situated at Kitt Peak National Observatory near Tucson in Arizona.

Since comets, sources of organic molecules, are irregular in appearance, as soon as radio telescopes that could receive signals from space at the correct wavelengths — in the centimetre and millimetre ranges — these were directed to areas of the sky containing dark nebulae. It seemed that in the cool regions of such dust and gas, the more complex organic molecules might well be found. This research began in the United States in 1969 and gathered momentum in the 1970s when a vast range of such molecules was discovered. Of the 40 observed during a period of nine years, some deserve particular mention.

In 1969 formaldehyde (H_2CO) was discovered at the NRAO. This was a significant step forward because here was a molecule with two comparatively heavy atoms, carbon and oxygen, and a molecule of a substance that

takes a very energetic part in organic chemical reactions, especially those associated with proteins. Water molecules had been discovered in interstellar space the year before and with the detection of formaldehyde hopes were high. 1970 saw the discovery, also at the NRAO at Green Bank, West Virginia, of formic acid (HCOOH). This is an acid associated with some bacteria, although its presence cannot be taken necessarily to indicate that bacteria have been found in space. Another significant discovery, which occurred at the same observatory, also in 1970, was methyl alcohol or 'wood alcohol' (CH_3OH) which is a basic component of many more complex organic substances. In 1974, the NRAO astronomers also found ethyl alcohol (CH_3CH_2OH) which is the more familiar and less poisonous form.

So far, no long-chain organic molecules have been discovered but enough research has been done to show that the complex organic molecules of modern chemistry are to be found in the depths of space. This fact is extremely significant to the specialist astronomers, who are concerned with the physical conditions in interstellar dust and gas clouds, and also to biologists interested in the possible existence of life elsewhere than on earth.

SECRETS OF THE GALAXY With its 100ft (30m) dish, the radio telescope at the National Radio Astronomy Observatory, Green Bank, West Virginia, is the largest equatorially mounted telescope of its kind in the world. It has detected many of the complex organic molecules we now know exist in space, so opening up a new field of astrochemistry.

Earth Sciences

In the Western world, the scientific study of the earth and its climate is a product of enquiries that were first made during the Renaissance or still later; in China, however, developments began much earlier. The delay in the West seems to have been due to two factors. In the first place, the Greeks and earlier civilizations had no general theoretical interest in the earth as a physical body. Certainly they were interested in its shape, but any physical or chemical analysis of its surface appears to have elicited only a modicum of enthusiasm. Minerals and metallic ores were known and were used for both ornaments and for practical purposes. Mining flourished in Greece, Rome and other European countries but the miners and those who employed them were mainly concerned with the commercial aspects of what they brought up from beneath the earth's crust. Minerals that appeared in crystalline form were thought by some to 'grow' and were placed in the scheme of nature with living things; alchemists considered them as objects which developed or 'gestated' inside the earth and imitated these changes in the hot, closed conditions of their ovens. Mineralogy was a science that lay far in the future.

The second factor in the West that contributed to the delay of a scientific approach was the strong belief throughout Christendom in a literal interpretation of the Scriptures. This involved the concept of a 'once-and-for-all' Creation coupled with a later universal deluge. The fact that the remains of marine life were visible inland was interpreted as an indirect result of the Flood, while mountains and other features were considered to have been formed during the seven-day Creation. Subsequent folding and other changes seemed likely to have occurred after catastrophes such as earthquakes or volcanic eruptions and little serious investigation was made into such happenings. It was not until the Renaissance gave rise to the 'scientific revolution' during the sixteenth century that a productive, reasoned attitude of mind could blossom in the West.

The Chinese were not, however, restricted by religious ideologies and took a scientific attitude to geological features probably as early as the second century AD, while interpretation of fossils as animal remains was made at least as early as the first century BC. The Greeks made an appreciation of their nature even earlier but they did not pursue the matter. It is generally the case that while the Greeks made some brilliant insights, between the second century and about the fifteenth century AD the Chinese were extraordinarily advanced in their general scientific outlook and application of ideas.

China lies in an earthquake belt and for centuries the feudal bureaucracy required reports and records of everything affecting the ruler, the court and the people to be made. This led not only to some unusual geological knowledge and to a method of recording earthquakes, but

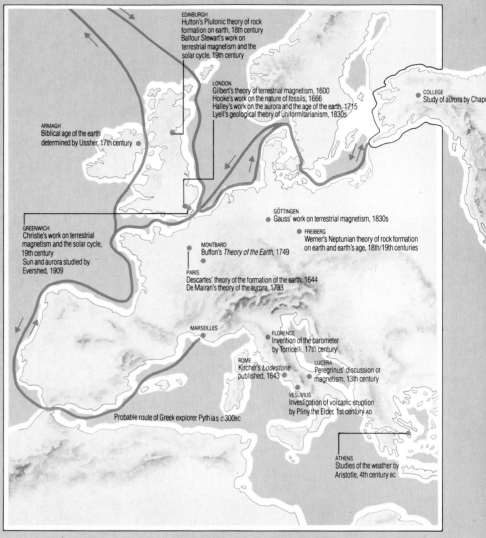

also to an interest in meteorology and the recording of weather conditions. Tides also came in for careful consideration, particularly since China has an extensive coastline — some 3,000 miles (5,000km) — and because one of the two largest tidal bores in the world is situated on the Quian-Tang (Ch'ien-Thang) River near Hangchou (Hangchow). The other is on the Amazon River. Interest in the tides evolved later in the West, due in all probability to the fact that the subject was not one to arouse much curiosity in Greece and Rome, as tides on the shores of the Mediterranean are slight, and a connection between the moon and the tides was only explained after Newton's time.

Mapping the earth was a challenge for the Greeks, however, particularly in Alexandria, and much useful work was done. But after the fall of the Alexandrian museum and library, the mood of enquiry declined and scientific map-making was pursued in China, not the West. Until the trade expansion that occurred during the

DISCOVERIES AND CENTRES OF LEARNING While the Greeks made some contribution to map-making and exploring, as with the travels of Pythias in the fourth century AD, (shown *above*) it was in China that major developments took place. Hampered by a belief in the literal truth of the Bible and a lack of interest shown by the Greeks, Western thinkers did not begin to look scientifically into questions raised by studies of the physical earth until after the scientific renaissance. Even then, meteorology, studies of the aurora and other earth sciences were comparatively late developments in Europe and the West.

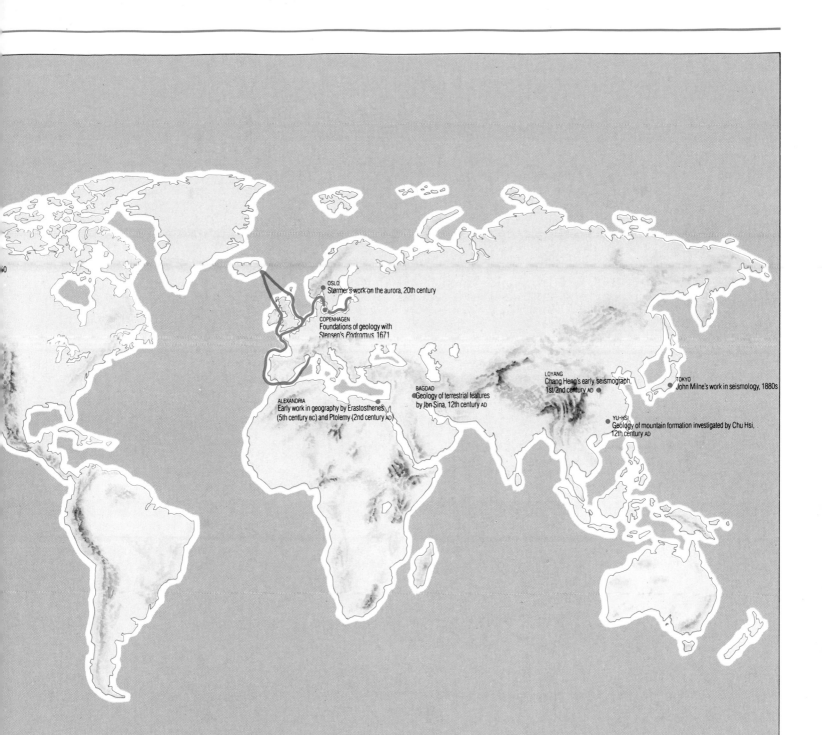

OSLO
Størmer's work on the aurora, 20th century

COPENHAGEN
Foundations of geology with
Stensen's *Padromus* 1671

LOYANG
Chang Heng's early seismograph,
1st/2nd century AD

TOKYO
John Milne's work in seismology, 1880s

BAGDAD
Geology of terrestrial features
by Ibn Sina, 12th century AD

ALEXANDRIA
Early work in geography by Erastosthenes
(5th century BC) and Ptolemy (2nd century AD)

YU-HSI
Geology of mountain formation investigated by Chu Hsi,
12th century AD

Renaissance, when new coastlines and new countries were explored, the Chinese led the world but then the map-makers of the West gained importance out of necessity.

Once the Renaissance had arrived, the development of the earth sciences began, although in most fields there was slow progress. In geology, the first real advance was not made until 1668 and it was another century before theories of the formation of geological and geographical features came to be formulated and discussed. Then two different approaches appeared: there were those who followed the so-called Neptunian theory, which claimed that all rocks were originally formed from deposits beneath the water, and the Plutonists who believed that many, but not all, rocks were formed by heat and pressure underground. This led in due course to a deep questioning about the period of time such formations would have taken to occur and the rate at which such changes happen, the answers to which had a

profound bearing on various ideas of biological evolution.

Terrestrial magnetism was another subject in which considerable growth appeared after 1600, although it was the Chinese who discovered the magnetic compass. In the seventeenth and eighteenth centuries, theories of terrestrial magnetism were proposed, although it was only in modern times, after the early experimental work in electricity and magnetism had been made, that really satisfactory explanations became possible. In the West, meteorology and studies of aurora were late developments, despite the fact that some meteorological instruments had been designed from the seventeenth century onwards.

It may be seen that studies of the earth as a physical body were slow to become a truly experimental science but they have now reached a highly developed stage, initiated for the most part during the sixteenth-and seventeenth-century upsurge in natural science.

Analyzing Earthquakes

In some regions of the world earthquakes have been known from time immemorial, often surrounded by superstition and certainly by dread. Severe earthquakes are probably the most disastrous natural events, and can affect a very large area at any one time. The loss of life from a single earthquake has been known to reach hundreds of thousands. Major earthquake activity is, however, confined to comparatively narrow belts across ocean floors, although on the large continents there are broader belts of activity. It seems to be associated with what are now thought to be the younger of the world's mountain ranges.

One of the greatest areas of earthquake activity from the earliest times lies in China and, because of their bureaucratic tradition, detailed records of these events exist and now form the longest complete series in the world. The statistics from these are impressive and terrifying. Until 1644, a total of 908 recorded earthquake shocks or seisms were noted and, among the earliest of these, in 780 BC, the courses of three rivers were interrupted. The main areas of earthquake devastation always lay north of the Yangtse and in the western provinces of the country, and the records show there were 12 peaks of activity between about AD 450 and 1644; these peaks show a 32-year cycle. One such earthquake in February 1556, in the pro-vinces of Honan, Shansi and Shensi, is recorded as having a death-toll in excess of 800,000.

In China little progress was made in formulating any theory of earthquakes, nor was there any theory in the West; such explanations had to wait until after the Renaissance and the new science of geology, with its concept of the earth's crust. In the first century BC, an explanation was given in terms of an imbalance between yin and yang but the upsetting of normal conditions seems to have been given as a reason universally. In Ancient Greece, in the sixth century BC, Anaximenes stated the cause as masses of earth falling down into cavernous places and, a century later, Anaximander explained the cause as water bursting into subterranean areas. Aristotle, in the fourth century BC, favoured the idea that earthquakes were the result of vapours, generated when the sun dried moist earth, becoming unstable and meeting with difficulties in escaping. Interestingly enough, the Chinese had an equivalent idea during the second century AD.

Truly scientific theories did not emerge for more than 1,500 years, but still it was the Chinese who invented and built the first earthquake detector or seismograph. It was made by the astronomer, geographer and mathematician Chang Heng (Zhang Heng) (AD 78-139) and contained the essential parts of all later in-

EARTHQUAKE ZONES An earthquake occurs as the result of a build-up of stresses in the earth, which cause a fracture and a sudden release of energy in the form of 'elastic' waves. These reflect off and bend through different materials. There are clearly defined belts of seismic activity, separated by large regions almost devoid of earthquake centres *(below)*. The map also shows areas likely to be affected by earthquakes. The waves are recorded by seismographs which measure shocks in the ground. The earliest *(above)* dates from the second century AD.

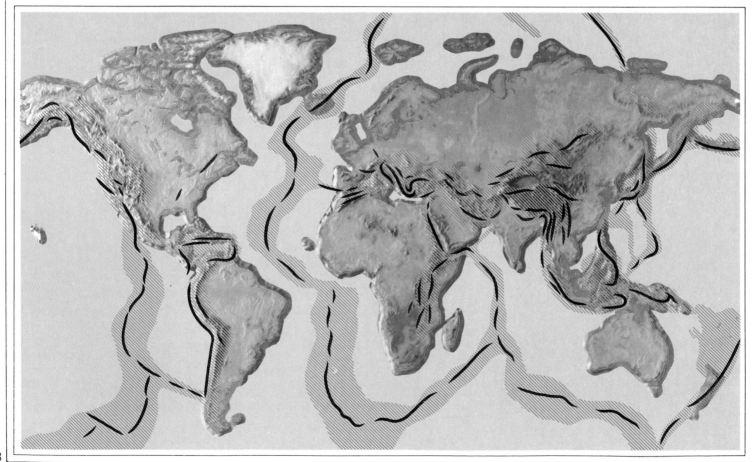

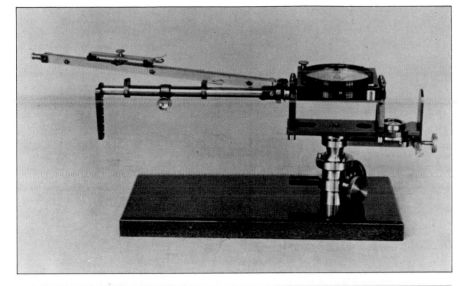

DETECTION OF SEISMIC ACTIVITY Twentieth-century instruments are designed to measure tiny rumbles within the earth. The magnetometer *(top)* is capable of detecting the magnetism of rocks while other instruments are used for the prediction of earthquakes and volcanic eruptions. A great deal more is now known about the earth than in the seventeenth century of Kircher's *Monda Subterranea (above)*.

near the jar. There were also eight sets of dragon jaws, so it was usually possible to record the general direction in which the shock had been moving.

The three essential parts of the seismograph were the heavy pendulum, the locking mechanism and the recording system. The pendulum needed to be heavy so that it responded only to the very low frequency of the rumbles of an earthquake shock, ignoring any slight, local disturbances. The locking method was a vital component because every shock, which comes in the form of a longitudinal or 'to and fro' wave, is accompanied by transverse or 'side-to-side' waves which can sometimes be severe enough to move an unlocked pendulum and set it off in a different direction. For this reason, it was essential to lock the pendulum as soon as it moved to obtain a true picture.

It seems possible that some Chinese seismographs were taken westwards, at least as far as the Middle East, for seismic instruments were recorded at the Maraghah Observatory in Persia in the thirteenth century. Yet there seems to have been little advance, and none whatsoever in the West until the beginning of the eighteenth century, when Jean de Hautefeuille (1647-1703) set up a primitive seismograph using an overfilled dish of mercury as the 'pendulum'. But if measuring instruments did not improve substantially in the eighteenth century, theory did, and in 1760 the British scientist John Michell (c 1724-1793) suggested that earthquakes were due to subterranean fires suddenly heating subterranean waters until evaporation occurred. The steam caused shocks, then the ground above fell in, causing the actual earthquake which itself released more shock waves. Until there was a better understanding of the interior of the earth and of geological change this theory was not satisfactorily replaced.

Substantial improvements in seismographs were made in the 1880s, when the British scientists James Ewing, Thomas Gray and John Milne, working in Japan, began a study of earthquakes. Milne, in 1883, designed a horizontal pendulum seismograph that became widely adopted, especially in an improved form devised by his pupil Omori Fusakichi. In the twentieth century, some more elaborate compact designs have been built, including the electromagnetic transducer seismograph of 1932 which the American Hugo Benioff designed. Such instruments are now used not only for earthquake recording but also for the detection and prediction of volcanic eruptions, for the detection of nuclear tests and for oil and gas prospecting, using artificially generated seisms to show up discontinuities under the earth's crust. Precision is a vital component of all such measurements, particularly now, and universal use is made of a magnitude scale devised in 1935 by the American seismologist Charles F. Richter (b 1900).

struments. The basic structure was a large bronze vessel, 'resembling a wine jar', which was some 6ft (2m) in diameter. Inside, a heavy pendulum, free to move in any direction, would be set in motion when an earthquake shock arrived. The direction in which the pendulum swung depended on the direction of the shock and, having swung once, it would be locked immediately in position by a lever inside the jar. This locking mechanism also operated the upper jar of an ornamental dragon, fashioned on the outside of the jar; the movement of the jaw released a ball which dropped into the mouth of one of eight bronze toads placed on the ground

The Earth as a Magnet

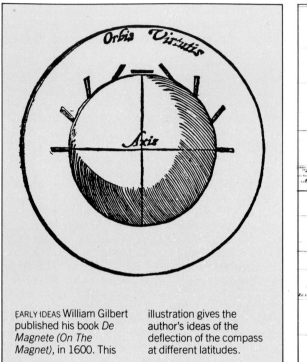

EARLY IDEAS William Gilbert published his book *De Magnete (On The Magnet)*, in 1600. This illustration gives the author's ideas of the deflection of the compass at different latitudes.

HALLEY'S MAP OF VARIATION By 1700, knowledge of the earth's magnetism was further advanced and Edmond Halley published what he called 'A New and Correct Sea Chart of the Whole World Shewing the Variations of the Compass' *(above right* and *far right)*. This is an optimistic title taking into account a note in the top righthand corner that reads: 'The Coast and Seas between Japon, Corea and Yedso are hitherto undiscovered...' However, Halley's attempt to account for the difference between true and magnetic north was an impressive combination of observed fact and a possible explanation. He explains that the 'double lines', ie the thicker ones, divide the areas of east and west variation, and under these the compass is true.

The concept of the earth as a giant magnet, familiar enough now, was realized comparatively late because it required both a knowledge of magnets and also an appreciation of the fact that it was possible for the earth itself to exert a magnetic pull. This theory was first announced in 1600 by William Gilbert (1544-1603) but the research and discovery that led to this came not from previous Western science but from China. The reasons that led to this conclusion show an interesting interplay between magic and science in many different parts of the world.

All early civilizations practised magic in various forms and the Chinese were no exception. Various magical techniques were used for different purposes and in China there developed a special kind of geomancy. Originally a form of divination using the patterns formed by throwing down earth on a flat surface, in China it became associated with the siting of houses and tombs so that they harmonized with the 'lines' of cosmic winds and forces of life to be seen in streams, in outcrops of layers of minerals and in the results of prevailing winds in an area. One result of this was to lead the Chinese to a particular sensitivity and appreciation of local terrain. To apply the art of geomancy, the expert used a 'divining board', which was in fact composed of two boards, one square to symbolize the earth, and one round, symbolizing the heavens. The Chinese had a basic belief in the entire universe as an organism of which earth and heavens were both a part. In addition, Chinese astronomers were, for various reasons, interested in the celestial pole, the ap-

parent pivot point of the northern heavens, and the upper board was marked with the constellation of the Plough or Dipper (part of the constellation of the Great Bear), that appears to rotate about it. The position of the Plough's handle can be used to indicate the time of night. In due course, the upper plate was replaced by a spoon to represent the constellation. At first this spoon was made of wood but, some time during either the first or second centuries AD, the wood was replaced by lodestones. The shape of the spoon was such that it rested easily on its bowl with the handle quite free from the board; it was in fact like a large pointer fixed at the centre of the lower divining board. What soon became evident was that the handle of the spoon always pointed in one direction, south, however the lower divining board was orientated. The spoon had an inherent facility to point in that direction, regardless of how it was first placed on the board.

In the centuries that followed, it was discovered that the directional property of the lodestone could be transferred to small pieces of iron that had been in contact with it and were subsequently floated on water. By the seventh or eighth centuries, pivoted iron needles were introduced. This led to greater accuracy, from which the Chinese learned that the needle did not point to true (geographical) south but to what we now call magnetic south, and this was centuries before the West was even aware of the lodestone's directional property. By the early twelfth century the magnetic compass was being used by Chinese mariners; from them it passed to Arab navigators and thence to the

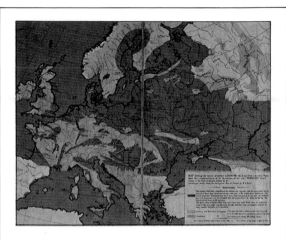

LYELL'S MODERN VIEW This is a page from the second volume of Charles Lyell's famous *Principles of Geology* (1832). The author's aim in the book was to demonstrate that slow-acting natural processes can explain all geological phenomena, as long as enough time is allowed.

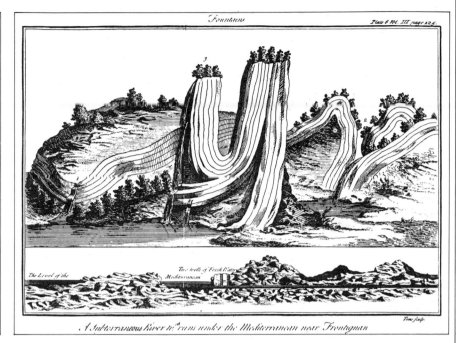

GROUNDWATER FLOW Labelled 'A Subterranean River which runs under the Mediterranean near Frentignan', *(above)* the lower illustration from *Nature Display'd* (1740) shows the river running through rock in a straight line and the upper picture describes imagined cross-sections through rocks, with subterranean channels of water feeding the sea. It is only due to modern instruments and information that we are able to discover the exact formation of rocks beneath the ground and how water passes through them; it is known, for instance, that the groundwater flow is closely related to surface topography and available drainage. Although the ideas illustrated in this diagram reflect this generalization, they seem a little crude and far-fetched to the modern eye.

mammals were found and recognized from the sixth century AD onwards. In the West any such remains were either taken as evidence of the Flood or ignored.

The advent of scientific geology in the West is usually taken to have been with the publication, in 1671, of *Prodromus (The Messenger)* written by the Danish physician Niels Stensen (sometimes known as Nicolaus Steno). It was a forerunner, as its title implies, of all later work on stratigraphy, for it described the way in which layers of rock, formed originally from deposits underwater, could collapse and so give rise to valleys and mountains. His approach, to look back into the earth's history by way of the order and shape of the layers of such rocks, was both novel and of fundamental importance. It was all part of the new spirit of scientific enquiry into the nature of things concerned with the earth itself. Indeed, five years before Stensen's book appeared, Robert Hooke had been describing fossilized wood and commenting on petrified bodies, suggesting that both were formed naturally over a long period of time.

Stensen was concerned with changes in what we would now term the outer crust of the earth but already some conjectures had been made on the earth's internal constitution, based on the experience of miners and travellers, as well as evidence from volcanoes, earthquakes and hot springs. As early as 1644 René Descartes (1596-1650) in his *Principia Philosophiae (Principles of Philosophy)* suggested that the earth was once molten, as he believed the sun to be, and that although the earth had now cooled and shrunk on the outside, its central regions were still very hot. He believed there was an incandescent central core around which was a very dense layer of material and a metallic

layer above this. Subterranean water together with a layer of mud and sand lay, he thought, underneath the surface on which we live. Later writers suggested the waters causing the Flood were drawn from this layer.

Variations on Descartes' scheme were made as the years passed, each in an attempt to better account for the evidence. The German, Athanasius Kircher (1602-80), published *Mundus Subterraneus (Subterranean World)* in 1665, in which he adopted the fiery centre theory but filled all subterranean cavities either with fire or water, believing this could be the only really satisfactory way to account for volcanic eruptions. Gottfried Leibniz (1646-1716) agreed with the suggestion that the earth had originally been incandescent, but went on to make the valuable suggestion that rocks formed under heat (ie igneous rocks) made up the original crust of the earth and that sedimentary rocks came later. But his views were not published until 1749, some 33 years after his death.

In the second half of the eighteenth century, a major controversy started in the attempts of the followers of Neptunian and Plutonic schools of thought to ascertain the truth about how rock were formed. The German geologist and mineralogist Abraham Werner (1749-1817), who was trained in the art of iron founding and who was to become the most noted geologist of his time, espoused the Neptunian view. Although Werner's support of this opinion was quoted by those who believed in the historical truth of the Flood, he never took part in the religious aspect of the argument. Werner's theory had two major points; on the one hand, he thought that the entire earth had been an enormous ocean and, on the other, that all the important rocks in the earth's crust either precipitated out of that ocean or were formed from sediments swept down by the ocean. He classified rocks into five groups according to how he believed them to have been formed, claiming that their characteristics depended on the depth and conditions of the universal ocean at various times and on the contents that were being laid down. The classification was, therefore, primarily historical, although Werner's time-scale was not the gigantic scale in use today. Nevertheless, at a time when many people were still thinking of a creation in 4004BC, Werner was thinking in terms of a million years, a period 'in contrast to which written history is only a point in time'.

Werner's theory incorporates various periods: an early time of calm, periods of storm when life first appeared, then a break-down of some of the older rocks, followed by periods of volcanic eruptions and floods.

The Plutonic view which opposed Werner's Neptunianism was championed by the Scotsman James Hutton (1726-97), who had a medical training but who also studied and practised agriculture and who became more interested in geology while travelling in Britain and France. Hutton's most important geological contribution was his theory of the earth which he first announced in 1785, although he had been working on it for more than 20 years before that. In this theory he concluded that sedimentary rocks are composed of fossils and of material from the seashore; in consequence they could not have formed part of the original crust of the earth. This implied, he believed, that while the land we live on was forming, there must have been a previous land which also supported life; this earlier land must also have been subject to erosion at a time when there was abundant marine life. All this necessitated sedimentary material being consolidated on the sea bed and later being uplifted out of the water. Heat was the agent of both consolidation and elevation.

Hutton went on to consider the strata he had seen, how breakages indicated a process similar to the one he suggested, and then discussed the appearance of mineral strata across other stratas which were quite different and concluded that heat had been the cause. He mentioned volcanoes and the occurrence of 'subterraneous lavas' ie igneous extrusions.

The Plutonian theory was revolutionary, so much so that Hutton has sometimes been called the founder of modern geology. His field work was similar to that produced by geologists now and it was he who brought about the realization that igneous rocks form a major rock group widely distributed over the world. His explanation of the mechanisms of consolidation and uplift were not correct but that was not important; the real signficance lay in the fact that his theory explained the features that could be observed on a process of cyclic change — erosion, followed by consolidation, expansion (due to heating), elevation of the material, to be

followed by more erosion and the other events as the cycle is repeated. Geological change is a continuing process.

Hutton's theory had its opponents. There were the Neptunists and others, notably the French zoologist Georges Cuvier (1769-1832), who believed his own not inconsiderable research into fossils showed them to be the products of catastrophes and not, as Hutton suggested, the results of slow and gradual change. New and weighty evidence was required to support the concept of slow geological change, for Cuvier had a great international reputation. It took the work of another Scotsman, Charles Lyell (1797-1875) to provide it.

Lyell was introduced to geology while at Oxford and was much influenced by the suggestion that rock strata could be determined by the fossils embedded in them, a view put forward in 1816 by William Smith (1769-1839). This was an important idea because so often rock strata are twisted and folded, and the final order may bear little, if any, resemblance to the order in which the strata were laid down. Later, Lyell made visits to various places and noted the geological features; in particular he was impressed by the slow erosion of the coastline in Norfolk in Britain and then on a visit to Paris he was shown the geology of the region by Louis Prévost (1787-1856). Prévost claimed that Cuvier and others were wrong in thinking that the strata with marine and freshwater fossils had been laid down by periodic incursions by the sea; they were, Prévost argued, formed within a single saltwater gulf similar to the English Channel. Other research that he carried out in the next five years convinced Lyell that slow change was the essential process of geological change, even though odd catastrophes — earthquakes and volcanic eruptions — did occur. Some of his contentions were supported by evidence obtained by Charles Darwin on his famous five-year voyage in the *Beagle*, but before Darwin embarked, the first of Lyell's three-volume *Principles of Geology* was published. The second and third volumes appeared in 1832, while Darwin was away.

Lyell's *Principles* contained a thorough survey of current geological processes which are continuously altering the earth's surface and then gave supporting evidence from the distribution of animals and plants. These, he claimed, had grown up in particular centres, spread out from these, persisted for a time, and then became extinct. This view of gradual change became widely accepted and the doctrine of 'uniformitarianism', as it came to be known, absorbed into the general outlook of geology.

Since Lyell's time, the science of geology has developed on the basis of gradual change. The theory of continental drift — the separation of the earth's land masses into units which have since drifted apart — was forwarded by the German geologist Alfred Wegener (1880-1930) in

1915; it was later rejected only to be reinstated in the 1950s in the light of new evidence. It is also during the twentieth century that detailed studies in seismology and in the earth's magnetism have provided evidence for a picture of the inside of the earth. Evidence now points to the view that the earth has a central metallic core, surrounded by a liquid iron outer core, which is itself overlaid by a mantle of very dense rock and then one of lighter rock. Over this is the earth's crust on which life exists.

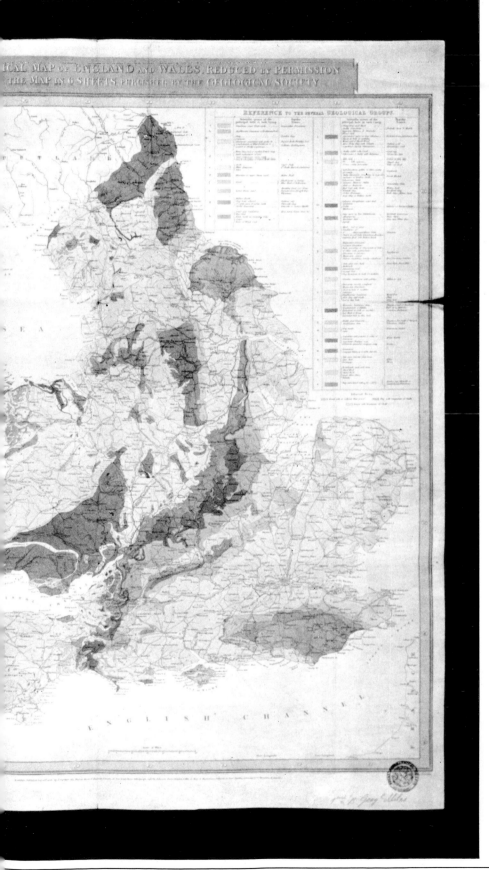

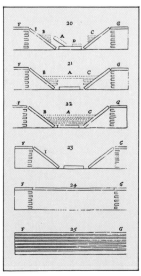

DEVELOPING THEORIES These diagrams *(left)* are taken from Steno's *Prodomus (The Messenger)* (1671), which describes how layers of rock could collapse to form valleys and mountains. In the nineteenth century, books on geology abounded; this map of England and Wales describes contemporary views of the region *(far left)*. In 1853 the ninth out of 12 editions of Lyell's *Principles* was published, with this picture of the Temple of Serapis at Pozzuoli as its frontispiece *(above)*. Despite being submerged during the second century, the temple columns had survived.

The Age of the Earth

The age of the earth has been the subject of many estimations at different times and in different cultures. The answer given has also varied: in early times the age of the earth was synonymous with the age of the universe but, since the scientific revolution, it has gradually become appreciated that the earth's age is shorter than the age of the universe or even the age of the sun.

Going back to the earliest recorded views, it may be seen that in many Asian countries, particularly those where Buddhism was the chief religion, there was a cyclic view of history. To the Buddhist philosopher the universe is un-created, without beginning or end, but it undergoes cyclic changes or 'origination, duration, destruction and annihilation'. These stages were each thought to be very long, which is perhaps due to the ability of Indian mathematicians to handle large numbers; a million was not an impossible concept for them. This was very different from some countries in the Middle East, where such numbers could be only hinted at, as the Hebrews did with their 'ten thousand times ten thousand'. The Hebrews, of course, had a seven-day Creation period, although how many years back in time this had occurred they did not specify in actual figures. Archbishop Ussher, in the seventeenth century, estimated the now famous date 4004BC using the ages of the patriarchs and other biblical persons.

Agreement on this, however, was not universal; the astronomer Edmond Halley (1656-1742) challenged it boldly and suggested a value obviously well in excess of Ussher's. In 1715 he derived his own figure for the date of the Creation from studies he had been making for some time on evaporation. Considering lakes without any natural outlets, such as the Caspian Sea, the Dead Sea and Lake Titicaca between Bolivia and Peru, he showed that, when forming, their waters must swell until such a time as the loss caused by evaporation just balanced the inflow from the surrounding countryside. Noticing that such lakes contain salt, not fresh water and pointing out that an ocean is really a large lake without an outlet, he then hit upon a method of estimating the age of the oceans. While the rivers feeding the oceans carry dissolved salts, the water that evaporates is fresh; Halley concluded that the salinity of the oceans must continually increase and the increase should be a proportion of their age, or at least of the time during which they have been fed by the surrounding rivers. There is a problem, which Halley did not fail to appreciate, that the oceans may have contained some salt to

BUDDHISM The Buddhist religion is one of introspection and its followers, like this young novice in northern Thailand, hold a strong belief in the essential unity and harmony of all living things. All creatures are in a state of development, continuously being born, dying and being reborn until a state of nirvana can be attained, which is the ultimate goal. The religion cannot therefore hold a belief that the universe began or will end at a certain time; its essence denies the possibility of either an initial void or extinction.

MINING SHAFT Taken from *De re Metallica*, by Agricola, which was published in Basle in 1556, this illustration depicts a cross-section of a mine, showing the shaft and galleries at two levels. On ground level, a man can be seen dowsing with a forked twig; he was supposed to be able to find hidden minerals with the twig which would dip suddenly when held over the right spot. At the time that this book was published, the strong biblical view of a seven-day Creation prevailed in Europe and mining was carried out not for any interest in geology, but to obtain minerals for building, cooking and making ornaments.

GREEK MINING This stylized illustration was drawn onto a clay tablet in the sixth century BC and depicts men hard at work beneath the earth. While the Greeks engaged extensively in mining activities, they were mainly interested in the commercial aspects of such work.

reached such a position by volcanic action, a type of event with which Italians were familiar in view of the ancient eruptions of Etna and Vesuvius, the sudden rise in 1538 of Monte Nuovo (New Mountain) near Naples and the recent appearance of a new volcanic island in the Greek archipelago. Moro suggested that originally the earth had a smooth stony surface entirely overlaid with a shallow ocean of fresh water. Later this surface was catastrophically disturbed from time to time by 'subterranean fires' to form dry land, a process which he thought would have taken a very long time.

The other important eighteenth-century view was proposed in 1749 by Georges Leclerc, the Comte de Buffon (1707-88) in his *Théorie de la Terre (Theory of the Earth)* which was published in an English translation in 1792 under the title *Natural History*. He also wrote a second book, *Époques de la Nature (Epochs of Nature)* which came out in 1778 and exerted a wide influence, especially among geologists. Buffon took a very broad view, connecting ideas about the age of the earth with the cosmic pictures of Kant and Laplace on the formation of the earth and the sun. Buffon accepted the idea that the earth was originally a hot, glowing molten body that only gradually cooled. As cooling occurred, hollows developed in the interior and depressions and ridges on the surface; these eventually became the oldest valleys and mountains. While cooling was taking place, the earth was surrounded by vapour but, once the process was complete, the vapour condensed to form an ocean covering the entire globe.

Buffon conjectured that such an ocean would originally have been too hot to support life and he thought that when living creatures did emerge, they would have been very different from those with which biologists were familiar; he suggested that a careful study of fossils would reveal the details. Gradually, he thought, the primeval ocean would erode the earth's surface, producing a sediment of clay then, as time went on, fissures would appear in the rocks of the still cooling earth; some of the ocean would then drain away, uncovering lower levels of the earth's crust as the sea-level fell. This water fuelled volcanoes which then began to appear and whose eruptions gave rise to the formation of very large valleys. Vegetation would by then have covered one percent of the land.

After all these upheavals, Buffon envisaged a period of calm during which land animals appeared; this was followed by a period when continents of the New World separated from the Old, Europe from Greenland and Spain from Canada and Newfoundland — a primitive form of the theory of continental drift. New islands also appeared in the Atlantic. Lastly, mankind arrived but would only survive for a limited time because, Buffon thought, eventually the earth would become too cold to support life.

Buffon attempted to put a time-scale to his stages of development. He thought the original

begin with, but he believed the method he proposed would provide some kind of scientific estimate. He realized the evaporation would be slow and that no records were available giving the sort of information he required but he appealed to his fellow scientists to make some appropriate measurements which could be repeated sometime in the future.

Although Halley had no firm evidence to provide even an estimate, he thought that this computation would be likely to provide a respectable age for the earth. He also pointed out that the arrival of man some thousands of years ago had no bearing on the age of the earth. People were apparently created on the 'sixth day' but Halley, for one, was not prepared to accept the biblical days as real days, particularly as the sun, the life-giver, was not created until the fourth. We now know, of course, that there are too many imponderables for his method of calculating the earth's age to give a satisfactory figure — we do not know, for instance, that the rate of river salt has been constant for any long period of time — but it was a bold attempt to apply scientific method to a problem.

Various other views were brought forward in the eighteenth century and all of them favoured a long time-scale compared with Archbishop Ussher's. In 1740 the Italian Anton Moro (1687-1740) criticized those who believed that fossil shells on high mountains were evidence of the Flood. Fossils could only have cooling would probably have taken some 3,000 years, the formation of hollows and depressions almost 10 times as long, and then 25,000 years for the cooling of the primeval ocean, production of clay sediments and the appearance of primitive marine life. To this total of 60,000 years had to be added the draining away of part of the ocean and the appearance of vegetation (10,000 years), the separation of the continents (5,000 years) and the arrival of mankind (5,000 years). All this gave a period of 80,000 years.

The next step was Abraham Werner's view that the primeval ocean was a million years old, which was an extension of Buffon's scale by more than a factor of 10. This was a time-scale which was, however, to be further expanded once James Hutton's cyclic views of geological history became accepted and then by the advent of Lyell's 'uniformitarianism'. But the problem of the earth's age only became a prominent issue after Charles Darwin (1809-82) expounded his theory of the evolution of animal species, because this vastly extended the period needed for human beings to develop.

However, the demand for such a long time-scale, measured in thousands of millions years, raised problems in astrophysics. Lord Kelvin (1824-1907) calculated in 1865 that the sun could not continue shining for as long as presumed in Darwin's theory, while he also worked out that the time taken by the earth to cool from an original molten state to its present temperature could in no way be more than 100 million years. Later research was, however, to show that Kelvin was mistaken on both counts. On the one hand, the discovery in the 1920s and 1930s of nuclear energy as a source of stellar radiation finally defeated arguments for a limited age for the sun, other earlier suggestions for supplying stellar energy having already undermined Kelvin's opinion. As for the cooling of the earth itself, the discovery of radioactivity in the early years of the twentieth century showed that such a process would, in fact, itself act as a source of heat supply, thus making a much longer time-scale possible.

The discovery of radioactivity and of the existence of radium in rock samples provided a new tool for the geologist and others who were concerned with the ages of rocks and rock strata, because it could provide a method of dating rock samples. This radiometric technique, based on the work of Rutherford and Soddy, depends on the fact that radioactive uranium and other naturally occurring radioactive substances decay to become lead and certain other non-radioactive substances at a particular rate. This rate is known as the 'half-life' of the material, the half-life being that period during which half the atoms of a sample will have decayed. The half-lives can be very long; in the case of uranium-238 (uranium of atomic weight 238), the half-life is 4,500 million years. As uranium is found in igneous rock or rocks that have been changed by heating within the

earth's crust, it is a useful indicator of the age of very old rocks. The method shows that the earliest rocks, the Pre-Cambrian, are very old indeed, so that the age of the earth on this evidence alone must be of the order of 4,600 million years, a time-scale quite long enough to incorporate the long periods required by Darwinian evolution.

Since the end of the Second World War, radioactive dating has been extended to living material by Willard Libby (b 1908), an American chemist who discovered that the production of natural carbon-14 (carbon with an atomic weight of 14 instead of the usual 12) was caused by cosmic rays bombarding nitrogen in the upper atmosphere. The resulting carbon-14 then combines with oxygen to make carbon dioxide, in which form it is absorbed by plants and thence into the bodies of animals feeding on those plants. It also dissolves in sea water and fresh water and is found in aquatic plants and animals. Results of carbon-14 dating fit in well with the evolutionary picture and thus with a long time-scale for the earth's age.

Studies made during the twentieth century by geologists have also given figures for the age of the earth derived from the speed at which rocks erode, while astronomers have been able to provide some ideas of age from purely astronomical ideas connected with stellar ages. All the present evidence seems to confirm the value of some 4,500 million years.

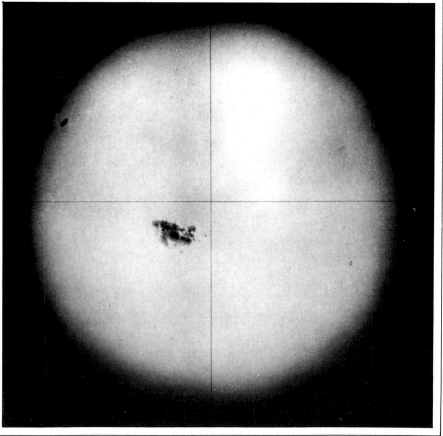

THE SUN The age and potential radiating time of the sun entered the debate about the age of the earth when Lord Kelvin suggested in 1865 that the sun could not continue shining as long as Darwin's theory presumed. Then, in the 1920s, nuclear energy was discovered to be the source of the sun's radiation, implying that the sun's age is very great indeed. This picture of our star was taken at Greenwich in 1905 while the debate was in progress.

Mapping the Earth

Map-making goes back to the time of the ancient civilizations of Egypt and Mesopotamia, although what remains from these civilizations is meagre. Egyptian 'theoretical maps', portraying imaginary journeys or places, usually in symbolic form, have survived; there is a route to Paradise — probably partly based on the course of the Nile — and a map of the Fields of the Dead. The Egyptians are known to have travelled on expeditions but no maps of their routes remain. The earliest true maps that still exist are Mesopotamian; there is one of the region dating from about 2500BC, another showing a small area of a city in the Nippur area (south of present-day Baghdad) and, perhaps the best known, a world map of about 500BC. In the last case Babylon is at the centre and the Euphrates flows from its source to join an encircling sea, presumably the sea surrounding the earth according to the Mesopotamian world view.

In Greece, map-making developed. As early as 550BC Anaximander drew a world map with the Mediterranean at the centre; at this time Greek knowledge of the world was limited. However, the Greek historian Herodotos (active around 430BC), who wrote about travels, did much to enlarge a general knowledge of Asia, while the conquests of Alexander the Great a century later and the travels of Pythias to the north, all contributed new evidence. By this time, a spherical earth had become accepted and its circumference was measured by Eratosthenes, who also divided up the earth; he followed the philosopher Dicearchos in dividing the earth into northern and southern regions, but also drew a meridian (north-south line) running through Rhodes at right-angles to this initial division.

Other Greek maps were prepared but the most important was to be that produced in the second century AD by Ptolemy. He did not however, use Eratosthenes' (correct) measure of the earth but a later incorrect and smaller value obtained by the scholar Posidonios (135-51BC) who, incidentally, had the Roman statesman Cicero as one of his pupils. But, of course, Ptolemy was not to know for sure which was the more reliable and clearly the later would seem to be preferable. Ptolemy's positive contributions to map-making were his descriptions of how to make map projections of the spherical earth on a flat surface using comparatively simple geometrical constructions, his suggestion of breaking down a world map into separate sectional maps, and providing a list of coordinates for some 8,000 places. The 'longitudes' of the places were obtained from the courses and times taken by ships and by those travelling overland; they could not have been very precise.

Ptolemy's work remained unsurpassed in the West for some 1,200 years, because no scientific or precise attitude was taken to map-making until after the Renaissance. Instead maps became religious and symbolic. One type used a circular disc with a circular ocean inside, in which the world was divided by a 'T' formed by the Don and the Nile (across the top of the T) and the Mediterranean (the vertical stroke of the T). The top half of the map represented Asia, with Jerusalem at the centre of the whole disc; Europe was at the lower left and Africa the lower right. Such 'T-O' maps had east at the top. A second type put north at the top and divided the earth into climes or zones, frigid at north and south, with a torrid zone in the centre and a temperate zone either side of this. Sometimes both were combined in one map. There were also other isolated variations. Similar methods were used in Islam. Not until the fourteenth century did the more realistic 'portolan' maps used by navigators appear, where ports and coast lines were connected by special sailing or 'rhumb' lines which always made the same fixed angle with a meridian. These made the task of navigation more straightforward.

Although scientific map-making may have ceased in the West between the time of Ptolemy and the Renaissance, in China a great cartographic tradition grew up. This was partly because of the demand for good maps by the feudal bureaucracy and records show that reasonably accurate maps were being prepared during the Han dynasty, that is from about 200BC. Further techniques to improve detail were developed especially during the Thang (Tang) dynasty (seventh to ninth centuries) and the Sung (Song) (tenth to thirteenth centuries). Here we find not only the use of a rectangular grid of lines, which goes back at least to the third century AD and possibly to the second, but the combination of these lines with celestial coordinates during the Thang. It was at this time that

MERCATOR PROJECTION
Gerardus Mercator (1512-94) did not invent the map projection named after him but was the first to apply it to a nautical chart. He produced the famous world chart in 1569 and designed it so that a navigator could lay off a compass course in a straight line making the same angle with all meridians.

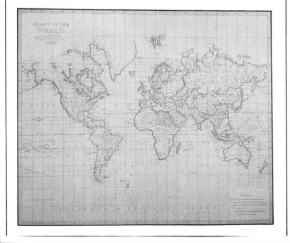

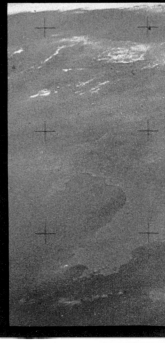

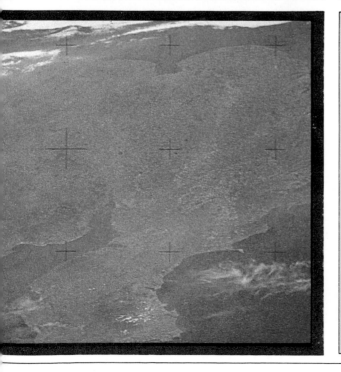

Ptolemy's contribution to map-making in the ancient world was his ability to make projections of a spherical world on a flat surface *(bottom)*. After this Greek achievement, symbolism and fanaticism reigned. The 'T-O' map *(below)* is an example of this retrogression. Map projections were, however, used and developed from the sixteenth century onwards, and in the twentieth century aerial photography *(below left)* became a valuable aid. Satellite pictures *(left)* and related technology have made mapping ever more precise.

the first use of contours to depict heights was made. During the Sung, progress continued and in 1137 a huge gridded map almost 3ft (1m) square was drawn up to display the travels of Yü the Great, a semi-legendary emperor. This was an extraordinary achievement. It shows a firm, correct coastline and accurate delineation of rivers and places, the whole covered with a grid of squares. No map of such precision — and it looks very like a modern map — was produced in any civilization anywhere else at this time, indeed, until centuries later. The Chinese adopted a 'Mercator' projection for celestial charts in the eleventh century AD and it was during this same century that they produced the first relief maps, marking hills, mountains and river valleys.

From the sixteenth century onwards, scientific map-making based on hard facts and accurate figures was revived in the West, due to the needs of an expanding worldwide trade. The method of triangulation (determining positions of inaccessible points with two fixed and known positions) was described by Gemma Frisius (1508-55) in 1533, and more precise instruments were invented for plotting and measuring. The difficult problem of measuring longitude at sea was solved in the eighteenth century and, by the nineteenth, accurate maps, geographical, geological and climatic as well as other types, were drawn up, often using new and specialized map projections. Aerial photography developed into a valuable mapping technique in the twentieth century aided, since the Second World War, by surveys from artificial orbiting satellites and still further improved methods of surveying using laser technology.

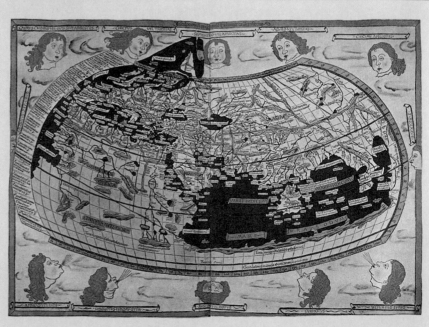

Studies of the Weather

METEOROLOGICAL INSTRUMENTS
The first barometer, a device for measuring atmospheric pressure, was invented by the Italian scientist Evangelista Torricelli in 1643. Torricelli used water as his measuring medium *(below)*, but this was soon replaced by mercury *(below right)*. Because of its greater density, this requires a smaller measuring column. Robert Hooke devised his hygrometer *(above)* to measure the moisture content of air; in meteorology, it is used to determine the relative humidity.

The subject of meteorology originated in the age of antiquity. The word itself is Greek; its literal meaning is 'things above the ground' and was first used in this specific sense by Aristotle, although his book on it also deals with other transitory phenomena such as comets and meteors which are not now so classified. In Greece the study had two aspects; on the one hand, it was concerned with weather forecasting, on the other, with the causes of wind and rain, rainbows, haloes and lightning. The forecasting was not highly developed and consisted of *parapegma*, which listed the seasons (usually by heliacal risings and settings) and the appropriate weather conditions likely to be experienced.

The causes of weather phenomena were variously explained. As early as the sixth century BC, Anaximander understood the 'water-cycle' — the evaporation of water to form clouds which return the water as rain — and in the fourth century BC Aristotle set down in his *Meteorologica* a series of explanations. Rain, mists and hot weather were all due, he suggested, to moist and dry exhalations emerging from the earth; if this sounds today a little too vague and even facile, it was a reasonable view for the fourth century BC because, put in more modern terms, it claimed that the causes were water vapour and radiant heat. No rain, mist or wind was to be found, Aristotle believed, at heights greater than some 4 miles (6 km). Then Geminos, in the first century BC, claimed that no wind or rain was present on mountains above about half this height. Rainbows and haloes round the sun or the moon received explanations connected with reflection of sunlight and moonlight, but these were only vaguely connected to weather lore.

For meteorology to become a science there was a need for a more precise approach, for measurement of such matters as rainfall, wind direction and speed, temperature and so on. In the West, such measurements were not made until the Renaissance but in China bureaucratic efficiency ensured they were made much earlier — from the thirteenth century BC onwards. In prediction, China never advanced beyond the Greek stage of weather lore, tying the prevailing weather pattern to the changing seasons.

The Anyang oracle-bones of 1220 BC record rainfall, the appearance of snow and sleet and the direction of both rain and wind. The water-cycle was recognized by the fourth century BC. It is evident from early annals that

China has experienced a long-term change of climate; contemporary observations between the fifth and third centuries BC show many annual biological phenomena occurring a month earlier than now, while there were elephants by the Yellow River (latitude 36°) until about the third century BC. The Chinese also noted humidity, using feathers or charcoal, both of which indicate levels of dampness, and measured it, for example, by weighing pieces of charcoal. Rain and snow gauges had come into use by the thirteenth century AD. By the fourteenth, kites were used to investigate winds, although the equivalent of weather vanes had been in use as early as the second century BC — Greece also had at least one such device at the same time — and the Chinese seem to have used a kind of anemometer for measuring winds.

Once the Renaissance had begun in the West and the spirit of enquiry was abroad, we find some studies of the weather beginning; in the fifteenth century the scholar Nicholas of Caus made measurements of humidity, weighing wool against stones. More sophisicated devices soon appeared; in the seventeenth century the members of the famous Italian *Accadamia del Cimento* designed an hygrometer that condensed and collected water from the atmosphere, thus giving a quantitative measurement. In the 1660s, Robert Hooke (1635-1703) designed a device that operated a pointer and a wind-gauge that could measure wind direction as well as strength. He attempted to design and build a 'weather-clock' to record as well as measure wind, temperature, pressure and humidity; he also constructed a successful rain-gauge.

The work of Galileo on the vacuum led his pupil Evangelista Torricelli (1608-47) to devise the principle of the barometer, although it was Robert Boyle (1627-91) who pointed out its use to measure changes in atmospheric pressure at a given place rather than just the heights of places above ground level (because, of course, atmospheric pressure varies with height). The concepts of height and atmospheric pressure were studied by Edmond Halley (1656-1742) who, like the French physicist Edme Mariotte (c1620-84), linked barometric pressure and wind with the weather. It was Halley, too, who suggested the causes of the trade winds and monsoons in the three great oceans and who studied the amount of solar radiation which he believed to be the primary cause of all winds.

During the eighteenth century, meteorological textbooks began to appear and the meteorological records begun in the the 1670s in Germany were continued on a wider scale. Instruments improved, based on new and more precise temperature scales; Henry Cavendish designed maximum-minimum thermometers in 1757 and also a recording thermometer. Wind-speed measurements were improved, as were hygrometers. Progress continued during the next century and national meteorological observations were established between 1820 and 1860 in Europe, to be followed by others elsewhere, and cooperation on an international scale began in the 1850s. An exchange of information internationally made weather forecasting more reliable, and in 1951 the World Meteorological Organization was recognized by the United Nations.

Ground-based meteorological observations continued in both the nineteenth and twentieth centuries but, from 1900 on, instrumented balloons made it possible to explore the upper air on a regular basis. Balloons equipped with radio (radio-sondes) and, since the Second World War, radar (observing radio echoes) have provided information on the movement and behaviour of clouds and upper air winds, so helping materially in short-range weather forecasting. Still more recent have been sounding rockets which soar to heights of between 19 and 63 miles (30 and 100km), reaching the upper atmosphere. In the 1950s and 1960s, artificial satellites like *Tiros*, launched in 1960, and in the 1970s onwards the *Nimbus* series, not only help immensely with forecasting but can also help to save life by giving advance warning of tornadoes. Electronic computers have also aided the process of forecasting.

WEATHER FORECASTING A weather balloon *(above)* carries meteorological instruments into the atmosphere to record temperature, wind speed and wind direction. Satellite scans *(below)* have been invaluable in developing the science of long-range weather forecasting. The white areas indicate areas of high humidity; the vortex shape is a depression.

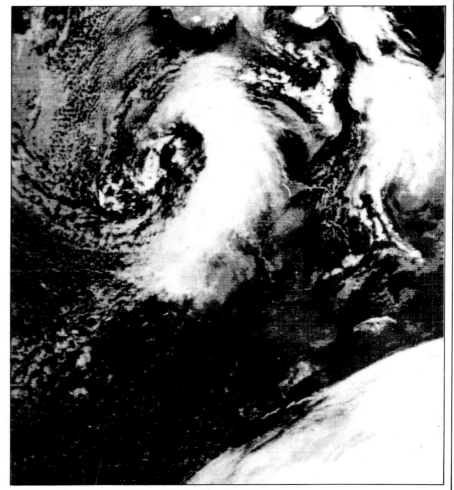

The Aurora

One of nature's more spectacular events is a display of the aurora. Although we now know that displays always occur simultaneously at both north and south magnetic poles, in earlier times only the 'northern lights' or aurora borealis was known. Generally speaking it is visible only from more northerly latitudes — usually above 55° — although high and bright displays are very occasionally seen at latitudes as low as 10°. We should not then expect the Greeks to be much concerned with auroras, although travellers to the north such as Pytheas may possibly have witnessed displays or at least heard about them. They were variously reported and many who believed in a bright heaven beyond the sphere of the stars thought the lights shone through gaps or cracks in this sphere. It would seem that some such idea lay behind Aristotle's description of them as 'chasms', in the fourth century BC. The Chinese described them as 'cracks in heaven' or as 'swords of heaven', while in medieval times in the West they were sometimes referred to as 'dancers in the sky' or as 'armies fighting in the sky', and some people even claimed to have heard the clash of arms. Since a large display is sometimes accompanied by hissing sounds, perhaps such reports show more misinterpretation than wilful imagination. Early descriptions of fireballs, meteorites and comets are not always clear and in the West it is difficult to be certain about the subject being described in each instance. Auroras are easier to identify and quite frequently included in reports from higher latitudes. The Chinese observed and recorded a few displays; their earliest report dates from 208BC and the last independent one, before the arrival there of Western science, was in 1639.

Scientific research into the aurora in the West did not begin until Edmond Halley (1656-1742) published a theory about its origin in 1716. In March and early April that year two notable displays had occurred and he described both in some detail. The March display showed a 'crown' of light above it but he realized that this was a purely optical effect caused by the 'concourse' of many auroral shafts of light which were almost vertical at the poles. After making sound recommendations about how the height of an aurora could be measured, the principle of which is still used, he went on to expand his theory. The auroras were, he suggested, due to the escape from below the earth's crust of a luminous 'medium' which, having once escaped, was governed by the earth's magnetic field. The medium became luminous 'after the same manner as we see the Effluvia of Electric Bodies by a strong and quick Friction emit Light in the Dark'. The word 'aurora' was not used by Halley but seems to have been adopted the next year, 1717.

During the eighteenth century, other attempts were made to account for the aurora, the French physicist Jean de Mairan publishing a book on the subject in 1733. He supposed the aurora to be an extension of the sun's atmosphere which at times, he thought, blended with the earth. In 1741 some Scandinavian scientists had noticed irregular movements of magnetic compass needles during auroral displays, and two years later the English schoolmaster John Canton confirmed this but explained auroras as the results of exceptional heating, of subterranean origin, of parts of the earth's surface. On the other hand, in 1746 the German-Swiss mathematician Leonhard Euler thought the auroral streamers were portions of the earth's atmosphere shot out by action of the sun, much in the same way as comets' tails.

The next stage in the investigation of the nature of auroras did not come until the nineteenth century. Then, in the 1850s and 1860s, Rudolf Wolf (1816-93) detected a relationship between the appearance of auroras and the degree of sunspot activity; clearly, there seemed to be a definite connection between solar activity and auroral displays. This was confirmed in the years that followed, especially by the Italian astronomer Pietro Tacchini, but it required a deeper understanding before the subject could be further extended.

In 1908 Hale, the American astronomer, discussed sunspots in some detail, collating their appearance with streamers seen in the dim hazy outer solar atmosphere or 'corona'. He noticed what seemed to be vortexes surrounding the spots and he concluded that electrified atomic particles were whirled into sunspots and created magnetic fields as they did so. The evidence of the corona seemed to support the idea. The next year, the British solar astronomer John Evershed showed, however, that there seemed to be an outward flow of particles from spots, although there was no doubt that the spots were magnetized. Indeed, theories about the sun were making it seem likely that the causes of such magnetism lay deeper down inside the sun. After this, it became evident from the appearance of auroras, the onset of magnetic storms which set magnetic needles awry and the fading of short-wave radio transmissions that all kinds of electrical and magnetic effects emanated from the sun at times of the appearance of large sunspots. But all these effects did not occur simultaneously and it became clear therefore that while some were due to radiation, others were due to the ejection of atomic particles.

The arrival of such corpuscles was analyzed by a number of scientists, most notably Kristian Birkeland (1867-1917), Carl Störmer (1874-1957) and Sydney Chapman (1888-1970). In 1950, Chapman was able to show in detail how a 27-day recurrence of magnetic phenomena on the earth fitted in with the sun's rotation period and how, if particles were emitted from the sun, they would react with the earth's magnetic field to give just the kind of paths that were seen in the auroral streamers. His work was confirmed

by later studies and, in particular, the discovery of two huge 'radiation belts' by the Americans, James van Allen and colleagues, using an artificial satellite launched in 1958. These, now known as the 'van Allen' radiation belts, were foreseen by Birkeland and Störmer. They act as traps to high energy protons and electrons from the sun, which spill over at the poles to give the auroras which, as had been proved from observations made at about the same time during the International Geophysical Year (1957-8), appeared simultaneously at both the north and and the south pole.

ATMOSPHERIC DISPLAY The spectacular flashing coloured lights of the aurora led to many fanciful theories. This sixteenth-century print *(left)* explains the phenomenon as two armies fighting in the sky Auroras are now thought to be caused by high speed protons and electrons, which, having been discharged by the sun and trapped in the Van Allen radiation belts high above the earth, are then drawn towards the poles by the earth's magnetic fields. When they enter the magnetosphere *(right)*, the outer shell of the earth's atmosphere, the electrical charges held by both sets of particles react with the molecules of the air to make them luminous. An auroral display is shown in the illustration *(below)*.

Biology and Medicine

It would be reasonable to assume that biology and medicine were developed as sciences before all the others. Biology — the science of living things — would surely be the most likely study for primitive people who lived directly off the land. Plants and animals of every type were part of daily existence and were utilized in multitudes of ways. The problem of treating the sick arose wherever human beings were to be found. Indeed, there is evidence that the operation of trephination (cutting a hole in the head) was performed with success in prehistoric times, while the use of plants for medical purposes goes back so early that it would be pointless to attempt to find its origin. However, biology and medicine only became true sciences after the Renaissance, despite being close to this stage of development during the Greek civilization.

That the blossoming of both studies into true science came so late was mainly due to the same reasons as also made chemistry late. Simply, there was too much material to be assessed and examined. As a result of this, both biology and medicine were purely practical studies for a long time. Biological theory developed at first into what we should today call 'natural history', the study of the habits and habitats of plants and animals, together with details of the plants and animals themselves. In many instances drawings were compiled from dubious evidence, including travellers' stories. These were probably embellished with imaginary detail and told, in any case, of creatures half-glimpsed or imperfectly observed, and of plants whose nature and functions were poorly understood. Sometimes the confusion was such that the dividing line between plants and animals became hazy. The mandrake *(Mandragora)*, being a fork-shaped root, was thought to resemble the human form and supposed to scream if it was dragged from the ground. Some plants were even believed to give birth to animals; for instance, there was the 'barnacle goose' *(Branta leucopsis)* that was thought to be hatched from barnacles; in medieval Christendom, such geese were classified as 'fish' and could be eaten on Fridays.

In spite of the difficulties, a few characteristic similarities between some animals and plants were recognized in Ancient Greece. In Ancient China, too, some investigations were made into plants and their environment, but no fully fledged biological science emerged. Relationships were sought but it was difficult in the early stages to know how to look, to decide which features were relevant and which were not. Relationships which seem so obvious today were not clear in the past. There was no overall embracing theory of the development of plants and animals over time — a theory of an emerging evolution — to bind disparate facts together. Aristotle drew up a scale of nature, but his was a hierarchy of forms, not an evolutionary sequence.

GLASGOW
First aseptic surgery by Lister, 1860s

CAMBRIDGE
Nervous system studied by Sherrington, 19th/20th centuries
Discovery of the double helix formation of DNA by Crick and Watson, 20th century

LONDON
Pioneer work in microscopics by Hooke, 17th century
Discovery of circulation of the blood by Harvey, 1628
Hales' pioneering work in plant physics, 1727

BERKELEY
First use of vaccinations by Jenner, 18th century

DOWNE
Darwin's theory of evolution, 19th century

PARIS
Belon's work on marine biology, 16th century
Pioneering study of microbes and disease by Pasteur, 19th century

AMSTERDAM
Swammerdam's use of microscope to study insects, 17th century

DELFT
Pioneer work in microscopy by Leeuwenhoek, 17th/18th centuries

HORNBACH
Botanical work by Bock, 16th century

UPPSALA
Botanical classification devised by Linnaeus, 18th century

BERLIN
Study of chromosomes by von Waldeyer-Hartz, 1888

LEIPZIG
Roux's work in experimental embryology, 19th/20th centuries

JENA
Schwann's cell theory, 1839

TUBINGEN
Botanical work by Fuchs, 16th century

BRNO
Mendel's work on plant genetics, 1866

ZURICH
Gesner's zoological studies, 16th century

VIENNA
Pioneer work in asepsis by Semmelweis, 19th century

MONTPELLIER
Rondolet's work in marine biology, 16th century

PADUA
New study of the human body by Vesalius, 1543

BERNE
Brunfels' work in botany, 15th/16th centuries

BASEL
Pioneering work in experimental embryology by Hiss, 19th century

MADRID
Ramón y Cajal's work in neurology, 19th/20th centuries

ROME
Malpighi and Eustachio's studies of the human body, 16th century

COS
Important Greek medical school, 5th century BC

EPIDAUROS
Centre of Greek Asklepian medicine, c 500 BC

ATHENS
Aristotle's study of zoology, 4th century BC
Theophrastos' study of botany, 4th century BC

It is only too easy to look back with hindsight and imagine that Aristotle must have had some idea of progression. To do this would be wrong. It is important to avoid presuming the existence of later, modern ideas in earlier times; one of the ever-present dangers of historical work, and especially studies in the history of science, is to look at the past with preconceptions. It is only too easy to imagine an idea of the past to have possessed a particular relevance that it simply did not have.

Some progress was made in Greek times, although much was lost in the West after the decline of Greek culture, including the ability to observe and see plants or animals objectively. During the Renaissance a fresh look was taken at plants and animals, and this outlook was linked with the newly emerging physical sciences and came to be coloured and assisted by contemporary experimental techniques. The arrival of the microscope in the seventeenth century opened up a whole new biological world which, in the nineteenth cen-

DISCOVERIES AND CENTRES OF LEARNING Biology and medicine remained practical studies for a long time, partly because of the sheer amount of material to be analyzed and assessed. The Greeks came close to developing these areas into true sciences but much of their important work was lost or ignored after the destruction of the library and museum at Alexandria. In China, medicine developed along quite separate lines, and is only now being appreciated in the West. The publication in 1543 of Vesalius' *De Humani Corporis Fabrica (The Fabric of the Human Body)* was the true beginning of modern medicine. The development of the microscope was another landmark.

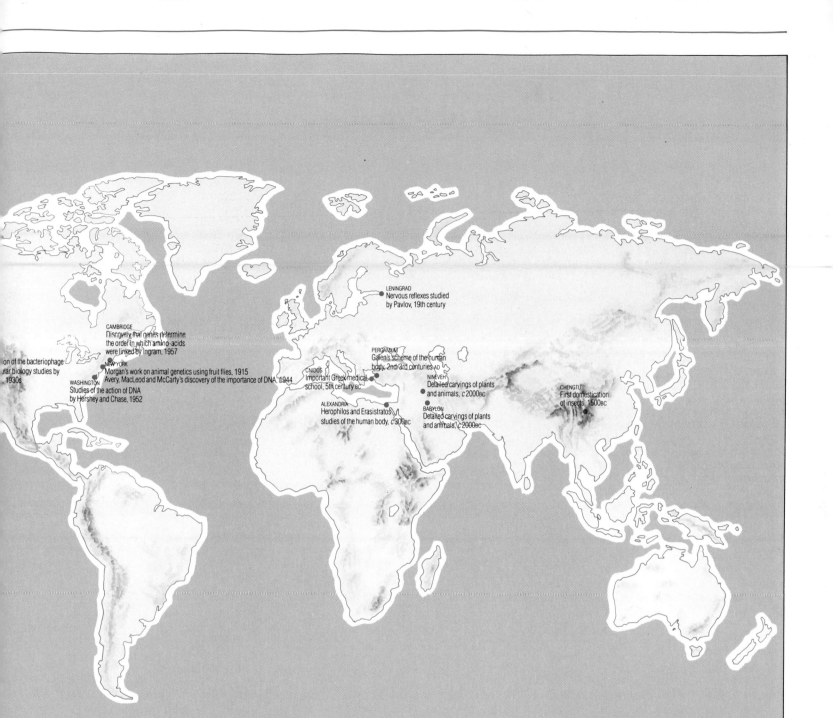

CAMBRIDGE
Discovery that genes determine
the order in which amino-acids
were linked by Ingram, 1957

...on of the bacteriophage
...ular biology studies by
...1930s

NEW YORK
Morgan's work on animal genetics using fruit flies, 1915
Avery, MacLeod and McCarty's discovery of the importance of DNA, 1944

WASHINGTON
Studies of the action of DNA
by Hershey and Chase, 1952

LENINGRAD
Nervous reflexes studied
by Pavlov, 19th century

PERGAMUM
Galen's scheme of the human
body, 2nd/3rd centuries AD

CNIDOS
Important Greek medical
school, 5th century BC

ALEXANDRIA
Herophilos and Erasistratos
studies of the human body, c 300BC

NINEVEH
Detailed carvings of plants
and animals, c 2000BC

BABYLON
Detailed carvings of plants
and animals, c 2000BC

CHENGTU
First domestication
of insects, 1500BC

tury, was to help most significantly with ideas of embryology. The new atomic theory of Dalton, once it had been developed by the organic chemists and the physicists of the late nineteenth and early twentieth centuries, was to prove vital to the development of molecular biology and the concept of the genetic code.

Regarding medicine, some basic investigations seem to have been made in Alexandria. The Greeks, it is interesting to learn, were concerned with psychological medicine as well as the treatment of physical ailments. In fact, at Alexandria some astonishing discoveries were made after research work was carried out on the human body, but the reports were lost and not rediscovered in the West until the scientific revolution. Interestingly, in China medicine developed along quite independent lines in many respects: they used non-vegetable drugs and also discovered acupuncture which is now receiving scientific investigation all over the world.

A great problem facing early investigative research in medicine was the fact that the dissection of human bodies was considered immoral, if it was not actually made illegal. In the West, between the time of the Alexandrian school of medical research and the Renaissance, a series of edicts was published to prevent human dissection. This, combined with people's strong belief in the validity of the analysis of the body by Aristotle (explained by the Greek surgeon Galen in the second century AD) meant that very little progress was made until the sixteenth century.

The new independent outlook, however, caused the Belgian surgeon Vesalius to overthrow the old ideas, his book *De Humani Corporis (The Fabric of the Human Body)* appeared in 1543, the same year as Copernicus' *De Revolutionibus*, and was equally startling. This marked the birth of modern medicine, with its wealth of discoveries and explanations. The high standards of modern surgery and medical treatment would not have been possible without this initial change of attitude.

Early Zoology

The study of animal life began in primitive times, as evidenced by cave paintings and carvings of animals, probably from some time in the Mesolithic Period (Middle Stone Age — about 8000BC to 2500BC) in the West. The paintings and carvings show that some animals were available for close study, although domestication may well have occurred 1,000 years earlier. In Ancient China, from about 1500BC, they began to domesticate insects beginning with the breeding of silk worms and, in Szechwan province, the scale insect *(Ericerus sinensis)* for its white wax, while other similar insects were cultivated for their dyes. The Chinese kept bees, as did most early civilizations, since these were a source of sugar, and also crickets, which were used for sport, rather as the West later used fighting cocks. It is to the Chinese that the credit must go for the earliest known method of biological plant protection, for by the third century AD they would hang bags containing ants (the species *Oecophylla smaragdina)* on trees against the depredations of mites, beetles and other pests — an ingenious method of control.

In Egypt and Mesopotamia, carvings and paintings make it evident that zoological knowledge was being accumulated all the time. For instance, when the Assyrians became the dominant power in Mesopotamia in the mid-eighth century BC, they soon began encouraging the sport of lion-hunting, and a bas-relief of this period shows a lioness whose hindquarters have been paralyzed by an arrow in the spine; the carving is clear evidence of careful observation. Other carvings illustrate the interest taken in animals of all kinds and in their behaviour, but so far it seems that the records of the time give no indication of any general ideas about animal species. By 1900BC, however, the Mesopotamians knew of over 30 different kinds of fish; they also made a basic classification of marine and land animals, the latter being divided into serpents, birds and four-legged creatures. These groups were then subdivided, which was a positive move towards the classification of species.

Zoology developed considerably during Greek times with many careful observations and also some intrepid generalizations about animals and their origins. Then, in the sixth century BC, the philosopher Anaximander suggested that all living creatures originated in the sea and, as time passed, some became surrounded by a husk or shell and found a new life on land, later shedding their shells and adapting to their new surroundings. This was an ingenious theory, based no doubt on observations; it was, in a sense, a primitive theory of evolution, although it must be noted that it contained no operating cause, no reason being given for the move from sea to land or for the change from one stage to another.

The greatest figure of Greek zoology was certainly Aristotle (384-322BC), although in medieval times and, indeed, until the nineteenth century, his biological achievements were almost forgotten, being overshadowed by his very important contributions towards an understanding of the nature of the physical world. The change from neglect to recognition seems to have come about in the 1850s, when the Swiss-American naturalist Louis Agassiz (1807-73) began to look more deeply into Aristotle's description of the habits of catfish *(Parasiluris Aristotelis).* Observing the breeding habits of this animal, Aristotle noted that once the eggs had been laid by the female catfish, she swims away and it is the male that remains behind guarding the eggs and the young 'for 40 or 50 days' until they are old enough to fend for themselves. Aristotle had also noticed that the

EARLY OBSERVATIONS Evidence in the form of paintings, reliefs and artefacts from the earliest civilizations show a strong curiosity about animal life. Favourite subjects were hunting scenes. This bas-relief from seventh-century BC Nineveh is a detail from Ashurbanipal's lion-hunt series *(below)*. Aside from the accurate depiction of the animal's physique, the relief also clearly shows the paralyzing effect of the arrows in the spine of the lioness. The reason for this was not known but the observation is correct.

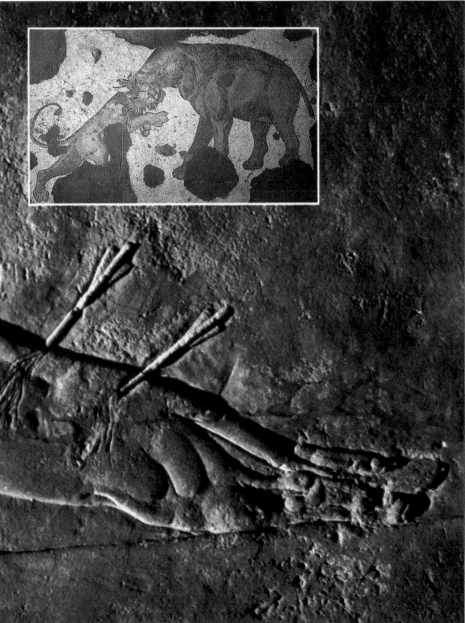

fish could emit 'a kind of muttering noise'. Yet European zoologists had not observed behaviour of this kind; the catfish they examined did not act in this way, although some could make a noise with their gill covers. Agassiz discovered that there exists a different species of catfish in the United States, and that these do behave just as Aristotle had described. Agassiz was also to show that the particular species observed by Aristotle was still behaving just as he had described.

Aristotle's study of the catfish was no isolated foray into marine biology; it was a subject that he pursued vigorously. He studied the torpedo (Torpedo ocellata) which gives electric shocks and was already well known in his own day, and the angler fish, giving meticulous descriptions of both, together with details of their behaviour. He also studied crabs and lobsters, observed the complete life cycle of the cuttlefish, and paid particular attention to octopuses, although, it was discovered in this century, he was mistaken over the behaviour of the closely related paper nautilus (Argonauta Argo). Whales, porpoises and dolphins he did not classify as fish, because they produce living young rather than eggs and are warm blooded; this was a penetrating decision that shows a considerable zoological insight. He noticed too that among the Selachii — a family of fish that includes sharks and rays — the female 'lays eggs within itself', the eggs being connected by an umbilical cord. Not until the nineteenth century was this observation confirmed, as was his discovery that among squids and cuttlefish — the 'Cephalopoda' — some males have an arm which is used for fertilizing the eggs of the female.

As for land animals, Aristotle was an expert on bees and their diseases, he discovered the compound stomach of ruminant animals, and it is clear that he carried out dissection himself. Moreover, Aristotle not only classified some 500 different kinds of animals, he also made some important biological generalizations — for instance, that no animal is endowed with more than one adequate system of defence, and that there is an inverse relationship between horns and teeth — as well as devising a scale of nature that started with plants and ascended by way of sponges, jellyfish, molluscs, fish, birds, reptiles and mammals to mankind. Obvious to us now, the scale was then an imaginative feat.

Aristotle came close to a true science of zoology, based on observation, dissection and a careful analysis of evidence leading to a general classification of living forms, coupled with ideas on the nature of life. Unfortunately, his monumental efforts were not followed up in the West after the collapse of Greek science. It is a mark of the failure of subsequent ages to arrive at efficient zoological methods of observation and analysis, that his stature in this field was not fully appreciated until comparatively recent times.

First Studies of Plants

The daunting variety of birds, fish and animals is well matched by the varied collection of plants worldwide. Even in one particular location the number of different plant species would have been quite bewildering to an early scientist. No attempt was made to classify or collate information for a long time, however; at first biological knowledge was simply a matter of survival. As tribes became settled rather than nomadic so they cultivated plants, and by selective breeding encouraged the production of strains that were suited to the environment and to their needs. This meant that there was an increasing awareness of plant life and of its wide variety. Evidence of careful observation in Egypt and Mesopotamia comes from paintings and carvings but, as plants also provided the main source of drugs used in medicine, knowledge about them had another dimension compared with studies of wildlife.

In Mesopotomia the date palm was important because it provided a staple diet, being rich, as we now know, in carbohydrate, protein, fat and mineral elements, and it is found frequently in carvings, often represented in a stylized way. With the vine, also shown frequently and with considerable accuracy, the fig and the pomegranate, the date palm was often associated with mystical and magical scenes, where these plants were shown with a king, and a priest or some other dignitary kneeling in attendance. One interesting carving of this type that appeared in various places depicted a stylized plant with mythical figures, half men and half eagles, on each side. These figures were shown holding out grapes or fruit or, in the case of the date palm, the male flower. Clearly, these symbolized fertility and the choice of the male flower of the date makes it seem probable that the Mesopotamians had some knowledge of the sexuality of some plants.

Other carvings display some careful botanical observation, especially those of pines and pine cones, one type of relief showing the general contour of the tree, another concentrating on the cones. The Madonna lily was frequently depicted, usually in a slightly formalized way, showing a stem with leaves surmounted by a triple-headed flower, while the lotus appeared in a variety of ways but always with an emphasis on the fruit.

In Ancient Greece we find a far more scientific attitude, with less emphasis on the magical qualities of fruit and flowers, especially from the latter part of the fourth century BC on. Aristotle did not confine his biological interests to animals, but embraced the 'vegetable kingdom' as well, although he did not advance botany as much as he did zoology. His system of souls — that everything alive either had a vegetable or nutritive soul, an animal or sensitive soul, or a human or rational soul — showed his interest not only in plants in general but also in their process of living and their place in nature. He noted that plants do not appear to

breathe and that they obtain their nourishment from the earth in, he believed, an already digested state (the earth acting as a 'stomach'). He saw no sex differentiation in plants, failing to appreciate stamens and pistils; the function of a plant was, he thought, to bear seeds and fruit, and some plants which did not do this aided others to ripen. Parasitical plants took no nourishment, or so Aristotle suggested. He considered that the longevity of trees was due to their low water content.

In botany Aristotle was outshone by his pupil Theophrastos (c371-c287BC), who took over the Lyceum, which Aristotle had founded. Indeed, Theophrastos is sometimes called 'the father of botany'. He is remembered now for his *Enquiry into Plants*, which in essence contains two kinds of material — tales about the uses of plants told to Theophrastos by travellers from distant countries and serious scientific work based on his own observations. The travellers' tales often contained fabulous and mystical overtones and are very different from the scientific approach of Aristotle, or even from that of Theophrastos himself when it comes to observation and classification.

To Theophrastos are due the technical terms 'carpos' (fruit), 'pericarpion' (seed vessel) and 'metra' (pith), while it was he who began a plant classification, dividing them into four groups — trees, shrubs, under-shrubs and herbs — depending on the number of stems and branches. In studying the germination and development of plants, he introduced two new terms which, like 'carp' and 'pericarp', are still in use today; these are 'monocotyledon' and 'dicotyledon' to describe those plants which sprout with one (mono-) or two (di-) seed leaves. Theophrastos also discussed the idea of plant sexuality, but his ideas on this were vague. Nevertheless, his separation of plants into

CHANGING ATTITUDES In Mesopotamia, certain plants, notably the date palm, were linked with mysticism. This bas-relief shows a magic tree bordered by two winged eagle-headed gods *(top)*. With the Renaissance, plant life was examined in a new, more scientific way. This illustration from Fuch's *De Historia Stirpium (The Natural History of Plants)* shows two artists drawing from nature *(centre)*. Another aspect of the new interest in botany was the popularity of herbals *(above)*.

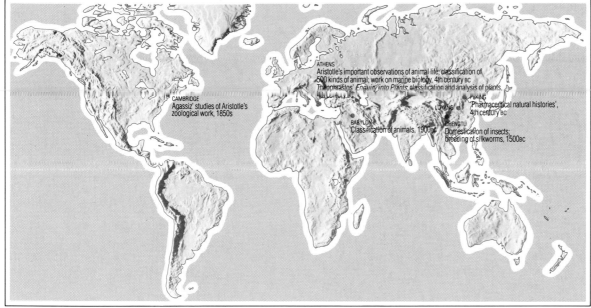

ATHENS
Aristotle's important observations of animal life; classification of
500 kinds of animal; work on marine biology, 4th century BC
Theophrastos' *Enquiry into Plants*, classification and analysis of plants,
4th century BC

CAMBRIDGE
Agassiz' studies of Aristotle's
zoological work, 1850s

PEKING
'Pharmaceutical natural histories',
4th century BC

LOYANG

BABYLON
Classification of animals, 1900BC

CHENGTU
Domestication of insects;
breeding of silkworms, 1500BC

EARLY BOTANY AND ZOOLOGY. The work of Aristotle and Theophrastos in Greece laid the foundations for the modern science of botany and zoology *(left)*. While extensive classifications of animals and plants were made in Mesopotamian civilizations and insects were domesticated in China as early as 1500BC, it was the Greek spirit of enquiry that first promoted a vigorous analysis of the observations that had been made.

RENAISSANCE APPROACH Albrecht Dürer (1471-1528), the German mathematician and artist, was influenced by the new observational attitude. His watercolour of grasses, *The Monumental Turf*, is as meticulously observed as any botanical illustration of the period *(below)*.

distinct parts was good; he recognized the root, stem, leaf, stipule and flower, although he did not distinguish between bulbs and tubers. Lastly, he not only discussed the medicinal uses of plants, but also described ideas on the geographical distribution of various species.

The distribution of plants and an extension of this, the association of different plants with underground mineral resources, were also studied in Ancient China. Part of the stimulation behind the work lay in the desire of the administration to know about all natural resources, a desire that also led to a study of the different kinds of soil best suited to different plants; the Chinese were thus the first to study soil science. In China, botany was aided by the very wide variety of plant species to be found there, far greater than anywhere in Europe.

The Chinese also took a scientific attitude to plants, breaking each plant down into separate parts, rather as Theophrastos did, and prepared many botanical writings, especially from the fourth century BC onwards. From the second century BC a vast number of 'pharmaceutical natural histories' appeared, setting out the medicinal uses of plants and minerals and even describing some medical products. Printing, invented in China in the tenth century AD, led to the publication of books containing fine and scientifically accurate drawings of plants; such progress was not made in Europe until the sixteenth century.

In China, with its vast, expanding population, two unusual aspects of botanical study were carried out. One concerned the investigation of the possibility of growing crops in regions outside their normal habitats — this began during the tenth century AD — and the other was the examination in the fourteenth century of which wild food plants could be used in times of famine.

The Microscopic World

The invention of the microscope is shrouded in at least as much doubt as surrounds that of the telescope. Magnifying glasses were familiar at least from the thirteenth century when the first spectacles appeared, but a magnifying glass is limited in the degree of magnification it can provide. However, as soon as the idea of combining lenses had arrived, the use of a magnifying lens to magnify the image of another lens seemed to catch on. Galileo (1564-1642) constructed these devices and by 1612 had presented some instruments to notable people.

The problem of the compound microscope (ie a magnifier with two or more lenses) was that it suffered very badly from chromatic aberration, so that everything observed was surrounded by coloured fringes; this made it extremely difficult to study minute detail. Attempts to minimize the defect led to the use of diaphragms to limit the area of the multiple lenses used; however, this technique reduced light available to the eye and limited the useful power of magnification. Not until the late 1820s was this problem overcome. Nevertheless, compound microscopes were used in the seventeenth and eighteenth centuries and some astonishing research carried out. This was partly due to Robert Hooke (1635-1703), who constructed a compound microscope and published his discoveries with it in his *Micrographia* (1665); this contained not only a lively text but a wonderful set of copperplate engravings of insects, plants and inanimate objects that he had examined. Hooke's book stimulated the new study of insect anatomy that was impossible before the advent of the microscope.

Medical men soon began to make use of the new instruments, and three of the first were the Italian Marcello Malpighi (1628-94), the Englishman Nehemiah Grew (1641-1712), and the Dutch physician Jan Swammerdam (1637-80). Malpighi made some medical advances with the microscope but, on the biological side, he studied the early development of the chick in a way not possible before. He also dissected the silkworm under the microscope with immense skill, and discovered that it had no lungs but breathed through tubes distributed throughout its body, which is a characteristic of all insects. He made some pioneering discoveries on the stems of plants. Grew spent a great deal of time investigating what can best be called vegetable anatomy. He saw that the tissues of the plants are really cellular — the existence of cells in cork had been discovered by Hooke who, incidentally, first used the term 'cell' in this context — but Grew's greatest discovery was that flowers are really the sexual organs of plants. He discovered the calyx, corolla, stamens and pistils and noticed that when the fertile part of the stamen opened it scattered 'many perfect globes..., sometimes of other figures, but always regular'. Thus he was first to observe pollen grains. He also gave details of the anatomy of the bean, publishing his results in his *Anatomy of Plants* in 1682.

Swammerdam was a superb dissector and practised this art under a microscope with conspicuous success. He discovered red corpuscles in the blood of frogs and also found that if a nerve were cut and the end stimulated then the muscle could be made to contract. However, he noticed that, contrary to popular opinion, the muscle's increase in volume was not due to the nerves containing a fluid that ran into the muscle on contraction. Study of nerves with the microscope confirmed the absence of fluid in the nerves, which he saw were not hollow tubes

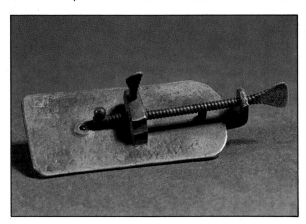

THE LOUSE Comparing the louse from Hooke's *Micrographia (below)* with one photographed (x80) under a modern microscope *(right)* reveals the precision of Hooke's observations.

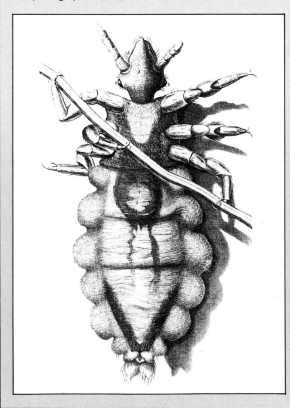

THE DEVELOPMENT OF THE MICROSCOPE Leeuwenhoek's contribution to microscopy was his design for single lens instruments, so bypassing the optical problems encountered in the design of compound microscopes *(far left)*. Despite their difficulties, compound microscopes were used in the seventeenth and eighteenth centuries to make some remarkable discoveries. Edmund Culpepper's microscope of 1730 is such an example *(left)*. Modern technology has produced microscopes of immense power, notably scanning electron microscopes, which are not limited by the power of optical lenses but use a stream of electrons controlled by electric or magentic fields. Instruments such as the giant electron microscope at Cambridge University have been used to reveal genetic material *(right)*.

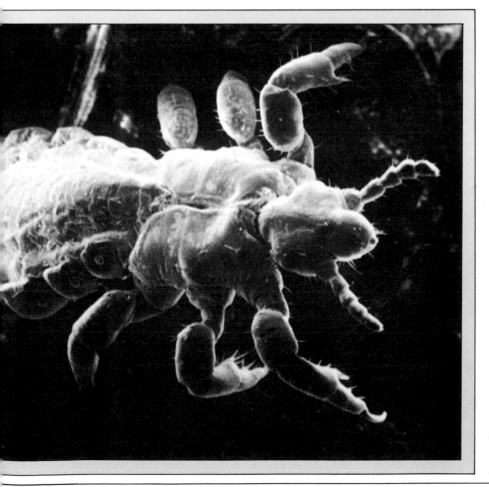

as was believed by most of his contemporaries.

Swammerdam's greatest achievement lay in his studies of insects. He dissected and examined wasps, ants, gnats, dragonflies and mayflies, describing their anatomies and comparing one with another. Although he published some of his results during his lifetime, his main work *Biblia Naturae (Bible of Nature)* only came out between 1737 and 1738, almost 40 years after his death. This book is still the finest collection of microscopic observations ever produced by one man, and contains an astonishing description of all the internal organs of the bee, as well as of the other insects he examined. It traces the development of the frog with further descriptions of his dissections of tadpoles. Swammerdam's work is the more remarkable considering the optical defects of the compound microscopes he used.

In an attempt to overcome the drawbacks of the compound microscope, the Dutch civil servant Antoni van Leeuwenhoek (1632-1723) designed his own single lens microscopes and with their use made the greatest impression on his contemporaries of all the early microscopists. He solved the optical problem by constructing single lenses that looked rather like pebbles. They had very short focal lengths which meant that they gave high magnifications, of the order of 270 or 300 times, sometimes more. With these instruments, van Leeuwenhoek was not only able to confirm Malpighi's work on frogs' blood, but also discovered red corpuscles in his own blood and then found that these were different, being circular, from the oval corpuscles in the blood of other mammals, birds and fish. Indeed, his microscopes were even able to show up the tiny nucleus in each corpuscle. He also studied those tiny animals, protozoa, and described the hydra, the rotifers found in rainwater and the single-celled volvox, noting how the young escaped from openings in the parent. Leeuwenhoek studied aphids and their life cycle, the development of the flea, and examined spermatazoa. Perhaps his most important discovery was that of bacteria; he described some as 'minute rods showing movement'.

After the enthusiasm of these early microscopists, work of this kind virtually ceased. Only with the advent of the achromatic or 'colour-free' microscope in the nineteenth century did things change. In the twentieth century the electron microscope was developed, the first complete instrument of this kind being made by L.L. Marton in Belgium in 1932; this made it possible to identify tiny particles of specimens. The reason for using electrons instead of a beam of light is to obtain higher magnifications and detect objects too small to be detected by light-waves. Whereas an optical microscope is limited to magnifications of the order of 2,500, the modern electron microscope can magnify 250,000 times and more, thus showing up basic genetic material.

New Ideas about Living Things

BOTANY AS A SCIENCE In the seventeenth century the new botanical observations were used as a basis for analysis and classification. John Ray produced an encyclopedia describing and classifying more than 17,000 varieties of plants *(below)*. The publication of Stephen Hale's *Vegetable Staticks* in 1727 saw the application of physics to botany *(below right)*.

Once the Renaissance was under way and the scientific revolution had channelled some of the new independence of outlook into the study of the natural world, biologists began to look afresh at both animals and plants. They rejected most of the fabulous stories surrounding living things, which so many medieval minds had accepted uncritically, and moved away from stylized pictures, preferring to record things objectively. The herbals, which had begun to appear in the fourth century BC and contained descriptions of plants from a medicinal point of view, became a vehicle for a revival of botany in the sixteenth century. First of all, as in the *Great Herbal* published in London in 1526, the first printed herbal in the West, the evidence was a hotchpotch of tradition and observation, drawing on Greek and Islamic sources, as well as western medieval descriptions. Yet it contained some useful material and accurate descriptions and was aimed at a wide readership, which had not been the case with the French *Le Grand Herbier* on which it was based. A second printing of the *Great Herbal* was called for within three years. Another aspect of the revival of interest in botany was the establishment in the mid-sixteenth century of botanical gardens by some universities, where a study of botany became independent of the art of medicine. The universities of Padua and Pisa were the first to do this, but the idea soon spread; the ready examination of plants themselves rather than reliance on second-hand descriptions was made possible in this way.

Into this new botanical climate came a host of botanists, among them a German school — the 'German fathers of botany' — composed of Otto Brunfels (c 1489-1534), Jerome Bock (1498-1554) and Leonhard Fuchs (1501-66). Brunfels, who became town physician of Berne, produced in 1530 the famous *Herbarum Vivae Eicones (Living Illustrations of Plants)* which drew heavily on the work of the Greek botanist Dioscorides (who lived in the first century AD), and if not original in some aspects, it created a stir because of its illustrations. Drawn by Hans Weiditz and his assistants, the illustrations described exactly what was visible, not what the herbalist thought a reader should or might see, and so made public a truly observational approach. Bock (or Hieronymus Tragus as he was often known), a school-teacher turned medical man and then preacher, was also a spare-time botanist, and he is also known for a herbal, the *Neue Kreütterbuch (New Plant Book)*, which came out first in 1539 without illustrations and then seven years later in an illustrated edition. Although its pictures were not as fine as those in Brunfels' *Herbarum*, the text was far superior, Bock trying to discern some relationships between different plants, noting their habitat and giving brief life histories. His book was also written in German and could therefore reach a far wider readership than Brunfels'. Fuchs, the third member of the trio, is perhaps the best known, for the *fuchsia* is named after him. The results of his work were enshrined in *De Historia Stirpium (The Natural History of Plants)* in 1542. This was based to a great extent on Dioscorides, but is notable both because of its outstanding illustrations from life and the fact that in it Fuchs tried to establish a basic botanical terminology.

Other botanists were at work besides the 'German fathers', extending the knowledge of species and broadening the interest from just the medicinal uses to a wider more purely scientific viewpoint. In consequence, by the early seventeenth century, a vast new corpus of material was ready. This, together with his own observations, was used by John Ray (1627-1705) to try to find a new way to classify plants; between 1686 and 1704 he produced the encyclopedic *Historia Generalis Plantarum (A General Account of Plants)*, describing more than 17,000 varieties and classifying them according to fruit, then flowers and, lastly, leaf. Meanwhile, the Englishman, Nehemiah Grew had broadened botanical studies by using the newly-invented microscope, and early in the

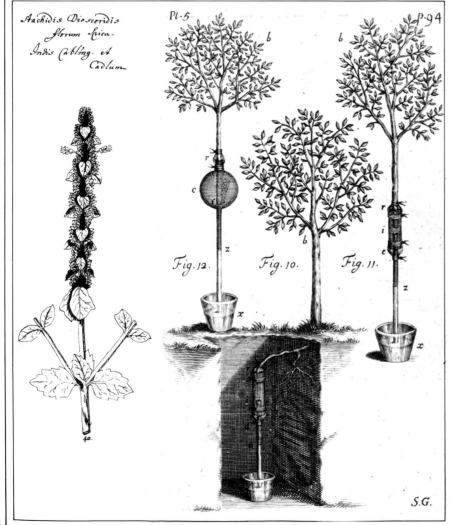

next century Stephen Hales applied basic physics to botany with his *Vegetable Staticks* (1727), in which he discussed sap pressure and other physical matters that opened up new light on plant life.

John Ray's attempt to find a new classification was not confined to plants. He also classified animals according to whether they had blood or not, or, as we should say, into vertebrates (possessing a backbone — mammals, birds and fish) and invertebrates (without a backbone — insects and shellfish). He certainly had much new material on which to draw, for during the sixteenth century a school of 'encyclopedic naturalists' — notably Pierre Belon (1517-64), Guillaume Rondelet (1507-66) and Conrad Gesner (1516-65) — had amassed a great deal of information. Belon wrote extensively on marine biology and also on birds, his *L'Histoire de la Nature des Oyseaux* (1555) becoming famous because it was the first book on comparative anatomy, in this case discussing the skeletons and organs of birds and human beings.

Rondelet was also concerned with marine biology and extended the number of marine animals known. Equally important, he realized that they all require air whether they have lungs or gills, and was the first to describe the swim bladder in fresh water fish. He made the first dissection of an invertebrate sea creature — the urchin — and made some comparisons between dolphins, pigs and human beings.

Of these three naturalists the most important was probably Gesner, who collected and collated a vast amount of material which, duly discussed, appeared in 1587 in his five-volume *Historiae Animalium (Account of Animals)*, 22 years after his death. He also prepared a companion *Opera Botanica (Botanical Works)* which again came out posthumously.

In both his vast treatises Gesner made new attempts at classification. This was important if proper relationships between living things were to be established; it had another importance during the sixteenth, seventeenth and eighteenth centuries because of the general opinion was that there was only one 'correct' classification, and this would echo God's own divine design. It was a view fervently held by that greatest of all classifiers, the Swede Carl von Linné (Linnaeus) (1707-78), who in 1735 published the first edition of his *Systema Naturae (System of Nature)* in which he proposed a system that, in 1758, he had developed into a binomial (two-name) system. Here, each animal or plant is assigned to a particular 'genus' and 'species'. Thus the genus *Elephans* tells us that the creature is an elephant of which there are now two different species, *Elephans Indicus* (the Indian elephant) and *Elephans Africanus* (the African elephant). This system is still in use today, although its divine nature is not now accepted.

TAXONOMY Classification of living things is not just a way of organizing information; it reflects what is known about relationships between different forms of life. The system devised by Linnaeus in the eighteenth century is still used today. Linnaeus devised a hierarchy based on shared physical characteristics; the fundamental unit being the species. A species is usually defined as a particular group whose members, if they mate together, are capable of producing fertile offspring. Each different animal or plant is assigned a name consisting of a genus name followed by a species name. In the case of the elephant, two different species are now recognized, both members of the genus *Elephans*: the African elephant *(Elephans Africanus)* *(above left)* and the Indian elephant *(Elephans Indicus)* *(above)*.

Theories of Evolution and Heredity

Not all biologists accept the view that the ultimate classification system would reveal the divine plan of nature. To begin with, the chief rebels against this opinion were to be found in France, where the eighteenth-century Enlightenment questioned the whole concept of divine intervention and promoted a mechanistic outlook. Many doubted whether species were fixed once and for all, the leaders of this opinion being the mathematician Pierre Maupertius (1698-1759) and the notable biologist, the Compte de Buffon (1707-88). Both based their arguments on ideas of embryology and on genetics. Buffon was a great observer of nature and he amassed a vast amount of biological material which was published in his *Histoire Naturelle (Natural History)* that appeared between 1749 and 1788, in no less than 36 volumes. In this he suggested not only that species changed but that there might be some common

ancestor for apes, quadrupeds and mankind. To support his contention he pointed out that there were certain organs in humans as well as animals which seemed to have no use and, he thought, therefore indicated some kind of change. To decide the matter more evidence was, however, required.

At the turn of the nineteenth century two men, Erasmus Darwin (1732-1802) and Jean Lamarck (1744-1829), published books supporting an evolutionary outlook. Darwin was a practising physician, a naturalist and, incidentally, a poet who was taken with an evolutionary outlook. He argued that the structure of an animal determined the way in which it could act and then, since all creatures possessed 'lust, hunger and a desire for security', they would be bound to alter behaviour and thus structure if their physical surroundings changed. It was a novel approach which he published in two

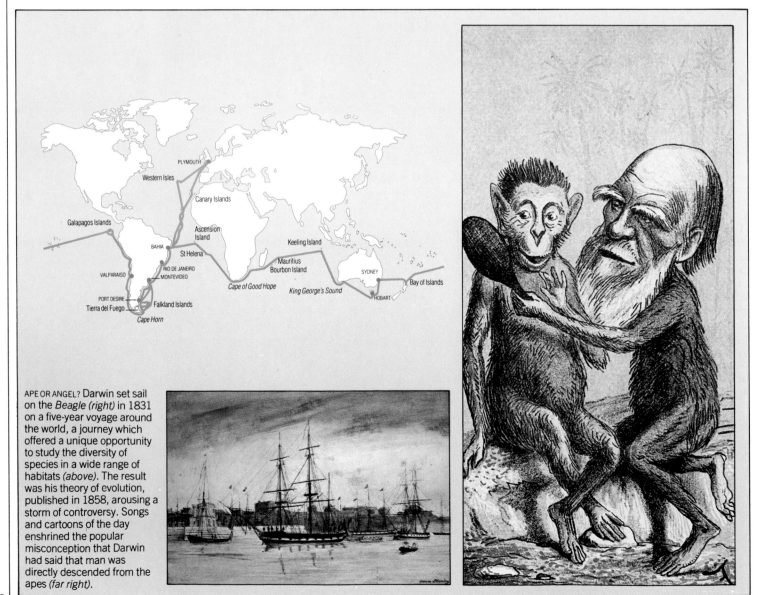

APE OR ANGEL? Darwin set sail on the *Beagle (right)* in 1831 on a five-year voyage around the world, a journey which offered a unique opportunity to study the diversity of species in a wide range of habitats *(above)*. The result was his theory of evolution, published in 1858, arousing a storm of controversy. Songs and cartoons of the day enshrined the popular misconception that Darwin had said that man was directly descended from the apes *(far right)*.

volumes in 1794· and 1796 under the title *Zoonomia, or the Laws of Organic Life.*

Jean Lamarck was forced by circumstances to work in a bank in Paris rather than take up a medical career. He did, however, take up botany and became so interested in the subject that he managed to study at the Jardin du Roi, the royal botanical gardens; from there, 10 years later, he was able to present an immense list of French plants to the *Academie des Sciences,* which elected him a member. Botany was in fashion in Paris, and Lamarck was given a position in the Jardin and, after the French Revolution, in the new Museum of Natural History. His duty was to classify the Museum's collection and in this he had the help of Georges Cuvier (1769-1832) who was an expert in comparative anatomy, but who firmly believed in the fixity of species.

Led by the differences between fossils and modern forms of animals, Lamarck became convinced that species did change, and he then set himself the task of discovering why they did so. Soon after Lamarck's appointment to the Museum, Hutton's theory of slow geological change was published. Lamarck readily accepted this, concluding that animal species changed according to ordinary physical laws as a result of their response to changing conditions in their environment. The giraffe had a long neck, he pointed out, because previous generations had stretched for leaves almost beyond their reach. What is more, he believed each generation inherited the new characteristics acquired by the parents. He published his views in two books, *Système des Animaux sans Vertèbres (System of Invertebrate Animals)* (1801) and *Philosophie Zoologique (Zoological Philosophy)* (1809). But when he died 20 years later, Cuvier, whose own reputation had become immense, wrote an unsympathetic obituary and in due course Lamarck's ideas, which had already received criticism and even ridicule, became ignored.

To become generally accepted, evolutionary theory required some deep rethinking, especially in view of the attacks of Cuvier and others, and it was Charles Darwin (1809-82), the grandson of Erasmus Darwin, who was to achieve this. Sent to Edinburgh to read medicine, he found the subject distasteful and moved to Cambridge to prepare for the Church. However, he seems to have spent much of his time there collecting beetles, of which he discovered many rare species, and in studying botany and geology. When in August 1831 a request came for a naturalist to sail on the *Beagle,* which was to survey the South American coastline, the university's professor of botany recommended Darwin as a suitable person. He set sail at the end of the year.

Taking the first volume of Lyell's *Principles of Geology* with him, Darwin studied a wealth of phenomena in both geology and biology over the next five years, and was convinced, on his

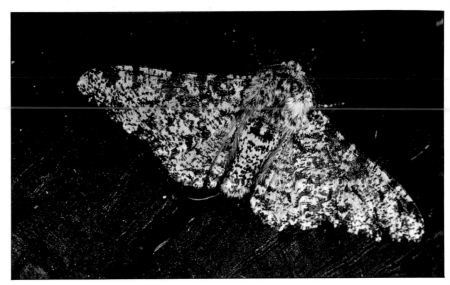

return, of the truth of the doctrine of gradual change. One important study he made was that of coral reefs. Due to his knowledge of the way in which corals build, he found enough other evidence to show that slow subsidence is a geological fact. There was also biological evidence of animals, basically similar but showing slight differences, replacing each other as he travelled from south to north, and the variations in the finches of the Galapagos islands made it clear that they had developed from one common ancestor.

Darwin became certain in his own mind that species did change. Selective breeding of the fittest would produce similar results to natural evolution, he decided, and he realized that a species of animal will become extinct if not well adapted to the environment. Since changes will occur from one generation to another, only those best adapted to the surrounding conditions will flourish and multiply. Later, in 1838, while still considering the problem, Darwin read *An Essay on the Principle of Population* by the Reverend Thomas Malthus in which the author argued that, unchecked, a population would double every 25 years, thus bringing a pressure on resources greater in degree than Darwin had ever imagined. He realized then that there was a natural selection process at work; it chose those creatures most fitted to survive or live in changed surroundings.

Darwin's famous *On the Origin of Species* came out in July 1858. In it he traced the origin of species back in time and suggested four or five original types of animal from which the rest could have evolved; he also showed how these changes could have come about. Darwin gave a physical cause for the variation of species which no other evolutionist had been able to do. The immense variety of nature was at last seen to be governed by a basic scientific principle which, in spite of criticisms and objections, has unified the whole of biological science.

ADAPTATION AND HEREDITY The peppered moth *(Biston betularia)* is a good example of adaptation. The original light form *(above)* has a protective colouration which acts as camouflage when the moth rests on lichened rock surfaces. Since industrialization, a dark form of the moth has also evolved, in response to blackened, polluted surfaces. Lamarck was one of the first to put forward the idea that acquired traits are inheritable — for example, giraffes have long necks because they and their forebears reached up to browse on trees *(below).*

Genetics

The whole concept of the evolution and change of every species brought to the fore a number of biological questions that had been simmering for some time. Jean Lamarck (1744-1829) had suggested that a change caused by the environment would then become an inherited characteristic, while Charles Darwin (1809-82) believed that only the changed species survived. All the same, discovering precisely what it is that is handed on from one generation to the next, and indeed deciding what it is that causes an animal to reproduce its own kind and not offspring of some quite different species, or why children display family resemblances, proved a fascinating source of enquiry.

The publication of Darwin's *On the Origin of Species* gave a truly scientific basis for an evolutionary outlook and stimulated much work in animal and plant morphology (the study of their form and structure). This occurred because it was thought that an understanding of evolutionary and genetic processes would benefit by this kind of approach; one of the leaders was the German zoologist Ernst Haeckel (1834-1919). Haeckel, even though a dedicated Christian, became a staunch supporter of Darwin's theory; he was not one of those who had vociferously attacked the theory because it did

not accord with the description of a once-and-for-all divine Creation as given in the Scriptures. Haeckel was a strong believer in the attitude which looked on living things as biological machines. Support of Darwin set him off on a close study of the comparative anatomy of human and animal species, with the result that he devised a 'pedigree' of living things. This began with protozoa like the amoeba, moved up through invertebrate animals — worms, molluscs, sponges, insects etc — thence to vertebrates — snakes, reptiles, fish etc — and on to mammals, crowned by man at the top. It was a kind of family tree and, in fact, was drawn out as such in his book *(Generelle Morphologie der Organismen (General Morphology of Organisms)* which came out in 1886, only 12 years afer Darwin's *On the Origin of Species*.

Studying comparative anatomy was, however, only one way to delve deeper into the consequences of the new theory of evolution. Another approach was to study the changes that occurred in experimental animals and in plants. One of the most famous workers in this field was the Czechoslovakian monk Gregor Mendel (1822-84) who in the 1850s and 1860s carried out a series of experiments in plant hybridization. Mendel had become dissatisfied with current ideas to explain all the varieties and changes he observed in plants, and it was this that set him off on his research programme of pea hybridization. He took strains of the ordinary edible pea and crossed them. To understand his astonishing results it is most convenient to consider one characteristic in isolation — the factor of tallness. When he crossed a tall and a dwarf type, the offspring were all tall like the tall parent and not small in size as was the expected result of such cross-breeding. Tallness seemed to be the dominant characteristic. However, in the next generation of pea, which he bred from the hybrids, about one quarter were short and three-quarters were tall; the 'recessive' characteristic of shortness had reappeared. The dwarfs went on breeding dwarf peas but the tall plants bred offspring one-third of which were tall and remained tall through subsequent generations, but the remaining two-thirds again gave dwarfs (one-quarter) and tall peas (three-quarters). These divisions continued in still later generations of the peas.

Mendel explained the results by saying that each pea can contain two inheritance factors — tallness and dwarfness. If these are one dominant and one recessive or two dominant, then offspring will show the dominant factor, but if both factors are recessive then the offspring display the recessive factor. But whichever result occurs, the various characteristics are handed on unchanged.

Mendel published his work, which covered the study of seven characteristics, in 1866, but they remained buried in the pages of an obscure book until the beginning of the twentieth century. One of those who brought them to light in

HUMAN CHROMOSOMES Each cell, except the ovum and sperm, contains 46 chromosomes in 23 pairs. One chromosome of each pair comes from the mother; the other comes from the father. The twenty-third pair determines sex: in men, this pair consists of a large X and small Y sex chromosome; in women, the pair consists of two large X sex chromosomes. Chromosomes are the means by which genetic information is stored and carried from one generation to the next.

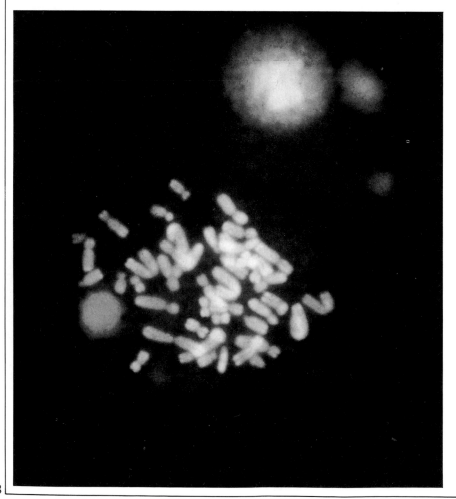

1900 was a Dutch biologist Hugo de Vries (1848-1935). De Vries had already carried out some biological research of his own, particularly on primroses. He noticed that two different strains appeared side by side in a field and he then bred from them; both bred the same but when crossed, three different types emerged which were different enough to represent a new species. He came to the important conclusion that small changes did not lead to a new species but that the change occurred in a large jump that he called a 'mutation'. He went on to publish these results during the period between 1901 and 1903.

Further evidence about inherited characteristics came in 1910 from New York where the American biologist William Morgan (1866-1945) had been breeding fruit-flies. The particular species he used — *Drosophila melanogaster* — breeds very quickly, one generation following another every 10 days, so they were excellent for observing hereditary changes, a year's experiments being able to provide valuable results. As Morgan proceeded with his studies some unexpected results emerged which were more complex than those of Mendel or de Vries: the inherited characteristics did not always seem to work in-

dependently but to be variously linked to the sex of both parents.

Morgan did not work alone and with his colleagues Alfred Sturtevant (1891-1970), Hermann Muller (1890-1967) and Calvin Bridges (1889-1938), he was able to conclude that Mendel's hereditary characteristics seemed to be actual physical particles; they then discussed just how these could be carried on 'chromosomes' which were to be found in the nucleus of germinating cells passed by parents to offspring. Morgan's team called these particles 'genes' (a name derived from the root of the Greek word for birth).

The gene seemed to most biologists an admirable explanation of all the results of the genetic experiments of Mendel, de Vries and Morgan's team, as well as those conducted by others, although there were some who did not believe in their existence, some who did not favour the handing on of inherited characteristics but preferred to put everything down to environmental factors. Certainly, the Morgan team's gene was only a theoretical possibility in 1915, the time it was proposed; it was not until 1960 that an actual gene was isolated experimentally and its physical existence proved.

MENDELIAN INHERITANCE This illustration, published in 1912, around the time when Mendel's work was rediscovered, shows the second-generation results of crossing green with yellow peas. Black represents the yellow peas; white the green peas.

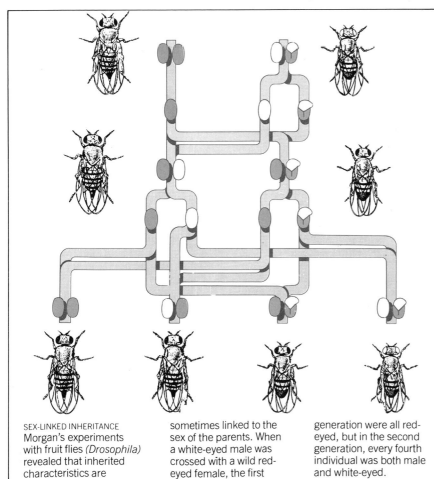

SEX-LINKED INHERITANCE Morgan's experiments with fruit flies (Drosophila) revealed that inherited characteristics are sometimes linked to the sex of the parents. When a white-eyed male was crossed with a wild red-eyed female, the first generation were all red-eyed, but in the second generation, every fourth individual was both male and white-eyed.

Molecular Biology

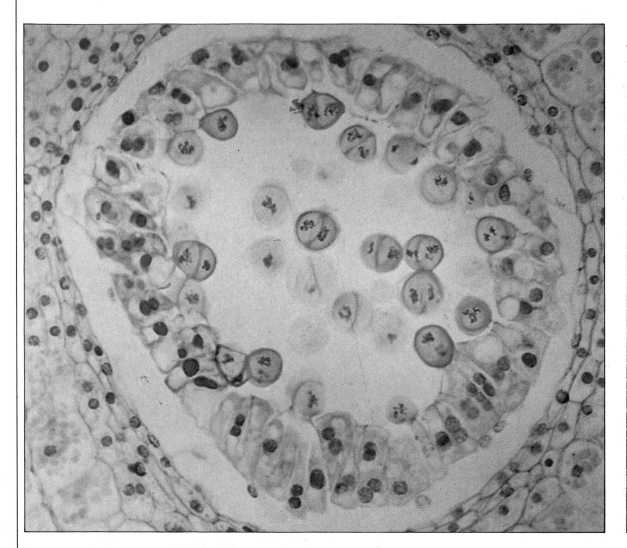

The realization in the latter half of the nineteenth century that organic materials were composed of complex molecules was a great step forward, while the appreciation that those molecules could be of immense size with huge molecular weights opened up new possibilities for understanding the chemical processes which occur in living things. The development during the same century of the achromatic microscope meant that high magnifications could be used without the image being degraded by the presence of coloured fringes.

The improved microscope brought about an important development in the 1870s and 1880s: those interested in germination were able to look in some detail on the complex nucleus of the cell. However, in doing so they faced a difficult problem: the components of the nucleus are transparent, with the result that it was difficult or impossible to pick them out. However a technique was developed of staining the specimen to be examined, so that the different components took up different amounts of stain and could be identified when observed through a microscope. When staining was done on the cells in question, one material in particular

became a strong colour; thread-like in appearance it seemed of considerable importance because the threads were seen to be transferred when cells divided during reproduction. In 1888, Wilhelm von Waldeyer-Hartz (1836-1921), an anatomist who had been investigating the nucleus, named the threads 'chromosomes' after the dye chromatin which had been used as the stain. Later research by Morgan and his team made it seem likely that genes were distributed along the thread-like chromosomes, although no microscope was powerful enough to show them up.

Assuming the real existence of genes, the British physician and biochemist Archibald Garrod (1892-1968), who was investigating human metabolism (the chemical changes in cells which provide energy for vital processes), suggested in 1909 that genes act by stopping certain steps in metabolic processes — in other words that genes affect what goes on in a cell — although nothing was done about this for the next 20 years. Only in the 1930s did the geneticist George Beadle and the microbiologist George Tatum take the matter up in the United States. Using a bread mould suffused

CELL THEORY At one time it was believed that the growing tip or bud of a plant was present inside the plant, microscopic in size, and then simply grew larger. With improvements in microscopes in the nineteenth century, it was realized that the tissue of the plant itself forms the bud, which subsequently grows, as shown in this photograph of cells at the tip of an onion *(above left)*.

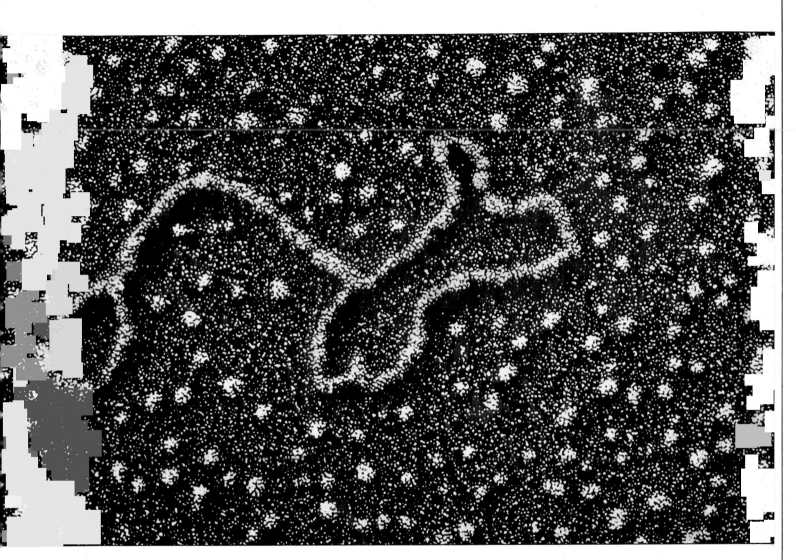

with the bacterium *Neurospora*, whose metabolism could be studied without too much difficulty, they not only confirmed Garrod's discovery but also found that each gene controlled the synthesis of a particular enzyme. Over a decade later, mainly in the 1950s, further studies were made elsewhere on sickle-cell anaemia, an illness which affects the red blood corpuscles, and it was finally found in 1957 by Vernon Ingram, again in the United States, that genes determine the order in which amino-acids are linked together.

By the late 1950s it was becoming clear that the complex molecules of living things were responsible for all vital processes and that genes, whose existence by then seemed virtually confirmed, could exercise powerful controlling functions. This subject of molecular biology — a combination of biochemistry and genetics — was also helped by two quite separate discoveries. One was the use of the technique of X-ray analysis of crystals devised by the Braggs, the other due to research carried out in the later 1930s by the German Max Delbrück, an atomic physicist turned biologist. Working in the United States, Delbrück introduced the

'bacteriophage' — a creature that attacks bacteria — as a research tool; he did this for a number of reasons. First of all the bacteriophage is easy to grow — many millions can be cultured in a small space — and it breeds rapidly, one generation following another every 20 or 30 minutes. But the bacteriophage has other advantages as an 'experimental animal', which arise from its chemical nature. It is a virus and thus an extremely simple creature because it consists of only two molecules — one a protein molecule and one a nucleic acid — and this means that the behaviour of these substances can be followed in detail during processes like its reproduction.

Nucleic acids are polymers, (substances whose component parts are smaller molecules or 'monomers'), and are composed of 'purines' (two-ringed structures of carbon and nitrogen with some other atoms) and 'pyrimidines' (molecules with a single carbon-nitrogen ring structure). They had been discovered in 1869 by the German organic chemist Friedrich Miescher, but it was not until well into the twentieth century that their significance in matters of heredity began to be appreciated. Instead,

GENETIC ENGINEERING The techniques which have brought genetic engineering into the realm of possibility have only been developed over the last decade. This photograph shows the molecule of DNA used in the first successful experiment in this field, carried out in 1973 by Professor Stanley Cohen and colleagues at Stanford University. The loop centre is a plasmid. This can replicate itself and can be used to carry genetic information from one cell to another. In this crucial experiment, two plasmids were cut up, a composite code constructed and the composite then placed back into a living cell.

THE DOUBLE HELIX OF DNA
Chromosomes are composed of tiny strands of protein wrapped in spirals of the nucleic acid DNA (deoxyribonucleic acid). The discovery of the structure of the DNA molecule was made by Crick and Watson at Cambridge University in 1953. The DNA molecule was found to be similar to a spiral staircase, with four types of 'steps'. The steps are chemical bonds which can be repeated in any order and in any number, making a string of different combinations. Each combination is a gene; each gene plays a role in the function of the cell.

proteins had been the substances on which chemists and particularly biochemists had concentrated their attention, because their component amino-acids, which could be arrranged in a wide variety of ways, seemed ideally suited to be carriers of genetic information. Miescher thought that the nucleic acids had great potential as information carriers but his ideas were largely ignored; it was only in the 1940s, after these acids were at last seen to be polymers with nitrogen playing a part in the ring formation of the component molecules, that interest in their possibility as genetic information carrying was appreciated.

Returning to the use of bacteriophages, research began to show many interesting things when their action in killing bacteria was investigated. Each bacteriophage was built up with a protein 'skin' inside which was the nucleic acid. All were shaped like a syringe, the smaller end of which becomes attached to the outer skin of a bacterium, after which the bacteriophage inserts its nucleic acid into the bacterium itself. This foreign nucleic acid then takes over; bacterial cells are no longer generated and, instead, viruses in the form of new bacteriophages are produced. These burst out from the bacterium to wreak havoc on the other bacteria. While studying the action, it was also discovered that the bacteriophage's nucleic acids undergo changes and that different strains are produced; these are capable of recombining.

All this was of greater significance than those immediately concerned were able to realize, because in the 1930s interest in proteins as genetic carriers was still paramount among the scientists concerned with bacteriophage research. By the 1940s, however, new research by three American biochemists was beginning to point to the significance of nucleic acids. Following up some work of the British microbiologist Frederick Griffith, who in 1928 discovered that if a benign type of bacterium is injected into an animal at the same time as a dead virulent type, some of the bacteria become virulent. Those concerned were Oswald Avery, Colin MacLeod and Maclyn McCarty, and it was they who, in 1944, made an important discovery when they tried to find what it was that passed from the dead virulent bacteria to infect some of the living benign ones. With proteins still in mind, for they knew that most of the material of chromosomes was protein, they isolated proteins from the dead but virulent strains of bacteria and placed these into cultures of the living benign bacteria. Yet none had any effect; the benign bacteria flourished. However, in the end, they isolated an active agent that transformed some of the benign bacteria, and chemical analysis showed it was not a protein but a nucleic acid. It was the now famous deoxyribonucleic acid, DNA. They found this was the material capable of transforming one type of bacterium into another. Only

then did the three scientists concede that DNA might be the 'fundamental unit' of transformation, but they could not go so far as to say that it was the substance of which genes were composed. Only in the 1950s, when it was discovered that the bacteriophage left its protein skin untouched but made its killing by inserting DNA, did the bias change.

Further detailed studies of what happened to the DNA during the bacteriophage's action were then carried out. The American biologists Alfred Hershey and Martha Chase examined precisely what happened to the molecules involved and in 1952, after showing that the protein skin remained unchanged, they discovered that the DNA behaved by processes already known to biochemists. The molecule of DNA was able to act as a catalyst — a substance aiding a chemical reaction despite not being a part of that reaction — in the first place aiding some of the early stages of the formation or self-duplication of DNA molecules, and then, secondly, helping the formation or breakdown of other but different molecules. Thus the DNA from the bacteriophage was able to duplicate itself many times. It was also able to assist in the build-up of the bacteriophage skin proteins. The exact details of how these processes occurred was, however, not yet known.

Meanwhile, some important work at Cambridge University was being carried out on two related proteins, the substance haemoglobin (the chief molecule for carrying oxygen within red blood cells) and myoglobin (a molecule of similar shape that carries oxygen in the cells of muscle tissue). John Kendrew (b 1917) and Max Perutz (b 1914) examined these substances using the X-ray crystallographic techniques devised in the very laboratory, the Cavendish, where they worked. However, using the technique for very complex molecules, they faced considerable problems because the patterns of atoms shown up by X-rays could be interpreted in a number of ways. Kendrew and Perutz had to use knowledge of the chemical details and chemical reactions of the substances in order to supplement the X-ray information; only in this way could they fathom out the structures. By the early 1960s, they were able to show that these two proteins were immensely complex, that there existed not only a flat ring of atoms to which oxygen became attached, but also that this group was tucked away in a fold on the molecule's surface. Clearly, the whole of their research in the 1950s had shown that recognizing the three-dimensional structure of the molecule was vitally important to understanding its behaviour.

All this research — the significance of three-dimensional structure and the importance of nucleic acids, particularly of DNA, in genetical results — began to come together. In the early 1950s the English biophysicist Francis Crick (b 1916), who had done some work with Kendrew and Perutz, and a young American biologist,

James Watson (b 1928) decided that the evidence of Avery and his colleagues as well as other work, led to some exciting conclusions. A gene, they thought, must be some kind of molecule and DNA a hereditary material. Their problem was to determine the full nature of the gene molecule, see where DNA came into the picture, and find out its precise biological function. In this way they were helped by some research being conducted in London University's King's College. Here, from the mid-1940s, the biophysicist Maurice Wilkins had been examining X-ray diffraction patterns of DNA, a difficult task because it is not easy to prepare crystals from DNA.

From the evidence available to them, Crick and Watson began to try to build up a model of the DNA molecule that would satisfy two requirements: first, it should fit in with the X-ray diffraction picture and, secondly, it should account for the chemical behaviour shown up in the experiments on bacteriophages and bacteria. Regarding the structure given by X-rays, it was already clear that the molecule seemed to be built up in layers stacked in a spiral fashion on top of each other. Indeed, a spiral scheme for proteins had already been discovered in 1950 by the American chemist Linus Pauling (b 1901). It was also evident that there was a 'spine' of sugar-phosphate molecules running throughout the entire length of the DNA molecule.

In working out the details of the molecule, Crick and Watson had also to determine the forces between the atoms in order to be sure that the molecule they devised would actually hold together. In this they were helped by the mathematician John Griffith, who worked out that the chemical bases (ie water-soluble compounds capable of turning acids into salts) of different but not similar kinds attract one another. By 1952 Crick realized that the pairing of unlike bases was to be the fundamental structure of the DNA molecule, and then he and Watson worked out possibilities which they tested against the X-ray diffraction results. By early in 1953 it was evident that the molecule could be composed of two strands and, after a discussion with the American chemist Jerry Donohue, they realized that the bases were bonded by hydrogen atoms, and that the purine and pyrimine bases were the links. Their picture was complete and in April they announced their results. The DNA molecule was a double helix, rather like a spiral staircase, with paired bases for the 'steps'.

It was also realized that each DNA strand could act as a holder or jig, on which a 'message carrying' nucleic acid could be formed and, within the next decade, the actual 'coding' process and the part played by the nucleic acid RNA (ribonucleic acid) was discovered. The chemical basis of genes, and so of genetics, had been uncovered.

MODERN LABORATORY Today biochemical research is carried out using a variety of sophisticated equipment. In a modern laboratory this is likely to include chromatographic and other analytical equipment including spectrometers, microscopes and delicate weighing apparatus.

Embryology

One long-standing question facing biologists has been the way in which creatures bring forth their offspring. As Aristotle (384-322 BC) was well aware, some creatures produce their young by laying eggs and others produce their young live and developed; what takes place in an egg for some animals occurs in the womb of the mother in others. This much and more had been discovered by Aristotle himself, who had opened hen's eggs at various times after they had been laid, in order to observe the development of the chick. Others became intrigued by the question, and during the Renaissance the developing chick was once more a centre of interest. In the sixteenth century, Ulisse Aldrovandi (1522-1605) examined it at Bologna and this work acted as a stimulant to Volcher Coiter (1534-76) who studied the chick with even greater care, opening an egg daily to watch progress. But it was Hieronymus Fabricius (often known as Fabricius of Aquapendente after his birthplace) (1537-1619) who carried out work that began scientific embryology. In 1600 his *De Formatu Foetu (On the Form of the Foetus)* appeared, to be followed 21 years later by the posthumous publication of his *De Formatione Ovi et Pulli (On the Formation of the Egg and the Chick)*. The last broke new ground, dealing with earlier stages than any previous writing on the subject, while the first dealt only with the later stages when the foetus resembles the new-born creature to a great extent.

During the eighteenth century some more books on embryology appeared, but many were more concerned with philosophical questions raised by the subject. However, the famous English physician William Harvey (1578-1657) published *De Generatione Animalium (On the Birth of Animals)* in 1651 and this contained some important conclusions, the main one being the phrase 'All creatures come from an egg '. Care should be taken not to interpret this in the modern sense, for Harvey did not know of the eggs of mammals. A second significant point of his work is that he rejected the idea of 'preformation' — that the embryonic young creature was to be found at the moment of conception and only grows larger with time. Such a view was accepted, however, by Malpighi even though he used the microscope; in spite of this, his book *De Formatione Pulli in Ovo (The Formation of the Chicken in the Egg)* (1673) was significant because it presented a number of sound observations which acted as a basis for much subsequent research. His description of the development of the heart was particularly good.

Anton van Leeuwenhoek (1632-1723) looked at male spermatozoa through his microscope, and his observations fuelled strange 'preformationist' ideas, that very tiny examples of the new-born were discernible within the sperm itself. This view tended to hold back further development for a time. However, in 1759, the German anatomist Caspar Wolff (1738-94) published *Theoria Generationis (Theory of Generation)* in which he showed that something such as a leaf develops from uniform tissue at the tip of the growing shoot, so the appearance of a bud is not just a process of unfolding, but that the leaf or flower grows, emerging first as tiny lumps in the ordinary tissue. This process of emergence became known as 'epigenesis'; it was a totally different view from preformation.

The next important stage arrived in the nineteenth century when the Estonian physician Karl Baer (1792-1876), who spent much of his time on embryology, published a very important book *De ovi mammalium et hominis generi (On the Origin of the Mammalian and Human Egg)* (1827) which, as its title implies, enshrined the discovery of the mammalian egg so bringing the reproductive process of mammals into line with that of other creatures. He also described layers in the embryo from which various organs develop, and proposed what later became known as the 'biogenetic law', namely that the embryos of animals are alike in their earliest stages and develop in the same kind of way.

Another important nineteenth-century field of work was that concerned with the actual development process within the embryo itself, and led to a study of animal cells. This was started by the German physiologist Theodor Schwann (1810-82), who in 1839 published his

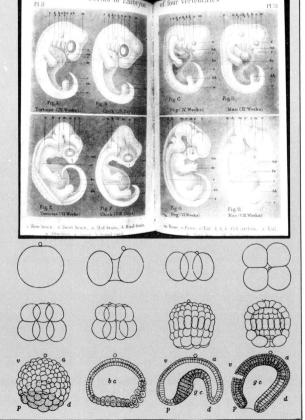

PIONEERS OF EMBRYOLOGY
Work carried out at the end of the nineteenth century led to the study of the development of embryos being placed on a truly scientific basis. One of the scientists whose research was important in this respect was Ernst Haekel. The possibility that all vertebrates might follow the same process of development aroused considerable interest and striking comparisons were made, as shown in this illustraton after Haekel (*right*), comparing the development patterns of the tortoise, chick, rabbit and man. E.G. Conklin (1863-1952), an American biologist, also made valuable researches in embryology. The illustration is taken from his *Heredity and Environment in the Development of Men* (1915-21) (*below*).

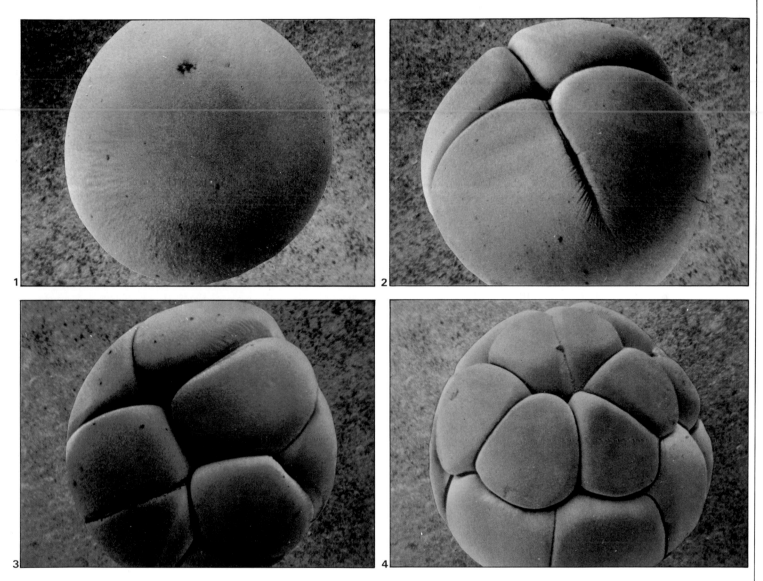

microscopic research on 'the similarity and growth of animals and plants'. Mainly devoted to animal tissues, which are more difficult to observe than those of plants, Schwann explained that they originated from 'cells' which he thought corresponded in every way to those of plants, and which behave in a similar manner. In animal cells he saw a nucleus surrounded by other material; those of mammals are, as he observed, very small indeed. Yet all contain the same basic elements. In essence, then, there is no difference between the animal and vegetable kingdoms as had previously been thought; all are living things based on the same processes of generation. Schwann also saw that the development of the egg in the young animal proceeds by division; thus the animal cell is really a germinating cell. Schwann's views, together with those of the botanist Matthias Schleiden (1804-81) who studied plant cells, became the basis for much later work, among which was the discovery of chromosomes in cell division.

As to the development of the mammalian embryo, the nineteenth century saw the final rejection of the idea of preformation and the acceptance of epigenesis due to the work of many scientists and especially of Ernst Haeckel, the early believer in Darwinian evolution. This was followed in the 1880s by the growth of experimental embryology, initiated primarily by Wilhelm His (1831-1904) and Wilhelm Roux (1850-1924). Thus it was that the whole study of the formation of young in eggs and as living embryos in the womb began to be fitted in to natural science, with physics and chemistry brought in to examine and probe the development. Whereas, in the past, philosophical considerations had led to observers seeing effects that were not there — the preformation theory was a notable case in point — with cell theory and the achromatic microscope a different and more truly scientific approach took over. As in other branches of natural science, observation and experiment were to be the touchstones of embryological research.

DEVELOPING FROG'S EGG This sequence shows the stages in development of a frog's egg: single cell (1), four-celled stage (2), eight-celled stage (3) and 16-celled stage (4).

Physiology of Animals and Man

It is a sign of general attitudes in the twentieth century that the body is looked on as a machine. This view had been prevalent in the eighteenth century, especially in France during the period of the Enlightenment when the physician Julien La Mettrie (1709-51) published his *L'Homme-Machine (The Man Machine)* (1747), but in this century it was taken up in experimental science. In 1911, at a meeting in Paris, organized by Haeckel (1834-1919) of those who held the view of the unity of all knowledge, the German physiologist Jacques Loeb (1858-1924) gave an address on 'The Mechanistic Conception of Life'; the next year it was published as a book.

Loeb, who began to study philosophy in order to discover as much as he could about the freedom of man's will to do as he pleased, became disappointed at what he saw as verbal confusion. He came to the conclusion that he could only reach his aim by studying the function of the nervous system — neurophysiology — and in 1880 had begun to study the functions of part of the brain at Strasbourg University. After other work at Würzburg University he produced his book which concentrated on two studies: on living cells and on the causes of animal behaviour, particularly their reflex actions. Both of these involved physical and chemical work.

Loeb's views were sometimes rather extreme, as when he expressed the opinion that eating, drinking and reproducing are functions carried out through no exercise of will but by compulsion, people essentially being machines. Naturally enough, there were reactions against this outlook, and an opposing school of biologists arose which thought that ex-periments on isolated parts of the body were insufficient; it was important to consider the organism as a whole simply because its parts are interrelated. This 'holistic' approach claimed that no one kind of physical and chemical explanation would suffice for all species. The school claimed that Loeb's outlook was too restricted and, by not allowing a creature to be more than a physico-chemical machine, ignored matters like perception and actions which could not be wholly studied so logically. The British anatomist Edward Russell (1887-1954) was a strong supporter of this opposing view.

The study of nerves, the way they conduct information and the organization of the nervous system was crucial in this debate. By and large, during the nineteenth century, German scientists like Hermann Helmholtz (1821-94), a physicist and physiologist, took the mechanistic approach, while the French and English, with men such as the physiologist Claude Bernard (1813-78) and the surgeon Charles Bell (1774-1842) opposed it. They had taken many steps towards understanding the nervous system, so that by 1880 reflexes like knee-jerks had been traced to the spinal cord.

The differences between the German and Anglo-French schools of thought seem to have depended, to some extent, on their different experimental approaches. The Germans tended to study nerves outside the living organism whereas in Britain and France the whole animal was used, either in careful dissection or surgical operation followed by appropriate tests. The mechanistic approach coloured the work of the Russian Ivan Pavlov (1849-1936), the holistic that of the Englishman Charles Sherrington (1857-1952).

Pavlov was a pupil of Ivan Sechenov (1829-1905), a neurophysiologist who had been trained in Germany and had studied with Helmholtz, although he had also worked under Claude Bernard in Paris. Sechenov formed notable schools of study at Leningrad and Moscow, examining in detail the role of the brain and spinal cord in reflex actions. Pavlov, a brilliant experimenter, was himself attracted to the mechanistic view. His early work concentrated on the secretion of saliva; it was at this time that preparations made in the laboratory for feeding dogs caused them to salivate even before food had been served. He became intrigued by the question of how this could happen; food could cause salivation by reflex action, but what of the incidental stimulants? He concluded that they set up new connections — a new 'reflex arc' — in the body, and that this was the result of 'learning'. Such new 'conditioned reflexes' were an important concept because they formed a link between physiology and animal behaviour.

To some extent Pavlov's approach was bound to be limited because it dealt only with limited functions: those involving the whole

TWO SCHOOLS OF THOUGHT The struggle to understand the workings of the nervous system during the nineteenth century was characterized by two opposing schools of thought. One approach was the mechanistic, where the body was seen as a machine and experiments were carried out on isolated parts. The other — the holistic view — held that the organism must be considered as a whole, that single parts or systems could not be studied in isolation from others.

LENINGRAD Discovery of the 'conditioned reflex' by Pavlov, linking physiology and 19th/20th centuries

CAMBRIDGE Discovery of how nerve impulses transmitted; synthesis of research in *Integrative Action of the Nervous System* by Sherrington, confirming holistic view, 1906

LONDON Bell's work on nervous system, 18th/19th centuries

BERLIN Helmholtz' mechanistic approach to physiology, 19th century

PARIS La Mettrie's *The Man Machine*, 1747. Bernard's work on the nervous system; opposition to mechanistic view, 19th century

WÜRZBURG Study of cells and the causes of behaviour in mechanistic terms, by Loeb, 19th/20th centuries

MADRID Discovery that nerves composed of sections of neurons, separated by gaps, by Ramón y Cajal, 19th/20th centuries

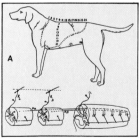

REFLEXES Pavlov, shown with his staff demonstrating the conditioned reflex *(top)* is best-known for this discovery. He found that if a bell was rung just before food was offered to a dog, eventually the sound of the bell alone could trigger salivation. Sherrington's holistic synthesis of neurophysiological research forms the basis of our understanding of the nervous system today. The illustration shows one of his experiments on simple relexes *(above)*.

animal were not part of the research. This was not the case with the work of Sherrington, who took an attitude that embraced the whole organism. His studies were aimed at finding out how nerve impulses are transmitted. The basis of the work was founded on research by the Spanish tissue expert Ramòn y Cajal (1852-1934), who had discovered that the nerves of all animals, whether they run through the spinal cord or out from it to all parts of the body, were built up in sections composed of individual 'neurons' each separated by a gap. The neurons were nerve cells and their existence posed a new problem. Previously, nerves had been thought of as fine continuous strands not in the form of cells, but now, presuming the existence of neurons and the gaps between them, it was necessary to find out how messages pass from one neuron to another in the central nervous system and do not go along the wrong route. This was needed because preliminary work by Sherrington had already shown that pathways for the neurons involved many groups of muscles, which meant that the impulses had to be fed over coordinated paths that were related to one another.

As a beginning, Sherrington found that in a reflex action there is not only stimulation, but also what was called 'inhibition'. For one muscle to contract, another has to relax at the same time. This control, he saw, must operate in the spinal cord. He also noticed that neurons do not touch, so he studied the gaps or 'synapses', as he called them. He then discovered that there are connections across the synapses, but that these vary in number; the synapses with the greatest number were most frequently used, while those with fewer needed repeated stimulation. By 1906, in his *Integrative Action of the Nervous System*, he had gathered all the strands of research together, noting that there is, besides the physico-chemical level of action, a level of action that involves the whole organism as a thinking individual, and a level at which mind and body interact. These were important conclusions that affected later physiological research, especially in the United States, both on how the chemical balance of the body is regulated, and on the response of the body to shock. This later research also confirmed the holistic view, the belief that all the different parts of the body are interdependent.

The Human Body

The human body has been a source of interest and wonder since the earliest prehistoric times, but it was only slowly that people began to learn what went on beneath the surface. Such information was probably gained from observation of wounds caused by accidents or war. Certainly the importance of blood was appreciated very early, but this is perhaps not surprising since severe loss of blood can lead to fainting and to death. It was similarly true of animals which, when cut up for food or sacrifice, provided evidence that the liver contains more blood than any other organ. Thus it was that the liver gained a special mystical significance in some civilizations, the Mesopotamians using it to help them in divination.

The Egyptians came to their knowledge of the human body mainly, it seems, through the practice of embalming. It led them to recognize the main cavities of the body occupied by the organs, since these had to be removed and stored separately before the rest of the body was mummified. They also knew that the surface of the brain was convoluted and covered with a thin, tough but transparent membrane *(dura mater)*, and appreciated that injury to the brain could lead to paralysis, the parts paralyzed depending on which part of the brain was damaged. However, it was the Egyptians, who, in spite of this, thought that the heart, not the brain, was the seat of intelligence as well as of the emotions.

The Greeks developed a more elaborate understanding, which later on in Hellenistic times became astonishingly modern in some respects. As early as the sixth century BC, Alcmaeon of Croton, one of the earliest Greek anatomists, described the optic nerve and even described the 'Eustachian tube' that runs from the middle ear to the upper part of the throat. This discovery was later lost and the tube was only rediscovered in the sixteenth century, by the Italian anatomist Bartolomeo Eustachi.

Of all the early Greek studies of the body, it is the work of their medical schools and especially of Hippocrates that is remembered or known today. The earliest school was that of Asklepios, who in Homeric times was not a god but a blameless physician; indeed his two physician sons, Podaleirios and Machaon, are mentioned in the *Iliad*. However, by the time of Hesiod, later in the ninth century BC, Asklepios was already spoken of as the son of Apollo and Coronis; the cult of Asklepios seems to have developed much later, beginning possibly in Epidauros near Athens sometime after 500 BC. Once the cult had started, a great number of centres grew up of which more than 300 are known; the chief ones were at Cnidos, Cos, Rhodes and Cyrene. Treatment at these temple centres consisted of a purifying bath and then sleep; the dreams of the patients were then interpreted by the priests from a psychological point of view — a forerunner perhaps of the modern relationship between a patient and

medical advisor or psychiatrist. Such a procedure seems also to have been practised in Egypt. Drugs may have been administered at the temples but surgery and other forms of treatment would have been practised elsewhere.

Centres of Greek medical study arose later at Croton — the work of Alcmaeon has already been mentioned — but the two main developments took place at Cnidos and Cos, both in the same region off the west coast of Turkey. At Cnidos, physicians paid most attention to obstetrics and gynaecology and it would seem that they developed some special knowledge of the female reproductive organs. At Cos a more general medical interest was to be found and it was here, in the fifth century BC, that the physician Hippocrates taught and wrote a series of treatises that have come to be known as the 'Hippocratic Corpus'. Although it is certain that he could not have been the author of all the treatises, because they cover a span of at least 100 years, he was the inspiration behind them.

What is so important about the Cos school is that it established biological reasoning and observation as the basis for medical work. As a

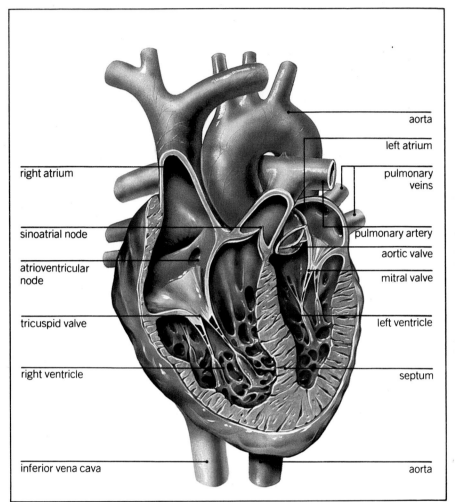

right atrium

sinoatrial node

atrioventricular node

tricuspid valve

right ventricle

inferior vena cava

aorta

left atrium

pulmonary veins

pulmonary artery

aortic valve

mitral valve

left ventricle

septum

aorta

THE HEART Not until the seventeenth century was the working of the heart properly understood, when Harvey discovered that the blood circulates around the body. The heart beats constantly throughout life, at an average rate of 70 beats a minute. It is composed of four chambers, two on each side of the septum, a division which is impermeable to blood. Blood enters the right atrium from the vena cava, the main vein, and passes into the right ventricle which pumps the blood to the lungs. Oxygenated blood returning from the lungs passes into the left ventricles and is pumped into the arteries via the aorta. The sinoatrial node is the heart's pacemaker, sending impulses to the atrioventricular node, which conducts the impulses to the nerves, causing the muscles of the ventricles to contract.

LEARNING ABOUT ANATOMY
Practical experience — such as these operations by doctors on Roman troops, shown on Trajan's Column, Rome *(above)* — was the only source of anatomical knowledge in certain areas of the world. *Anathomia*, finished in 1316, was the only textbook on anatomy in the West for 100 years *(below)*.

result, any suggestion of divine causes for disease — held to be the case by Mesopotamian medical practitioners and even some Greeks when it came to the 'sacred disease' epilepsy — began to be purged from both medicine and biology. However, dissection of human corpses was disallowed, and such knowledge of anatomy as they had was based on external examination and the treatment of wounds. The school was permitted to use skeletons, so the general bone structure of the body was studied, special attention being paid to the bones of the face, the feet and the hands. Some muscles and some of the larger glands were well described, but, although the liver and spleen were known, their functions remained a mystery. Members of the school also believed that the purpose of breathing was to cool the heart and the blood, since it was supposed that the heart had its own innate source of heat and that a person would die if cooling did not occur. The heart was thought to have blood on one side and 'pneuma', a 'vital spirit' (from the Greek word *pneuma*, meaning 'wind') on the other. The brain was considered as a gland, its purpose being to help cool the heart and blood. Knowledge of the eye was scanty and they seem to have

been aware only of parts of the ear.

It was at Cos that the doctrine of the four bodily fluids or, as they later came to be called, the 'humours' (from the Latin word *humor*, meaning 'liquid'), was developed from the four elements (earth, water, air, and fire) and the four qualities (coldness, wetness, hotness and dryness). These humours were melancholer (black bile), phlegm, choler (yellow bile) and blood. For a healthy body the four humours had to be in balance; an excess of one or more than one would lead to illness. It turned out to be a powerful although mistaken explanation of bodily function and malfunction, but satisfied people in the West for the next 2,000 years.

The next stages in understanding the human body came from the medical school that grew up at the museum and library at Alexandria in the second century BC. The school was founded by the anatomist and physiologist Herophilos, whose date and place of death are still unknown. It seems that he was a native of Chalcedon, on the Asiatic side of the Bosphorus, and studied at Cos, but whatever his early life, he made his mark at Alexandria, both as a teacher of medicine and as a research professor. Here he had the freedom to dissect the human body, which was an immense advantage since it was forbidden to medical men in Greece. He made such good use of this facility that he has often been referred to as the 'father of anatomy'; some of the terms he introduced are still in use. He was particularly interested in the reproductive organs and the brain and, to a lesser extent, the liver and the eye.

Herophilos gave excellent descriptions of the reproductive organs, particularly those of the female. He discovered the ovary and what are now known as the Fallopian tubes leading from it; this result was to be lost and only rediscovered some 1,800 years later by the sixteenth-century Italian anatomist Gabriele Fallopio (1523-62). Herophilos also seems to have had some knowledge of the lymphatic glands. The brain, it is interesting to find, he thought to be the centre of the nervous system — quite a different theory from Aristotle's which subscribed to the heart as the centre — and he described the cerebrum and cerebellum (the large forward upper part and the back protruding portion of the brain). He was also interested in the main cavities and described not only the membrane enclosing the brain but also the spinal fluid.

Over other parts of the body, Herophilos was the first to differentiate between motor and sensory nerves, and realized that the reason for respiration was to take in fresh air, distribute and then expel it; he also distinguished between arteries and veins. He described the optic nerve, and also the optic chiasma (the crossover point of the eye's nerves), he introduced a term from which the word 'retina' (the back of the eye) was derived, and coined the equivalent of the term 'duodenum' for the small gut.

The Alexandrian library and museum boasted another eminent researcher, the physician Erasistratos, who again had been a pupil at the medical school at Cos. Having spent most of his working life as a successful medical practitioner in Alexandria, Erasistratos moved into the museum where he carried out the research that has earned him the title of 'father of physiology'. He took an interest in almost every part of the body. He made an improved division of the motor and sensory nerves of Herophilos, realizing that they split into very fine branches. He studied respiration and believed Aristotle's undefined 'pneuma' passed into the body through the nose and mouth and thence to the lungs by way of the bronchial tubes, next to the heart and then to the rest of the body through the veins and arteries. But his most astonishing realization was that the heart with pneuma one side and blood on the other, acted as a pump. Unfortunately he did not follow the argument through to its conclusion and discover the circulation of the blood. He appreciated that both veins and arteries were divided up into ever smaller branches and said that tissues were composed of very fine arteries, veins and nerves.

Erasistratos also considered the digestive system, concluding that food is ground up in the stomach, although he went on to say that it was mixed there with pneuma from the veins. Lastly, Erasistratos developed a crude idea of metabolism, understood that growth was continuous and also that a constant wastage occurs.

It is more than unfortunate that the work of Herophilos and Erasistratos did not become the first stage of a new medical and physiological outlook but, when the Alexandrian library and museum were destroyed, their research went into eclipse. The man whose medical outlook permeated Western medicine was the Greek physician Galen (c 130-200AD), who spent some time at Alexandria before becoming a surgeon to the Roman gladiators in Pergamum and later a court physician. However, he strongly disagreed with the followers of Erasistratos, which was probably a result of not being able to dissect human corpses. Galen had to make do with the bodies of animals, particularly the Barbary ape (Macaca sylvana), the only wild monkey in Europe.

Galen's description of the skeleton was good — many of the terms he adopted are still in use — but his general physiology was so firmly centred on the pneuma that it led to errors which, unhappily, were perpetuated for centuries. Briefly, Galen taught that pneuma — part of the world soul — was drawn in during breathing and passed to the lungs and thence through a vein-like artery (now known as the pulmonary vein) to the left side of the heart. Meanwhile, when food was digested in the intestines, the nutritive matter was carried in a white substance called 'chyle' (from the Greek word khulos, meaning 'juice') to the liver where the chyle was turned into blood, and at the same time became endowed with a type of pneuma known as 'natural spirit'. The blood and natural spirit were

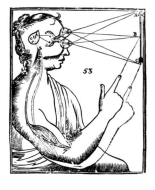

THEORY OF VISION This illustration from Descartes' *Opera Philosophica* (1692) depicts his idea of vision. A nervous impulse passes from the eye to the pineal gland, and from there to the muscles.

CIRCULATION OF THE BLOOD Harvey's *De Motu Cordis* (1628) includes this demonstration of the existence of valves in the veins. Labelled, B, C, D, E and F in figure 1, valves show up when a tourniquet is applied to the upper arm. In figure 2, the vein between the finger and valve O disappears when cut at H, although it remains distended at OG.

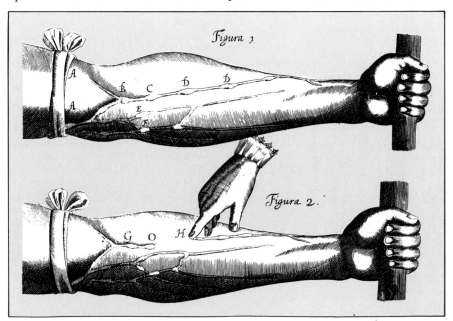

distributed by veins to the whole of the body, including the left side of the heart. In the right side of the heart, Galen claimed that some purification of the blood occurred and that 'waste vapours' were carried away by an artery-like vein (now the pulmonary artery) to the lungs and exhaled. The purified blood then went into the veinous system.

In addition to this, Galen taught that blood passed from the left side of the heart to the right, where it was endowed with yet another pneuma called 'vital spirit'. The blood then carrying natural spirit and vital spirit went into the arteries and so into the body where it ebbed and flowed. Finally, when this blood and its spirits reached the brain, the spirits were converted into 'animal spirit' which was distributed over the whole body by means of the nerves.

Galen's physiological picture was in error, due primarily, it seems, to the restriction on human dissection, for there is evidence that he was a fine experimenter. His belief that blood passed from one side of the heart to the other was wrong, and this, together with the doctrine of the humours and the belief in three types of pneuma, dogged studies of the body and medical treatment in the West until the sixteenth century. Only then was a new look taken by the brilliant Belgian anatomist Andreas Vesalius (1514-64) who trained at Louvain and Paris. Returning to Louvain, he reintroduced the practice of the dissection of human bodies which, although by then permitted, had not been exploited.

THE RENAISSANCE OUTLOOK A new attitude to the human body came with the Renaissance. Leonardo da Vinci (1452-1519) made extensive studies of human anatomy, filling many notebooks with the results of his observations, such as this drawing of the muscles of the back and legs *(below left)*. The brilliant anatomist Vesalius also made dissections. His *De Humani Corporis Fabrica (The Fabric of the Human Body)* appeared in 1543. This illustration of muscles is taken from Book II *(below right)*.

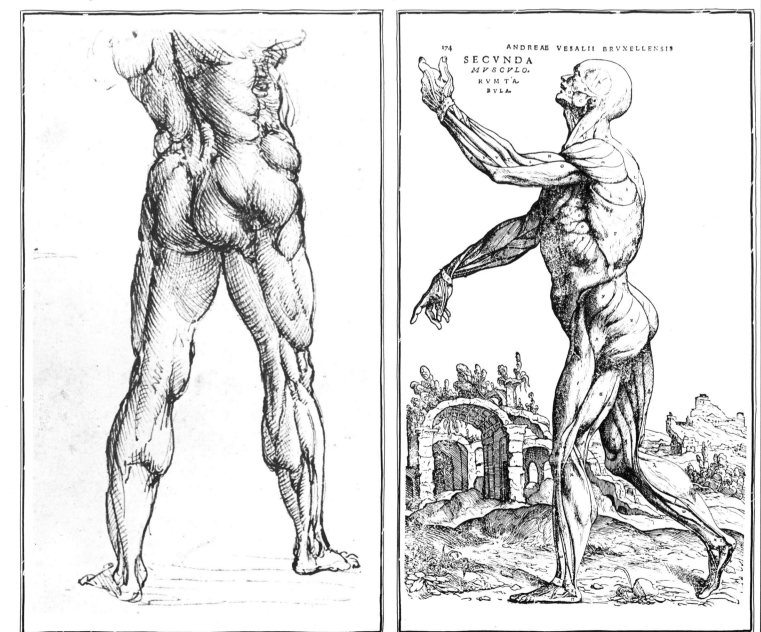

In the sixteenth century, the greatest European medical school was at Padua in Italy, and Vesalius decided to go there after qualifying at Louvain. His brilliance was recognized at once and he was appointed lecturer on anatomy and surgery. Immediately, and with no objections raised, he initiated a new approach — he carried out all dissections himself instead of leaving them to 'demonstrators', whose task was to point out the parts referred to by the lecturer. Vesalius also had large anatomical charts drawn to help his students. So far he had not progressed from Galen's teaching, as his publications of tne time clearly show. However, he was later able to make many comparative dissections and gradually came to realize that Galen was not always correct. By 1539 Vesalius had enough evidence to challenge Galen's system publicly, and then he set about preparing his own book, using the best illustrators and printers.

In 1543 his monumental *Humani Corporis Fabrica (The Fabric of the Human Body)* appeared, with magnificent illustrations and 17 full-page pictures. He described the bones and joints, compared the human skulls of different races — the first man ever to do so — and then described the muscles, the heart and the blood vessels. He still showed the Galenic idea of the passage of blood from left to right in the heart, although his text shows he was doubtful about the truth of this. He noted the nervous system and pointed out that nerves are not hollow as Galen supposed. Next there is a section on the abdomen and one on the thorax. This last contains his view that the heart is very like a muscle. Finally there is a section on the brain where, again, Vesalius corrects errors of Galen and even of Erasistratos. A second edition of the book appeared 12 years later, in 1555, and in this Vesalius claimed that nothing could pass across the heart, clearly breaking once again with Galen.

Vesalius' book heralded a new outlook in anatomy and medicine, as *De Revolutionibus* by Copernicus also broke with an age-old tradition. Although criticized at first, *Humani Corporis Fabrica* gradually had its due effect, especially on Vesalius' successors at Padua — Gabriele Fallopio and Hieronymus Fabricius.

The next important state in the understanding of the human body came in the seventeenth century. First, the 'lesser circulation' of the blood between the heart and the lungs was found; this had been noted by Islamic anatomists in the mid-thirteenth century and was later observed by Michael Servetus (c 1511-1533). Servetus was a medical practitioner, burned at the stake in Geneva for his religious unorthodoxy, who seems to have come upon his discovery more for religious rather than scientific reasons, and whose achievement remained virtually unknown. The great step — the discovery that the blood circulates throughout the entire human body —

was taken in 1628 by William Harvey (1578-1657), with the publication of his *Exercitationes Anatomicae de Mortu Cordis et Sanguis (On the Movement of the Heart and the Blood)*. A student first at Cambridge University, he moved to Padua where he worked under Fabricius. In 1603, Fabricius published a book, *De Venarum Ostiolis (On the Little Doors of the Veins)*, which described an experiment showing how, when an arm is bandaged to prevent the flow of blood, little knot-like swellings appear. These swellings act as valves and slow up the backflow of the blood.

Harvey made a thorough study of the heart and concluded that it is a hollow muscle, also that it does not beat as a whole, the ventricles or lower chambers beating after the aurioles or upper chambers. He also saw that there was a valve between the upper and lower chambers. Harvey noticed that the arteries expanded when contraction occurs (the pulse). In addition to this purely anatomical study, Harvey applied some simple physics — typical of the new scientific approach — for he found that although the heart only holds 2oz (60g) of blood, the left ventricle pumps at a rate of 540 lb (250 kg) per hour, that is about three times the weight of the average man. He concluded, and rightly, that the blood does not ebb and flow but circulates round the body, out through the arteries and back through the veins.

Harvey's momentous discovery completed the basic understanding of the human body although, of course, there was, and still is, a great deal to be discovered about metabolism, body chemistry, the nerves and the brain.

UNDERSTANDING THE BODY The story of the discovery of the workings of the human body is marked by discovery and rediscovery (below). With the destruction of the library and museum at Alexandria, much of the work of Herophilos and Erasistratos was lost or ignored. Instead, the teachings of Galen held currency until the sixteenth century, when such scientists as Vesalius, Fallopio and Eustachio took a fresh look at the subject in the light of the new Renaissance spirit of enquiry.

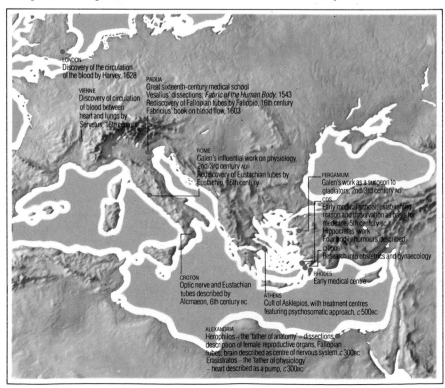

LONDON
Discovery of the circulation of the blood by Harvey, 1628

PADUA
Great sixteenth-century medical school
Vesalius' dissections; *Fabric of the Human Body*, 1543
Rediscovery of Fallopian tubes by Fallopio, 16th century
Fabricius' book on blood flow, 1603

VIENNE
Discovery of circulation of blood between heart and lungs by Servetus, 16th century

ROME
Galen's influential work on physiology, 2nd/3rd century AD
Rediscovery of Eustachian tubes by Eustachio, 16th century

PERGAMUM
Galen's work as a surgeon to gladiators, 2nd/3rd century AD

COS
Early medical school establishing reason and observation as basis for medicine, 5th century BC
Hippocrates' work
Four bodily humours described

CNIDOS
Research into obstetrics and gynaecology

RHODES
Early medical centre

CROTON
Optic nerve and Eustachian tubes described by Alcmaeon, 6th century BC

ATHENS
Cult of Asklepios, with treatment centres featuring psychosomatic approach, c 500 BC

ALEXANDRIA
Herophilos — the 'father of anatomy' — dissections, description of female reproductive organs, Fallopian tubes; brain described as centre of nervous system, c 300 BC
Erasistratos — the 'father of physiology' — heart described as a pump, c 300 BC

ANDREAE VESALII
BRVXELLENSIS, SCHOLAE
medicorum Patauinæ professoris, de
Humani corporis fabrica
Libri septem.

CVM CAESAREAE
Maiest. Galliarum Regis, ac Senatus Veneti gra-
tia & priuilegio, ut in diplomatis eorundem continetur.

DISSECTIONS The illustration (above) from *Fasciocolo di Medicina* by Johannes de Ketham (1493) shows an anatomy lecture at Padua before the time of Vesalius. The professor remains in his chair reading from a book, while a demonstrator points out the progress of the dissection with a stick. The students take no active part in the dissection — this 'ignoble' task is carried out by servants. In the sixteenth century, Vesalius revolutionized this procedure when he was appointed lecturer in anatomy and surgery at Padua. He carried out dissections himself and taught with the aid of large anatomical charts. In 1543, with the publication of *De Humana Corporis Fabrica (The Fabric of the Human Body) (left)*, Vesalius was able to challenge many of the views current at the time, most of which were derived from the teachings of Galen.

Microbes and Disease

Infectious diseases were familiar in early times and it was thought that they spread by contact, although no one knew precisely how this happened. Epidemics occurred and frequently spread — the Black Death (bubonic plague) in fourteenth-century Europe is a famous example — and this perpetuated the widespread belief in many civilizations that they were due to supernatural causes. Indeed epidemics were often considered to be divine punishments.

The first definite suggestion of a scientific cause came during the Renaissance from Hieronymous Fracastoro (1478-1553), who in his *De Contagione (On Contagions)* (1546), thought that diseases were transmitted by 'seeds of infection' either by contact, indirect contact (ie by objects that have been in contact with an infected person) or by transmission from a distance. These 'seeds', he thought, had the faculty of multiplying and propagating rapidly. It was a penetrating insight into the subject but, unfortunately, was not pursued until the seventeenth century, when Athanasius Kircher (1602-80) and Christian Lange (1619-92) also wrote about multiplying and propagating 'seeds' of infection. Anton van Leeuwenhoek (1632-1723), with his special microscopes, did indeed observe such seeds (later known as bacteria) but did not appreciate what they were. In the eighteenth century, Leeuwenhoek's work was followed up by Otto Müller (1730-84) who, in spite of the optical defects of the microscopes in his day, managed to use magnifications of 300 times and more to examine bacteria. Posthumously, in 1786, his *Animalcula Infusoria (Tiny Animals in Infusions)* appeared. The descriptions given in it can still be recognized, although it must be appreciated that Müller was writing as a zoologist, not as a medical man investigating diseases.

Another approach to infectious diseases arose at the close of the eighteenth century and the early decades of the nineteenth; this was the process of inoculation. Lady Mary Montagu, wife of the British ambassador in Turkey, introduced it to the West in 1718; while in Turkey she had had her six-year-old son inoculated against smallpox and on her return to England strongly advocated the practice. In 1721 a few condemned criminals were treated; when the results were successful the two daughters of the Prince of Wales (later King George II) were inoculated. The medical man behind the British investigation was the famous surgeon John Hunter (1728-93), one of whose pupils, Edward Jenner (1749-1823) was to take matters further. Jenner set up in practice in Berkeley, Gloucestershire, and while there came across rumours that anyone infected by cowpox (a disease sometimes caught from cows by those engaged in dairy farming) was immune to smallpox, which was then a terrible scourge. Jenner told Hunter and suggested inoculating the cowpox to counter the disease, but his ideas made little headway because the idea of using

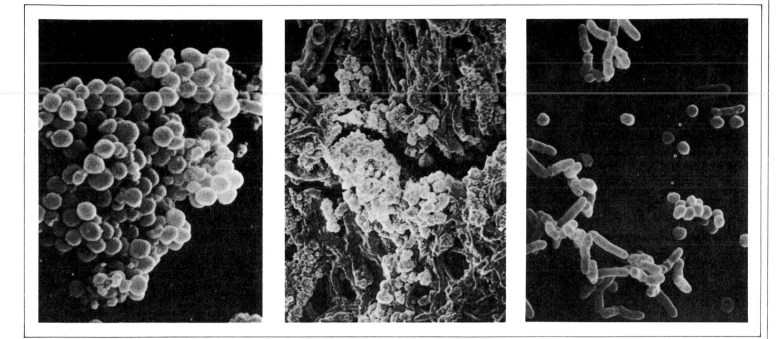

UNDERSTANDING INFECTION The investigations carried out by the French scientist Louis Pasteur *(left)* into the nature of bacteria led to the germ theory of infection. He showed, for instance, that fermentation and putrefaction are caused by air-borne organisms, using the apparatus *(below)*. The sterilized contents of the flask were protected from the organisms that Pasteur suspected were carried in the air by the ingenious S-neck of the flask. This would trap any such organisms in its bend. When, however, air was freely admitted, the contents soon reflected the change. The pictures *(above)* show three common bacteria. *Staphylococcus aurens (above left)* is responsible for infection in wounds, beta haemolytic *Streptococcus (above centre)* causes tonsilitis and scarlet fever, while *Streptococcus mutans (above right)* forms part of the plaque found on teeth, where it converts sugar to destructive acid.

an animal disease to combat a human one was repugnant to most people.

By 1780 Jenner had become convinced that the discharge from a cowpox sore could be used to inoculate against smallpox, providing the discharge was taken at the right stage in the development of the cowpox disease itself. Yet he could not be sure without a test on a human being and it was not until 1796 that he was able to do this. In mid-May of that year he inoculated an eight-year-old boy, James Phipps, with cowpox. The boy caught the comparatively mild disease but soon recovered and at the beginning of July was inoculated with smallpox, which had no effect. Jenner published his results in 1798, describing the matter producing cowpox as a 'virus' and the material used in inoculation a 'vaccine' (from the Latin word *vacca*, meaning 'cow'). The practice of vaccination soon spread, with beneficial results.

The process of inoculation was extended by the French scientist Louis Pasteur (1822-95) 70 years later. He wanted to apply the method to other dangerous diseases. Pasteur's problem was how to obtain a vaccine — he realized this must be material containing 'animalcules' or bacteria — which was less lethal than the disease being attacked. In 1880 he discovered that a lethal form of bacteria killing hens (it gave them a form of cholera), could be made less virulent if cultured differently. Injections of the less virulent strain were successful in preventing the disease. Indeed, Pasteur said: 'The disease is its own preventative. It has the character of virus diseases, which do not recur.' This was a great step forward because it led the way to the development of specially cultured vaccines against many infectious diseases, as Pasteur himself immediately appreciated.

Pasteur pursued this work, especially in the light of new research into the causes of other diseases which led to the recognition that many are due to the presence of bacteria. The leader of this new bacteriological research was the German Robert Koch (1843-1910), who in 1882 discovered the bacteria causing tuberculosis, and a year later those for human cholera; he then began to work to find the bacteria responsible for anthrax. In connection with the last, he managed in the end to obtain an almost pure culture, and was then the first to be able to follow the full life cycle of a bacterium.

Once the type of bacteria causing a disease was isolated, Pasteur set about trying to develop less virulent strains. He realized that timing was vital in the development of these bacteria and also that oxygen played a part. Auguste Chaveau (1827-1917) forwarded an alternative theory; he claimed that after the inoculation of a chemical substance, a new substance was released, killing any infection due to virulent bacteria. Pasteur thought otherwise. He believed the process to be an action between bacteria. Chaveau and a colleague had claimed to have a chemical 'vaccine' for anthrax, but this proved unsuccessful; Pasteur persevered and produced a bacterial vaccine, but he had difficulties because the virulent anthrax bacteria thrive on oxygen. In the end he discovered that it was necessary to apply heat in specific ways during the culture of the hopefully less virulent strain. In 1881 he applied his techniques to various other diseases, including rabies in human beings, and his ideas have been proved correct. Indeed, since Pasteur's time many successful vaccines have been developed, including those against poliomyelitis, whooping cough and diphtheria.

Discovery of Asepsis

In Ancient Greece it was believed that wounds would heal without supturation if their edges were brought together. This was accepted in the West until the fourteenth century, when the famous surgeon Guy de Chauliac (c 1290-c 1367) began to treat wounds with complicated lotions and salves. Since these applications contained bacteria, they allowed much pus to form.

With the arrival of gunpowder in the fourteenth century, wounds were always very infected and the one way available to deal with them was cauterization with a red-hot iron. Only in the sixteenth century was this treatment partly overthrown by the famous Renaissance surgeon Ambroise Paré (c 1510-1590), who discovered that when, on one occasion, he was forced to use a simple dressing instead of cauterization, this proved more beneficial. Even so, it was generally accepted that all wounds would supturate to some extent, but

why and how they did so could not be determined. It was only in the late nineteenth century that the causes and a cure were discovered, and this was due to research in fermentation.

We now know that fermentation is a bacteriological process. Although people had been familiar with it from the earliest times, no attempt to understand what occurred was made until the early nineteenth century. In 1810 the French chef and confectioner Nicolas Appert (c 1750-1841) described how to preserve vegetables and dairy products by bottling under heat. His results created some interest and the chemist Joseph Gay-Lussac (1778-1850) investigated the process, reporting that no free oxygen was present in the jars in which preservation was made. He concluded that oxygen was necessary for fermentation to occur.

The next stage came with the investigations of the behaviour of yeast, which is present in

HEALTH AND HYGIENE Building on the work of Louis Pasteur, the surgeon Joseph Lister used dressings impregnated with carbolic acid in his treatment of wounds to prevent bacterial infection *(below)*. His work laid the foundations of the principles of antisepsis.

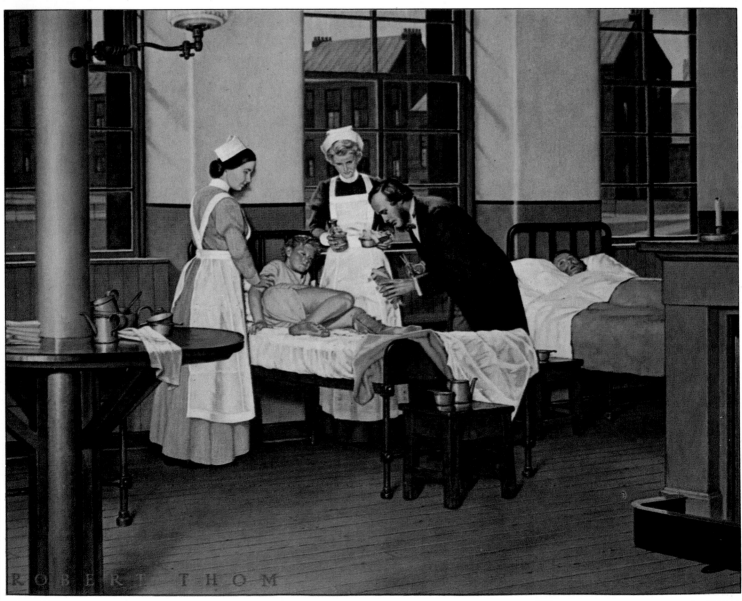

ROBERT THOM

many fermentation processes. In 1831, the German physiologist Theodor Schwann realized yeast was a living substance. This discovery was confirmed seven years later by the French scientist Charles Cagniard de la Tour who observed that it consisted of tiny globules capable of reproducing themselves. Although others confirmed these views, most chemists opposed them, still believing that fermentation was a purely chemical process.

When Louis Pasteur (1822-95) was asked to investigate the souring of beer and other alcoholic substances, his series of careful experiments demonstrated not only that alcoholic fermentation, but also souring, occurred because there were some microscopic organisms that could live without the presence of oxygen; he called these 'anaerobic' to distinguish them from those that were 'aerobic' and needed oxygen. By 1857 he was in a position to show that the fermentation of lactic acid — which is the commonest acid constituent of fermented milk products, such as sour milk and cheese — was due to the presence of small globules or very short segments which were different from yeast and lived on sugar. These were bacteria.

Pasteur regarded these microscopic animals or 'micro-organisms' as being airborne, a view which led him to new investigations and brought him face to face with the subject of 'spontaneous generation'. This subject had arisen not from fermentation but the putrefaction of dead flesh; maggots that appeared on rotting meat were traditionally thought to have generated 'spontaneously' from the rotting flesh. Although in the mid-seventeenth century a series of experiments by the Italian physician Francesco Redi (1627-97) had proved that maggots found on rotting meat had not bred there, the old myth continued. A century later the physiologist Lazzaro Spalazani (1729-99) showed that micro-organisms appeared in infusions (solutions of vegetable matter), and in 1836 the old ideas were again attacked when the German scientist Franz Schulze (1815-73) found that, if heated, the micro-organisms died and that none appeared unless fresh unheated air was subsequently admitted. In a careful set of independent experiments Theodor Schwann confirmed this. In spite of such evidence, in 1858 the French biologist Félix Pouchet (1800-72) sent a claim to the *Académie des Sciences* stating that he had proved the existence of spontaneous generation. Fortunately this stimulated Pasteur to work on the subject and, by a series of brilliant experiments, he was able to prove that micro-organisms were present in the air and this could account for all Pouchet's results.

In London in 1872, Henry Bastian (1837-1915), the anatomist, published *Beginnings of Life*, in which he also supported the traditional view that life could be generated from non-living matter. His work had a positive side, however, for he showed that some micro-

organisms are more resistant to heat than others. Micro-organisms were again shown to be airborne by John Tyndall (1820-93), the British physicst, but the most famous work was Pasteur's. This particularly impressed the English surgeon Joseph Lister (1827-1912) who was disturbed at the high death rate due to the onset of septic conditions, especially after amputations, both in army hospitals during the Crimean War and elsewhere. When Lister moved to Glasgow Infirmary in 1860 he found a similar situation, but he also noticed that no putrefaction occurred on wounds in the body.

While Lister was contemplating this problem, Ignaz Semmelweis (1818-65), a Viennese physician, noticed that in one ward 30 percent of the women having babies died from puerperal fever, and three percent in another. In a post-mortem examination on a medical friend, Semmelweis found the same kind of tissue as in the dead mothers and concluded the post-mortem room was the cause, especially as the ward with the high death rate was visited by students straight from the post-mortem room. Midwives who had not been anywhere near the room served the other ward. Semmelweis therefore insisted on a rule making all students wash their hands in carbolic and water before visiting patients; the death rate dropped to one percent. Yet Semmelweis' colleagues remained unconvinced and he met with open hostility.

Pasteur's work proved how important Semmelweis' ideas were, and in 1865 Lister had the air into the operating theatre filtered. Also, after an investigation of various liquids, he adopted carbolic acid as a bath for all surgical instruments, for washing the surgeon's hands, the patient's skin and for spraying the air. This all proved immensely effective and became accepted. Thus Lister initiated a new era of surgery governed by scientific principles. Without these aseptic conditions, the great achievements of twentieth-century surgery would have been impossible.

CARBOLIC SPRAY Lister devised this steam-driven carbolic spray *(above)* to produce a fine cloud of carbolic acid during operations.

THE FIRST VACCINATIONS By observing the effects of cowpox *(above)*, the English surgeon Edward Jenner (1749-1823) developed an effective vaccine against the killer disease, smallpox. He is seen here vaccinating his son *(top)*.

Index

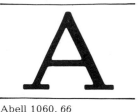

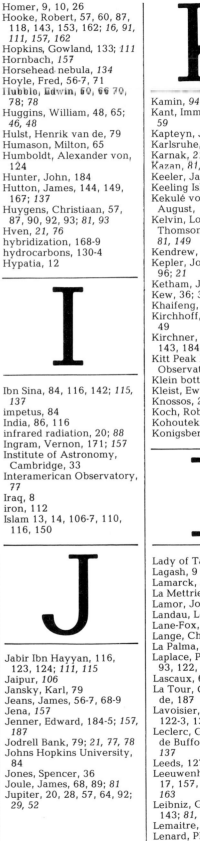

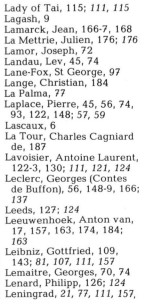

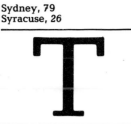

Acknowledgements

The illustrations on these pages are reproduced by courtesy of the following: **6** The Egypt Exploration Society; **7** Middle East Photographic Archive; **8(a)** Ann Ronan Picture Library, **(b)** National Museum, Copenhagen; **11** Trustees of the British Museum; **14** Ann Ronan Picture Library; **15** Trustees of the British Museum; **16** Ann Ronan Picture Library; **18** Austin Rover Group; **19** NASA; **23** Crown copyright — reproduced with the permission of the Controller of Her Majesty's Stationery Office; **24** British Library; **25, 26(b)** Ann Ronan Picture Library; **31, 32(al)** British Library; **32(bl)** Ann Ronan Picture Library, **(r)** Royal Astronomical Society; **33** Science Museum; **34** J.D. Waldron; **38(r)** Ann Ronan Picture Library; **39** Palomar Observatory, California; **40** Ann Ronan Picture Library; **42(a)** Don Trombino; **44(a)** Ann Ronan Picture Library; **45** Nature (Macmillans); **46-7** Royal Observatory, Edinburgh; **48(1), 49** Ann Ronan Picture Library; **51** Palomar Observatory, California, **(i)** Royal Observatory, Edinburgh; **52(1)** National Library, Florence (Scala); **52(r), 53(l)** British Library; **53(r)** Petworth House Archives (Lord Egremont); **54, 55** NASA; **56, 57** Ann Ronan Picture Library; **58(t), 60(a)** NASA; **60(b)** Ann Ronan Picture Library; **61(b)** NASA; **62** Colin Ronan; **63(l)** Dr R.L. Waterfield, **(r)** City of Manchester Art Galleries; **64** Ann Ronan Picture Library; **65** with special permission of the town of Bayeux; **66** Jodrell Bank, University of Manchester; **67(a)** Royal Observatory, Edinburgh, **(b)** Royal Astronomical Society; **69(a)** Palomar Observatory, California, **(b)** Ann Ronan Picture Library; **70, 71** NASA; **74(a)** John Sanford; **74(b), 75(a)** Ann Ronan Picture Library; **75(i)** Ann Ronan Picture Library and E.P Goldschmidt and Co Ltd; **76(l)** British Library, **(c)** Ann Ronan Picture Library, **(r)** National Maritime Museum, Greenwich; **78(l), (c)** Royal Astronomical Society, **(r)** Royal Observatory, Edinburgh; **79(a)** Ann Ronan Picture Library, **(b)** NASA; **82** Ann Ronan Picture Library; **83(a), (b)** NASA; **84, 85** Ann Ronan Picture Library; **86** Ann Ronan Picture Library and E.P. Goldschmidt and Co Ltd; **87(l)** Institute and Museum of the History of Science, Florence; **87(r), 88, 89** Ann Ronan Picture Library; **90(br)** Cavendish Laboratory; **91** Imperial College of Science and Technology; **93(a)** The Royal Society; **94(a)** A Shell Photograph, **(b)** Ann Ronan Picture Library; **96(ar), (br)** British Library; **97** Ann Ronan Picture Library; **98** Museum Boerhaave, Leiden; **99, 101, 102(r), 104(a)** Ann Ronan Picture Library; **104(br)** Albert W. Tucker; **106(a), (br)** Science Museum, **(bl)** Cambridge University Press; **108-9(c)** NASA; **109(tr)** British Library; **112(bl)** Robert Harding Picture Library; **113** Ann Ronan Picture Library; **114(l)** British Library; **114(ar), (br), 115(r), 116** Ann Ronan Picture Library; **117(al), (ar)** Ann Ronan Picture Library and E.P Goldschmidt and Co Ltd; **117(b), 118, 119** Ann Ronan Picture Library; **121** British Library; **121(i), 123** Ann Ronan Picture Library; **125** Science Museum; **126(c)** Ann Ronan Picture Library, **(r)** Science Museum; **127 (a)** CERN, **(b)** Science Museum, by courtesy of Professor Sir George Thomson; **128(l)** British Library; **129** Mary Evans Picture Library; **130(b)** Barry Finch Photography; **131** BP Oil Ltd; **132, 133** Science Museum; **134** Royal Observatory, Edinburgh; **135** National Radio Astronomy Observatory, West Virginia; **139(a)** Science Museum, **(b)** British Library; **140(l)** Ann Ronan Picture Library; **140-1(c)** National Maritime Museum, Greenwich; **141(r)** Institute of Geological Science; **142** Ann Ronan Picture Library; **143(l)** Royal Geographical Society; **(r)** Ann Ronan Picture Library; **145(l)** Royal Geographical Society, **(ar), (br)** Ann Ronan Picture Library; **146** Michael Freeman; **147** Ann Ronan Picture Library; **148** Staatliche Museum, Berlin; **149** Royal Astronomical Society; **150** Royal Geographical Society; **151(al), (bl)** NASA, **(ar)** British Library, **(br)** Royal Geographical Society; **152(a), (br)** Ann Ronan Picture Library; **(bl)** Ann Ronan Picture Library and E.P. Goldschmidt and Co Ltd; **153** Meteorological Office; **154, 155(b)** Ann Ronan Picture Library; **158-9(c), 159(t)** Trustees of the British Museum; **159(i)** Nigel Osborne; **160(t)** British Museum, **(c)** British Library, **(b)** Ann Ronan Picture Library and E.P. Goldschmidt and Co Ltd; **161** Albertina, Vienna; **162(al), (ar), (b)** Ann Ronan Picture Library; **163(a)** Cambridge University; **163(b)** John Watney Photo Library; **164** British Library; **165** Michael Freeman; **166(bl)** National Maritime Museum, Greenwich, **(br)** Ann Ronan Picture Library; **167(a)** Oxford Scientific Films, **(b)** Ann Ronan Picture Library; **168** Science Photo Library; **169(l)** British Library, **(r)** Ann Ronan Picture Library; **171** Professor S. Cohen/Science Photo Library; **173** Science Museum; **174** British Library; **175** Science Photo Library; **177(a)** BBC Hulton Picture Library, **(b)** British Library; **179(a)** Science Museum; **179(b), 180** Ann Ronan Picture Library; **181(l)** Royal Library, Turin; **181(r), 183, 184** Ann Ronan Picture Library; **185(a)** Science Photo Library; **185(b)** Ann Ronan Picture Library; **186(b), 187(t)** Donald Hay; **187(c)** Wellcome Institute Library, **(b)** Ann Ronan Picture Library.

Key: **(t)** top, **(a)** above, **(b)** below, **(l)** left, **(r)** right, **(i)** inset, **(c)** centre.